# Research on ESL in U.S. Community Colleges:
# People, Programs, and Potential

# Research on ESL in U.S. Community Colleges: People, Programs, and Potential

Edited by

■ Kathleen M. Bailey and Maricel G. Santos

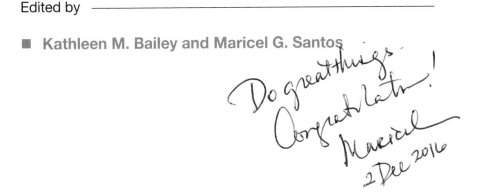

The Michigan Series on Teaching Academic English in U.S. Post-Secondary Programs

Series Editors: Patricia Byrd, Joy M. Reid, Cynthia M. Schuemann

Ann Arbor
THE UNIVERSITY OF MICHIGAN PRESS

♾ Printed on acid-free paper

ISBN-13: 978-0-472-03312-6

2012     2011     2010     2009          4     3     2     1

# Dedication

To the graduates of the TESOL and TFL MA Programs at the Monterey Institute of International Studies, who work to improve the lives of language learners everywhere, and particularly to those MIIS alumni who teach in community colleges. Special thanks to LaTesha Carbonnet and Larry Lawson, who served as the editorial assistants on this project.

—*Kathi Bailey*

To the many adult learners who pursue their educational goals at community colleges. Also, to the many teachers and students at Bunker Hill Community College in Boston, Massachusetts, who made my dissertation research possible.

—*Maricel Santos*

# SERIES EDITOR PREFACE

W<small>E ARE PLEASED TO WELCOME</small> ESL <small>TEACHERS, ADMINISTRATORS, AND RESEARCHERS</small> to this volume in the Michigan Series on Teaching Academic English in U.S. Post-Secondary Programs.

Because ESL and former ESL students are playing an ever more important role in the make-up of undergraduate classes in colleges and universities in United States, this series was designed to provide a venue to explore topical issues relevant to the teaching and learning of English for academic purposes (EAP). The books in the series are aimed at educators in undergraduate settings who are seeking insights based on both practice and research. Theorists will find the books to be useful for reference, while their tone, content, and organization embrace the larger audience of practicing teachers and administrators (both experienced and less experienced), pre-service teachers, and teacher trainers. The series is motivated by our belief that we can do a better job of helping ESL students transition to higher education, meet the challenging academic demands of undergraduate course work, and enjoy success as they graduate with two- and four-year degrees. College educators must become better informed about the needs and experiences of these students and their potential to contribute to society. Their diverse backgrounds bring strengths to undergraduate settings as well as challenges.

Enrollment figures for ESL and former ESL students in higher education are significant and continue to grow. We hope that the books in this series will encourage educators who work with these students to reflect on current practices, develop new understandings, and take action when change is warranted. Learning about instructional approaches informed by research and practical application benefits teachers, their students, and their institutions. In higher education, institutional missions include both teaching and research. In contrast to the research mission of most universities, most two-year and many four-year colleges give more weight to teaching in faculty workloads; consequently, teachers in such institutions have heavy teaching loads and limited resources or support for research. This series seeks to provide greater access to important investigations in this area and support practitioners in disseminating their works.

This collection, *Research on ESL in U.S. Community Colleges: People, Programs, and Potential,* compiled by Kathleen M. Bailey and Maricel G. Santos, sets forth a range of issues that now characterize EAP in the United States. This collection of studies—with its focus on community colleges—explores some of the most important challenges for EAP educators in a crucial area of U.S. higher education. Bailey and Santos have organized the studies into five themes: curricula, technology, retention and persistence, identity, and defining and assessing success. This approach provides a sampling of research in each area and represents varied voices and perspectives.

The volume's part on curriculum focuses on how EAP instructors can effectively blend language instruction with academic content relevant to college settings in California, Florida, Hawai'i, Illinois, Massachusetts, and Texas. The technology chapters are set in Arizona and California and confirm positive response to the use of technological tools in language learning with caveats. The part on retention and persistence explores influential student and programmatic factors in studies taking place in Massachusetts and Oregon. Identity construct, a variable of particular volatility for those experiencing self in multiple cultures and languages, is visited in settings in Arizona and Hawai'i. The collection's final part contrasts student and institutional perspectives on success in California and Florida. The struggle for ongoing reform in all five of these areas is endemic to ESL programs, and readers will gain insights into relevant practice while learning from studies that can serve as a basis for additional research. Part of the community college mission is a strong commitment to meeting local needs, and these studies serve to illustrate community connections and social implications while providing insights across common threads.

In their introduction, Santos, Charbonnet, and Bailey note that there is lack of research in the area of community college ESL for a variety of compelling reasons. At the same time, they express optimism about the spirit of those in these settings to overcome support limitations, carry out research, and publish their findings. As they say in the introduction, "In spite of these challenges, we know from experience that community college practitioners and administrators hunger for opportunities to exchange ideas and build the empirical base on community college ESL students." This book demonstrates the truth of that insight into the felt needs of community college educators—given the opportunity to carry out and publish research about their students and the education offered those students in their colleges, college teachers can do work that clarifies current problems and points the way to changes that correct those problems.

One former ESL student of Miami Dade College (Florida), Rafael Alonso, said about his ESL classroom experiences, "I think you encouraged me and my classmates to continue our education and break all the language's barriers." These words capture the spirit of this volume. "Continuing beyond barriers" is our goal for all ESL students and their educators; proposing and exploring systematic ways to achieve this goal is the purpose of this series.

Cynthia M. Schuemann
Joy M. Reid
Patricia Byrd

# CONTENTS

# Introduction

## New Contexts for Research in Community College ESL

■ Maricel G. Santos, LaTesha Charbonnet, and Kathleen M. Bailey

THE IDEA FOR THIS BOOK EMERGED AT THE 2006 TESOL ANNUAL CONVENTION when several of the contributors collaborated on a panel presentation highlighting research on the teaching and learning of ESL in U.S. community college contexts. We shared a common passion for working with community college ESL students, which includes a diverse profile of immigrants, refugees, and international students. Our research projects addressed a broad range of challenges facing community college ESL programs today, such as meeting students' academic, professional, and personal needs; measuring success in ESL programs; aligning curricular goals across departments; and the role of technology in ESL instruction.

We recognize that, at many community colleges, the research aspirations of most ESL instructors often are thwarted by obstacles, including heavy teaching loads, limited resources (time, funding, research assistants, access to library materials), and perhaps by an institutional climate that does not support practitioner research and its dissemination. Blumenthal (2006) offers a similar critique, citing several forces that tend to work against innovative thinking in the community college, including "funding decisions, government regulations, turf battles, and, most unfortunately, bias and discrimination" (p. 1). In spite of these challenges, we know from experience that community college practitioners and administrators hunger for opportunities to exchange ideas and build the empirical base on community college ESL students.

For these reasons, we are delighted to be able to present this collection of previously unpublished studies on ESL learning and teaching in the U.S. community college context. We hope that the volume will help fill the research gap in the knowledge base about ESL in U.S. community colleges. Strengthening the empirical base about the needs of community college ESL students is critical in light of the increasingly important role that community colleges play in providing language minority adults with opportunity to access post-secondary education.

The population of "immigrants, refugees, and international students who pass through the doors of community colleges" (Blumenthal, 2006, p. vi; see also Allison, 2006) is large, diverse, and growing. The "open access" policies of many community colleges attract students of various linguistic, ethnic, and cultural backgrounds, as well as students with a wide range of educational needs and goals and prior educational achievement (Aragon, 2001). Minority students—a diverse group that includes a large but undetermined number of immigrants and refugees—make up more than 30 percent of the total community college population (Phillippe & Patton, 2000). In 2004–2005, more than 84,000 international students were enrolled in U.S. community colleges, nearly a 20 percent increase from the enrollment four years prior (Institute of International Education, 2005). In addition, a study by Vernez and Abrahamse (1996) found that immigrant students are 10 percent more likely to begin and complete their educational trajectories at a community college compared to native-born students.

The phrase "community college ESL" refers to diverse instructional contexts, including credit- versus non-credit-bearing, non-academic, pre-academic, vocational, and academic, depending on the aims and aspirations of the institution and the ESL program (Machado, 2006). This diversity is a source of both strength and challenge for those charged with the task of providing instructional services to English language learners.

Increasing our understanding of the needs of community college ESL students is relevant in the broader discussion of U.S. economic and labor trends. Today, both strong English communication skills and some post-secondary training and education are increasingly regarded as essential (Carnevale & Desrochers, 2001; Murnane & Levy, 1996; Reder, 2000; Wiley, 1993). Without skills and credentials, many language minority adults are "locked out of full participation in the society in which they live and work" (Wiley, 1993, p. 1), unable to access well-paying jobs, economic advancement, and lifelong learning opportunities. While there undoubtedly are a myriad of social and political factors that restrict students' access to higher education (Saxon & Boylan, 1999; Wiley, 1993), community college ESL instructors can play a valuable role in ensuring quality academic preparation, the kind that supports ESL students' success in the classroom and, ultimately, their completion of educational programs and degree attainment.

While there remains a relative lack of research on community college ESL students, especially compared to research on ESL students in K–12 or in higher education contexts (i.e., intensive English programs, four-year colleges and universities), we have also witnessed an increased interest in evidence-based practice in community colleges. One notable effort is a series recently published by TESOL entitled *Perspectives on Community College ESL* (Carmona, 2008; Blumenthal, 2006; Spaventa, 2006). Other works that have contributed to the community college ESL knowledge base include *Beyond Access: Methods and Models for Increas-*

*ing Retention and Learning Success among Minority Students: New Directions for Community Colleges* (Aragon, 2001); *Adult ESL and the Community College* (Crandall & Sheppard, 2004); *Passing the Torch: Strategies for Innovation in Community College ESL* (Chisman & Crandall, 2007); and *Trends in Community College Curriculum: New Directions for Community Colleges* (Schuyler, 2000).

Collections such as the *Perspectives on Community College ESL* series represent a valuable contribution to the dissemination of "professional wisdom" in the field of community college ESL. By the term *professional wisdom,* we refer to the ways that publications, such as the TESOL collection, have promoted "the effective identification and incorporation of *local circumstances* into instruction" (Whitehurst, 2002, slide 4, emphasis added). The exploration of *local circumstances* in community college ESL programs enables us to learn from the experiences and perspectives of real teachers and students. As Blumenthal (2006) observes, inquiries into local practice "celebrate the successes of hardworking and dedicated students, teachers, and administrators in community college ESL programs, while challenging us [the readers] as individuals and institutions to better serve our college missions and better advocate for our students" (p. 2). We believe these inquiries into community college ESL programs enable us to make important connections between effective practices in specific contexts and broader understandings of the mission and purpose of "community college ESL" as a field.

In this spirit of celebrating "professional wisdom," it is significant that nearly all of the contributors to this volume are practicing community college ESL instructors and administrators who have been able to carry out formal research projects in the context of their own institutions or ESL classrooms. The primary goals of the volume, then, are (1) to disseminate recent research on community college ESL programs, (2) to promote communication and reflection among researchers and teachers about community college ESL learning and teaching, and (3) to inform teacher educators and future teachers about ESL learning and teaching in this important context.

To further these goals, the contributors report on studies that use both quantitative and qualitative data collection and analysis procedures. Conducted in a variety of settings across the United States, the studies include participants representing a range of first language backgrounds, cultures, countries of origin, ages, language proficiencies, and reasons for studying English. Each chapter follows a similar format: (a) a description of the research context and the issues that motivated the research, (b) a statement of the research questions and design, (c) descriptions of the data collection and analysis procedures, and (d) discussion of the study findings. Each chapter then concludes with a discussion of possible implications for practice and/or policy.

The volume includes five thematically organized parts. The first, "Research on Community College ESL Curricula," presents multiple perspectives on content-oriented courses. In Chapter 1, "Shifts in Focus: Examining Language Instruction in Content-Based ESL Lessons," Kathleen M. Bailey reports on an observational study of content-based instruction in ESL lessons she observed at community colleges in Chicago (Illinois), Honolulu (Hawai'i), Houston (Texas), Miami (Florida), and Sacramento (California). Bailey explores a central question about instruction in content-oriented ESL classes: How do ESL teachers manage to focus on language during content-based lessons? Her analysis highlights a range of teacher behaviors that enable students to gain language skills while deepening their content knowledge of a wide array of topics, including poetic imagery, biology and ethics, the American educational system, civil rights, biology and the environment, and the spread of lethal viruses as a public health issue. Bailey's vignettes of six content-oriented lessons help us understand how language use varies across subject areas. Her vignettes also highlight the dynamic nature of teachers' shifts between a focus on language and a focus on content within a single lesson as they simultaneously strive to make the linguistic input and the content comprehensible and engaging for their students.

In Chapter 2, "Content Teacher Perceptions of Content-Based Assignments in Writing Courses," Lara Ravitch addresses important questions about the alignment of content-based ESL composition assignments with the requirements of subject-area community college instructors. Based at Truman College in Chicago, Illinois, Ravitch's study is able to refine our understanding of the specific ways that content-based ESL instructors can prepare students to develop the language proficiency, critical-thinking skills, and academic vocabulary they need to succeed in college-level courses in the disciplines. In addition, her study demystifies the expectations about academic writing held by subject-area community college instructors, which often remain tacit. (For a similar discussion about academic aural/oral skills, see Ferris & Tagg, 1996.) Ravitch surveyed ten subject-area instructors about the skills they believed content-based ESL composition assignments should develop. In the discussion of her findings, she demonstrates how the subject-area instructors' feedback led to important improvements in the design of the ESL composition assignments.

Finally, in Chapter 3, "'A Long Little Story': Exploring the Experiences of Nursing Students as English Language Learners," JoAnn Mulready-Shick examines the complex challenges facing nursing students who are non-native speakers of English and who struggle with the communication demands of the nursing curriculum and the clinical setting. This chapter is unique in that Mulready-Shick is not a TESOL professional but rather a trained nurse and administrator of an undergraduate nursing program at University of Massachusetts–Boston. Mulready-Shick describes a study in which she uses interpretive phenomenological methods to analyze the experiences and perceptions of nursing students who self-identified as English language learners. In her discussion, Mulready-Shick weaves together reflections on her own experiences as a nursing educator of immigrant students over the past twenty years with insights about nursing students' identity, learning strategies, and academic needs.

Part 2, "Technology in Community College ESL Programs," includes two chapters that expand our knowledge base about the role of technology in the ESL classroom from the perspective of teachers and students (see also Brutza & Hayes, 2006). In Chapter 4, "Community College ESL Learners' Access to and Perspectives on Technology," Cristie Roe reports on survey research conducted at Phoenix College in Phoenix, Arizona. This chapter explores ESL students' responses to the use of computers in their ESL classes. Roe calls attention to the critical need for examining the meaning of technology from the perspective of students themselves, given that community colleges often attract large populations of refugees and other immigrants who may not have had access to computers in their early education or may have limited access outside the community college classroom. She found that her respondents were evenly divided in terms of their self-reported computer use prior to coming to the United States (i.e., they had never used a computer, used one a few times, or used one many times). Yet the students' attitudes about computer use were very positive.

To be able to gauge the impact of technology on ESL learning and teaching, we must first answer basic questions about the nature of technology use (i.e., which tools, which contexts, when accessed). In this regard, Chapter 5, "ESL Teacher and Student Perspectives on Technology in the Community College Classroom," by Marit ter Mate-Martinsen, helps to lay important groundwork in ESL research. Based at Santa Barbara City College, this survey-based study of ESL teachers' use of technology and ESL students' perspectives on the use of technology in their classrooms provides the ESL field with replicable survey tools and a process for documenting technology use at other community college campuses. Her findings highlight the variation in teachers' utilization and effective integration of technology in ESL classrooms. Her analysis also suggests that effective use of technology depends on the teachers' access to resources and their own level of confidence and familiarity with technological tools. With respect to the students' perspectives, ter Mate-Martinsen found that many low-level and part-time evening students relied on access to computers on campus due to limited access to computers outside school, a finding that positions the community college as an important gateway to technology for many ESL students.

Part 3, "Retention and Persistence Issues in Community College ESL Programs," includes three chapters. In Chapter 6, "Differences in Academic Vocabulary Knowledge among Language-Minority Community College Students: Implications for Transition," Maricel G. Santos raises questions regarding what we know about the academic vocabulary skills of English language learners who are making the transition out of predominantly English-focused instruction and entering academic content instruction. Santos explores the possibility that variation in academic vocabulary skills may be linked to the differences in academic integration level, referring to the degree to which students participate in the academic life of the college. In this study, which was conducted at Bunker Hill Community College in

Boston, Massachusetts, Santos finds that academic vocabulary development likely requires an investment of instructional resources over time, including while students are in ESL programs and during their early ventures into regular subject-area course-work. Santos reported unexpected findings about academic integration—namely, that academic vocabulary scores appeared to dip, not rise, at increased levels of academic integration. At first glance, this seems to suggest that academic integration does not benefit students' academic vocabulary knowledge; however, Santos argues that this trend should prompt further inquiry into the nature of academic integration experiences and the possible implications that these experiences may hold for academic language development.

Like Santos' chapter, Chapter 7 by Elizabeth M. Zachry and Emily Dibble also describes research conducted at Bunker Hill Community College. Zachry and Dibble's study, "Transitioning from ESL and the GED to Post-Secondary Education: A Case Study of a College Transitions Program," provides a descriptive analysis of Bunker Hill's innovative efforts to move General Educational Development (GED) recipients and English language learners beyond basic skills programs and into vocational/academic degree programs. By examining data collected throughout the program's six-year history, Zachry and Dibble are able to provide clear evidence that the program is meeting many of its transitional goals. For example, the study indicates that students in the Transitions program have matriculated into degree programs at greater success rates than students with comparable skills sets who did not participate in the program. Zachry and Dibble also describe the array of programming components that make up the program's transitional model, highlight-ing components that appear to be particularly beneficial to ELLs. This discussion demonstrates that supporting the transition of ELLs requires an investment of both human and institutional resources.

Finally, in Chapter 8, "Unlocking the Door: ESL Instructors' Diaries Examining Retention of Migrant Hispanic Students," Bengt Skillen and Julie Vorholt-Alcorn present a diary study that chronicles instructors' efforts to understand migrant students' low retention rates and to identify supports to student retention while teaching at a community college satellite campus in rural Oregon. Skillen and Vorholt-Alcorn explain that for many migrant students, regular attendance and completion of ESL courses are elusive goals, making it critical that community college ESL teachers identify and disseminate model strategies for working with migrant students. To this end, Skillen and Vorholt-Alcorn's reflective account over the course of a summer teaching cycle reveals promising practices in support of migrant student retention, such as inviting student input into retention policies and building class rapport. (See also Stasinopoulos, 2006, and Stone, 2006, who discuss the importance of building a good rapport with their students.) Notably, this study demonstrates how the authors' responsiveness to retention issues increased as they learned more about their students' everyday lives outside school (at home, at work) and their students' perceptions of teachers as authority figures. This shift in thinking is captured beautifully by Skillen, who writes, "my goal turned into a concerted attempt to understand my students before having them understand me as a teacher" (p. 115, this volume).

"Identity Construction and Development among Community College ESL Students," Part 4, presents chapters that showcase fresh new data on who community college ESL students are. In Chapter 9, Duffy Galda examines the experiences of three elderly Eastern European refugees studying ESL at Pima Community College in Tucson, Arizona. Galda's case study brings together a series of quotations drawn from in-depth interviews with the three refugees. Based on the interviews and classroom observations, Galda's study presents learner portraits that illuminate the experiences and perspectives that elderly (retirement age and above) ESL students bring to the community college culture. Galda documents five powerful and pervasive themes that emerge as important: their life experiences, literacy history, learning strategies, learning goals, and social identities.

In Chapter 10, Hanh thi Nguyen, Francis Noji, and Guy Kellogg address students' identity construction in a content-based instruction program. The subjects were international students attending ESL classes at Kapi'olani Community College in Honolulu, Hawai'i. Nguyen, Noji, and Kellogg draw on theories of language socialization to examine how utterances index the speaker's and hearer's stances toward what is being said (see Goffman, 1981). Specifically, they employ discourse analysis methods to examine electronic discussion postings throughout one semester in a content-based, pre-academic class focusing on civil rights in the United States. They document how students make sense of new academic concepts by relating such concepts to their personal lives, in the process gaining a sense of self relative to the second language they are learning. This chapter adds a unique perspective to a growing body of literature on content-based instruction in the community college context. (See also Crandall & Kaufman, 2002; Kasper, 2000; and Pally, 2000.)

Part 5, "Defining and Assessing Success in Community College ESL Programs," includes chapters that showcase diverse perspectives on the meaning and measurement of success for community college ESL students. Chapter 11 by Molly J. Lewis challenges conventional perspectives on the measurement of success among ESL students. The typical administrative view tends to prioritize passing a proficiency exam, completing a level or program, or transferring to a four-year school. Lewis' study seeks to deepen our understanding of how ESL students define success and how their shifts in goal orientation may reflect exploration of new identities as users of English. Lewis used survey data collected from a group of ESL students enrolled at Hartnell College, a predominantly Hispanic-serving institution in Salinas Valley, California. Her qualititative analysis began by coding for types of learner goals, followed by a thematic analysis of the data. After identifying patterns in her data, Lewis then used the chi-square statistic to examine variation in the students' self-reported motivations for studying ESL. She found that students at beginning levels of English tended to report language-focused learning goals (e.g., *I want to improve my English*), but at more advanced levels of English, students tended to report goals tied to their job or profession. Lewis' study sheds light on the evolving and dynamic relationship between identity development and English learning goals for community college ESL students at different points in their language development. Her findings also underscore the limitations of uni-dimensional and static approaches to gauging student success.

Chapter 12, "Access to Freshman Composition at Stake: Comparing Student Performance on Two Measures of Writing" by Cynthia M. Schuemann, is based on her work at Miami Dade College in Florida. She compared scores on two tests of writing—a standardized multiple choice sentence skills test and a holistically scored exam—taken by students in an advanced writing class at a large urban community college. The multiple choice instrument was the sentence skills section of the Computerized Placement Test (CPT), part of the College Board Accuplacer® battery (a high-stakes assessment instrument used extensively by colleges in the United States and Canada to evaluate student readiness for freshman composition courses). Using descriptive statistics and $t$-tests, Schuemann's analysis indicates that the CPT sentence skills test can be a valid and reliable placement instrument for advanced-level ESL students who intend to pursue community college degrees. The study also shows that the sentence skills test discriminated equally well among students, regardless of their gender and age. However, Schuemann also addresses situations in which ESL students who can do well on contextualized writing tasks do not perform as well on decontextualized sentence skills tests. Her study provides an important addition to our understanding of assessment issues for the ESL community college population. (See also Machado & Solensky, 2006, who investigated concerns with computerized placement testing for ESL students.)

In the final chapter, "Student Learning Outcomes and ESL Student Success in the Community College Classroom," Marit ter Mate-Martinsen highlights the variable interpretations of "student learning outcomes" (SLOs), referring to the "overarching specific observable characteristics" (Snowhite, Adams, Gilbert, Reilly, Welch, & Rheinheimer, 2005, p. 8) used to gauge learner progress and achievement. SLOs represent a source of innovation in curriculum reform in community college ESL as the expectation is that all stakeholders—teachers, administrators, and students—should be able to comprehend the scope and purpose of SLOs. The tensions around this expectation are highlighted in ter Mate-Martinsen's analysis of the experiences and perspectives of two ESL instructors who work at Santa Barbara Community College ("Jane" and "Barbara") as they learned to develop their own SLOs for course syllabi, assignments, and projects. In interview sessions with ter Mate-Martinsen, Jane (the ESL instructor) shared her struggle to write SLOs in English for students who are still learning English, by raising critical questions about the ultimate purpose and impact of SLOs: "Is there really a way to make SLOs clear and meaningful to a true beginning-level ESL community college student? Ultimately, for whom are SLOs being written at the beginning levels?" (p. 192, this volume). This chapter concludes by discussing what the teachers learned from the SLO writing process and providing the reader with suggestions on how to implement SLOs effectively to enrich classroom pedagogy and student learning.

This volume showcases a diverse range of research tools and methods, which seem to mirror the diversity of experiences, settings, and contexts under investigation in this collection. It is our hope that this collection will be immediately helpful to community college teachers and program administrators, as well as teacher educators and prospective teachers, in stimulating much-needed dialogue on what we know and inquiry into what we still need to discover about community college ESL students. As several chapters in this volume indicate, there is a need for conversations not only within ESL programs but also between ESL programs and other campus departments who enroll these students once they exit ESL programs.

We also hope that these studies will help to spark future research on ESL programs in the community college context. The contributors include both novice and established ESL researchers as well as experienced ESL researcher-practitioners—a dynamic that very much enriches the range and depth of perspectives reflected in this volume. We hope this richness sends an encouraging message to other community college practitioners—from all levels of research experience—to pursue their own lines of inquiry on ESL teaching and learning.

Because one of this volume's primary goals is to promote communication and reflection about teaching and learning practices in the community college ESL context, we encourage you to ask yourself questions as you read these chapters: What are the issues that motivated this research? Are these issues and study findings relevant to your work context? How do the contributors address their research questions? What tools did they use to gather data? Are there aspects of these studies you could replicate in your own context? What research questions would you want to ask about these topics? Questions such as these will enable you to interpret the merits of each study in light of your own community college context. We remain resolute that the capacity for practitioners to discuss (at the very least) and pursue their own lines of inquiry (ideally) is critical to the growth and vitality of the field of community college ESL.

# Part 1
## Research on Community College ESL Curricula

# Chapter 1

# Shifts in Focus: Examining Language Instruction in Content-Based ESL Lessons

■ Kathleen M. Bailey

THIS CHAPTER EXPLORES CONTENT-BASED INSTRUCTION IN THE CONTEXT OF U.S. community college ESL courses. *Content-based instruction (CBI)* is an approach to language curriculum design that entails "the integration of content learning with language teaching aims" (Brinton, Snow, & Wesche, 2003, p. ix). In CBI "support is provided for learners' linguistic development [and] language is contextualized through these relevant content areas" (Jourdenais & Shaw, 2005, p. 2). In addition, "the form and sequence of language presentation are dictated by content material" (Brinton et al., 2003, p. ix). That is, instead of having a syllabus based on pre-determined grammar or vocabulary items, the language elements to be taught arise directly from the materials used to study the content. This approach creates interesting and central challenges for ESL teachers. In fact, Snow (2001) has pointed out that "perhaps one of the greatest challenges in the ongoing expansion and innovation of content-based instruction is the search for the right balance of language and content teaching" (p. 314). In spring 2006, I visited CBI-oriented ESL classes at community colleges throughout the United States as part of my own "search for the right balance." As described in this chapter, this journey has yielded new insights into fundamental questions about the promise of CBI approaches in ESL teaching.

## Issues that Motivated the Research

What is unique about CBI is that it involves "the concurrent study of language and subject matter" (Brinton, 2003, p. 201). Students learn material from academic disciplines (history, chemistry, and so on) as they are developing their speaking, listening, reading, and writing and improving their pronunciation, vocabulary, grammar, and discourse competence. In the CBI approach, language learning is promoted through content learning, a benefit well documented in research (see Grabe & Stoller, 1997).

The balance between a focus on language and a focus on content has been discussed by van Lier (2005), who says that "CBI is a continuum, not an either-or choice" (p. 15). This continuum is depicted in Figure 1.1.

The dashed lines labeled A and B in this figure represent points of relative emphasis on language and content. As van Lier (2005) notes, "Taking just two arbitrary points on the continuum, A represents a class in which language takes precedence over content and B is a class in which content is regarded as more important than language" (p. 16). With this figure, van Lier notes that learning occurs at many points along the continuum, although the nature of the learners' engagement in these classes may vary. Sometimes learners may be focused on the study of linguistic elements with relatively little attention paid to subject matter (Point A), while at other times learners may be focused on learning subject matter with little overt attention paid to language (Point B).

While van Lier's model contrasts different courses, his continuum is also useful for understanding the varying levels of engagement with language and content that *occur within a single CBI lesson*. Starting from this understanding, we can view the content-versus-language issue as a pendulum, or a balancing scale. The continuum in Figure 1.1 thus could be used to capture within a given lesson the ways in which the instructional focus is sometimes more language-oriented and then shifts to being relatively more content-oriented. This view led me to wonder

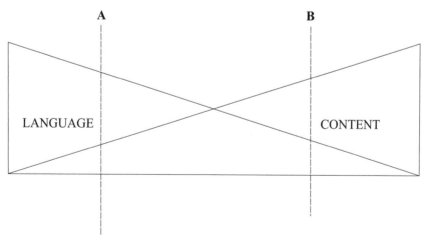

**Figure 1.1.**   Language and Content (from van Lier, 2005, p. 15)

how ESL teachers provide the linguistic input to learners in classes that emphasize content, and how they manage the shifts between language and content.

## Context of the Research

This discussion of CBI is grounded in six classroom observations conducted at five community colleges that vary in their demographic profiles and programmatic contexts: American River College, Sacramento, California; Truman College, Chicago, Illinois; Miami Dade College, Miami, Florida; Kapiʻolani Community College, Honolulu, Hawaiʻi; and Houston Community College in Houston, Texas. These vignettes are derived from observations in lessons on poetry, Biology and Ethics, the American educational system, Biology and the Environment, civil rights, and a reading/writing class based on *The Hot Zone* (a non-fiction account of human encounters with lethal viruses).

In these lessons, there was incredible diversity in the languages and home cultures of the students. In Miami, there were many students from Latin America, Europe, and the Caribbean, and students who were children of Cuban immigrants. In Sacramento, the classrooms were filled with Ukrainian and Russian immigrants. In Chicago and Houston, there was a rich blend of immigrant and refugee students from Africa, Latin America, Eastern Europe, and the Middle East. In Honolulu, the classes consisted mainly of international students who had come to Kapiʻolani College, largely from Asia, for summer ESL courses (see Nguyen, Noji, and Kellogg, this volume). The students varied widely in age: some were as young as eighteen, having just come from high school, and others were well into their eighties (see Galda, this volume).

## Research Question Addressed

The overarching research question guiding my exploration was: *How do community colleges ESL teachers using content-based instruction negotiate the balance between focusing on language and focusing on content?* Other related, more specific questions included: *What elements of language (e.g., discourse, vocabulary meaning, pronunciation) do teachers call attention to in addressing the content matter? What strategies do teachers use to teach language in these content classes?*

The lessons discussed here come from data collected in ESL classes in nine U.S. community colleges in six different states. The entire database involved observations of 28 teachers in 33 classes, for just over 51 hours of instruction. In this chapter, I will report on data from only six of the most content-oriented of those lessons. The database allowed me to examine the instructional practices of these community college ESL teachers as they managed the shifts between focusing on language and focusing on content.

## Data Collection and Analysis Procedures

These classroom observational data were collected by "opportunistic sampling," meaning I made no attempt to randomly sample classes for observation, or to construct a stratified sample based on known parameters of the population. Instead, I sought out community college ESL teachers around the United States who were willing to let me observe their content-based classes. This process began by searching community college websites for campuses with ESL programs in areas where I would be traveling. I contacted teachers and/or program administrators, explained why I wished to observe ESL lessons (particularly those using a content-based approach), and requested permission to visit classes. I was also able to reach teachers using a "snowball" process, whereby participating teachers introduced me to other potential participants. For each campus visit, I observed as many classes as possible in the time available without compromising the process of taking handwritten field notes and refining them after class. When the teachers' time allowed, I interviewed them before or after their lessons. Many gave me copies of the course syllabus, the lesson plan, and the day's materials. Some showed me examples of assessment instruments, textbooks, and students' written work.

As soon as possible after a class visit (typically immediately after), I fleshed out the handwritten field notes by elaborating on abbreviations, adding details in the margins, and noting questions to ask the teacher in a follow-up email discussion. Then, usually within 24 hours, I word-processed the handwritten field notes. (This electronic recording allowed me to search for key words as needed to locate specific incidents and identify patterns.) Then I sent an electronic copy of the field notes to the teacher for his or her perusal and input as a member check (Maxwell, 2005).

My analysis in this chapter is limited to 10.5 hours of classroom visits (20 percent of all the data collected). The records of these six lessons totaled 45 single-spaced field note pages. To address my specific research questions, I reviewed the field notes and located the lessons in the total data set in which a strong content focus had been most evident. I then reread each of those data sets many times, looking for the points where the teachers explicitly addressed language issues. These included episodes when the teachers drew attention to grammar, pronunciation, and discourse, but the most frequent language focus occurred when vocabulary items arose during the lesson.

## Findings

This section first presents vignettes of six lessons at five sites, focusing on how the teachers dealt with language issues during CBI. While these vignettes provide brief summaries (rather than exhaustive descriptions) of the lessons I observed, together they speak to the patterns in the ways that community college ESL teachers manage the presentation of language and content in CBI-based courses. After presenting the vignettes, I will summarize the instructional actions that characterize the teachers' shifts to language instruction in their content lessons.

## The Poetry Class (American River College)

In an upper-intermediate poetry class, the students had read Emily Dickinson's poem, "The Letter." The teacher elicited from the class the idea that Dickinson's poetry was different from that of her contemporaries, and that she didn't follow the traditional pattern of rhymes or the general style of poetry at the time. A student added that the poet was "not very sociable" and the teacher offered the more specific word *reclusive* to sum up the student's point.

To focus the students directly on the language of the text, the teacher said, "Let's look at the poem, because there are a few words—" and then wrote the following words on the board: *waded, moved, toiled, quibble, hinder,* and *neighing.* She explained both the connotations and denotations of these words. For example, she explained that *waded* conveys moving slowly and heavily through some kind of liquid. Then the teacher related *quibbled* to a discussion the students had had the previous week about their choice of poems to analyze for their projects. From this connection, the students apparently understood that *quibbled* means *argued* but conveys the idea of a minor disagreement. The teacher gestured with both hands as she explained the meaning of *hinder,* knocking her fists together. She asked the students if they knew the meaning of *neighing* and someone guessed it means being "like a neighbor." She waited for a few moments and then clarified that *neighing* is the sound a horse makes.

The teacher then read the poem aloud to the group. Her reading was expressive and emphatic. When she explained that a *coquette* is like a flirt, she made a flirty face by lifting her eyebrows and batting her eyelashes. The students laughed slightly at her portrayal, which suggested that they understood the meaning of *coquette.*

Next, the students quietly worked in groups to analyze the poem, while the teacher wrote part of a rap lyric by Talib Kweli on the board. It included these lines: "all those teenage dreams of rapping, writing rhymes on napkins, was really visualization, making this here happen." When the groups had finished analyzing the Dickinson poem, the teacher asked, "Do the lines rhyme?" There was a great deal of discussion about this point. The teacher contrasted "perfect rhyme" (such as *sun* and *fun*) with "slanted rhyme" or "off-center rhyme." She told the class slanted rhyme is now often found in rap music and she used the lyric on the board as an illustration. She pointed out the two syllables and the /p/ sound in *rapping* and *napkins* and *happen* as examples.

Next the teacher had the students look for instances of slanted rhyme in "The Letter." She used a general solicit pattern (i.e., questions directed to the class as a whole rather than to an individual). The students also volunteered their ideas. She noted the "command language" (the use of imperative voice) in the poem, and then gestured with her left hand, making two advancing motions, as she read the line "going to him."

The lesson ended with students once more getting into groups to prepare for their upcoming "poetry presentations." They had each chosen a poem they would like to analyze as a group project, and had to select one of those poems as the focus of the group project. The discussions were animated and intense as they argued for their choices.

In sum, this teacher focused on the language of the poetry with explicit reference to literary analytic terms (e.g., *perfect rhyme* and *slanted rhyme*), employing a context familiar to the students (rap music). This focus on the literary techniques helped the students to engage with and make sense of Dickinson's poem. In addition, the teacher highlighted lexical and grammatical features of the language in Dickinson's poetry, which also supported the students' ability to engage in the discussion of the poem's meaning and may have helped them learn the linguistic elements. Her facial expressions, tone of voice, dramatic reading, and gestures underscored the meanings of the words.

## The Biology and Ethics Class (Truman College)

I observed an intermediate-level lesson on Biology and Ethics, which was team-taught by an ESL teacher and a biology teacher. Prior to the class, each student had chosen an article about biology and ethics from the Internet. In groups of five, students gave oral summaries of their own articles and discussed which one would give the best focus for a "summary response" writing assignment (to be completed for homework). During these group discussions, the two teachers circulated and discussed the students' topic choices and selection criteria with them. The article topics included assisted suicide, stem cell research, measuring pain, and the use of laboratory animals in research.

While the content of the articles focused clearly on ethics in science, the teachers also directed the students' attention to the discourse of scientific articles—that is, the way ideas are presented in scientific writing. To do this, the teachers got the students to analyze their own approach to interacting with the readings. For instance, the ESL teacher asked the class, "You tell me. What did you use as criteria to select what you wanted?" The students murmured their responses, some talking about "fact and opinion." As they talked, the ESL teacher typed the students' selection criteria on her computer keyboard, which projected them on a screen at the front of the room. One student volunteered that she was looking for "clear statements of what was what." Another student said, "A specific issue—not generalizations." The ESL teacher repeated his statement and said, "That's an excellent point!" Another student offered "examples—major and minor supporting details" as a criterion. The ESL teacher responded with, "Ohhh! She said the magic words! Major and minor supporting details."

This lesson focused on discourse conventions used for academic writing in the sciences; thus, the content of this lesson was not limited to the topic of biology and ethics, but also encompassed the discourse of ethics discussions. The teachers gave students opportunities to talk about relevant discourse issues by structuring the group work and individual tasks, and by closely interacting with the students regarding the texts they had selected. In the small groups, each student talked to and listened to at least four classmates as well as the two teachers. The lesson seemed to help students understand the conventions that shape the way we write about science topics. By prompting the students to examine their selection criteria, the ESL teacher encouraged them to analyze and talk about science discourse, which represents a critical first step toward becoming good writers in the sciences (Eskey, 1997).

## The American Education System Class (Truman College)

I observed an intermediate lesson in a course on the American education system, in which the students worked in small groups to advise a fictional fellow student named Fred about plagiarism. Fred was described as a single father and a nursing student at Truman College, who also worked part-time. He was facing numerous time pressures and had a chance to buy a term paper rather than writing his own. From their comments it seemed that many of the students in the class could relate to Fred's life circumstances.

During the whole-class discussion the students shared several suggestions for Fred. Using the room's networked computer system, the teacher projected the groups' ideas on the screen at the front of the class and invited the students to clarify these ideas. The students thought that their suggestions for Fred were all clear, but the teacher said it might help if they would explain some parts more specifically. She did not deal with the minor spelling errors that appeared, but one student had written *perphrazi* and the teacher noted that that word might be a problem for Fred. She elicited more ideas from the students about paraphrasing and provided the correct spelling of *paraphrase*.

The teacher suggested, "Maybe Fred doesn't know what paraphrasing is." She elicited the meaning of *paraphrase* from a student, who said, "Your creative and thoughts." The teacher repeated the student's phrase and then elicited the related words *creativity* or *creation,* explaining that those would be the noun forms to use in this context. The teacher also elicited ideas from the class about when they needed quotation marks and where they should put quotation marks in writing a paper. As the class talked about paraphrasing, the teacher stressed to the students that they have to say "according to" or use some other form of attribution if they incorporate someone else's words.

One student used the phrase, "in the long run." The teacher asked, "What does that mean—*in the long run?*" Some students explained their understanding of this phrase—in this case meaning that although Fred might be tempted to buy a term paper as a short-term solution, it would be more "benefiting" for him over time to write his own paper. The teacher focused on the word *benefiting* and elicited the root word from the students. She commented that the *-ing* ending wasn't providing quite the right form of the adjective and then elicited the word *beneficial* from the students.

The teacher prompted the students to identify the grammar errors in a group's definition of plagiarism. She wrote on the whiteboard, correcting the projected text as the students suggested improvements. The students laughed about the suggestion that Fred should invite a displaced family from New Orleans (survivors of Hurricane Katrina) to live with him and help him take care of his children so he could write his term paper.

Thus, in this lesson, the teacher created a dilemma for Fred, who—like her students—had to learn about plagiarism. In small groups, the students gave Fred advice, which they then shared with the whole class. Their advice became the language samples they worked with, correcting spelling and grammar, and clarifying meaning. This strategy of highlighting problems and eliciting language seemed to help the students to notice the gap (Schmidt & Frota, 1986) between what they wanted to say and what they had said.

## The Biology and the Environment Class (Miami Dade College)

I observed a lesson in an upper-intermediate adjunct writing course on Biology and the Environment. (An *adjunct*, or *linked*, *course* is an ESL class connected to a course in the disciplines; the students are typically enrolled in both classes at the same time.) Before my visit, the students had worked in pairs to investigate conservation organizations, such as Green Peace, Conservation International, and the World Wildlife Federation. Pairs of students then co-authored papers on the organization they had investigated. On the day I observed, the teacher reminded the students, "Our last writing assignment was taken from the Tovar Declaration. Y'all know about that. Our college is one of the signers. So *sustainability* is the buzz word." She explained that government and businesses must figure out what to do to keep from destroying the earth.

Next, the teacher called on some students to come forward and read their papers aloud. As they did so, she displayed their compositions on the projection screen. The student writers' classmates listened, read along, and identified the features of the composition (e.g., the thesis statement, supporting evidence, etc.). After each presentation, the speakers' peers asked questions and offered comments, to which the writers responded. These discussions involved topics such as extinction, sustainability, migratory species, the Tovar Declaration, land ownership, and the existence of the Florida panther in the Everglades (the major national park near Miami).

There were a few grammar errors in one woman's paper, which she self-corrected as she read aloud. When she struggled with the word *bureau* (pronounced

/burayayu/), the teacher quietly said it correctly. The paper ended with, "In conclusion," and there was indeed a clear concluding statement. When the student finished reading, the group applauded her! She smiled and clapped with her classmates as she returned to her seat.

This lesson provided a forum to showcase the students' own research and writing. Their co-authored reports became the texts the student authors read aloud and their classmates analyzed. These analyses demonstrated and reinforced the writing issues they had been studying in the course, while generating the substantive reports and discussions led them to deepen and articulate their knowledge about the environment.

## The Civil Rights Class (Kapi'olani Community College)

I observed the second lesson of a low-intermediate ESL content course on civil rights (see Nguyen, Noji, & Kellogg, this volume). The various topics included the Bill of Rights, women's rights, gay and lesbian rights, disabled people's rights, and Hawai'ian American and Native American rights. The teacher began by putting the students into small groups and giving each group a printed statement (e.g., "Students have the right to sleep in class," "People have the right to buy as many guns as they want," and "People have a right to burn their national flag"). During the group work the teacher circulated and answered questions as they arose, mostly about the vocabulary in the statements.

After discussing the meaning of their given statements, the groups had to decide whether they agreed or disagreed with it. Each group chose a spokesperson who explained the group's position(s) to the whole class. In some cases the groups had reached a consensus and in others there was disagreement. Either way, the spokesperson was responsible for summarizing the group's thinking and giving supporting evidence for all perspectives. The class members asked follow-up questions and provided evaluative feedback. The brief printed statements focused the students on the task of agreeing or disagreeing, and the small group discussions seemed to scaffold the spokesperson's subsequent speech to the entire class.

In this activity, many low-level students were able to express complex issues with relatively basic English. For instance, in response to the statement, "Parents have a right to spank their children," a group of Japanese students agreed that parents could spank their children, but not in public. The problem, they felt, is that spanking a child publicly would be inappropriate because it would be embarrassing to the people nearby.

There followed an activity with scenarios about conflicting rights of the participants. One situation involved aggressive beggars in Honolulu asking pedestrians for money in front of shops. The customers and the shopkeepers objected to the beggars, and the students had to discuss the rights of each party. During the discussion, the teacher checked to make sure the students knew the word *pedestrian*. Some students said "walking" and the teacher repeated their idea in a full sentence, apparently in order to draw their attention to the fact that *pedestrian* was a noun, not a verb. She read the statement to the class, using two fingers to illustrate walking.

Three Japanese women asked the teacher for some clarification about a situation in which some college students were offended by tee-shirts that read, "Women are property." The teacher asked how they might feel if they saw a tee-shirt that said "Japanese women are dumb." She explained that the university was considering a dress code, because although some students feel they should be able to express themselves and wear what they want, other students might be hurt by negative tee-shirt messages. When she left, the group was moving ahead with the task, on task and speaking English.

When the full class discussed the statement about college students wearing tee-shirts with prejudicial slogans, the teacher again used gestures to clarify word meanings in the text. For instance, for the word *contradicting*, she lightly crossed the first two fingers of her right hand and rotated her wrist back and forth. When she explained the word *conflict*, she made fists and bounced the knuckles of her hands against each other.

Although this was only the second meeting of this course, the students were engaged in a serious discussion of civil rights and debating related issues of relevance to them and their situation in Hawai'i. The teacher's use of group work and appropriate tasks created a context in which these lower-intermediate students could express their ideas, debate their positions, listen to and question others, and learn vocabulary in context.

## The Reading and Writing Class: *The Hot Zone* (Houston Community College)

This lesson took place in an intermediate-level reading and writing class in an IEP at Houston Community College. The teacher began the lesson by asking the students how they felt, since they had just finished reading an entire book, *The Hot Zone* (Preston, 1994). The teacher congratulated them on reading more than 400 pages in English and said, "I'm really, really proud of you, and I hope you are too."

Next the teacher told the class about the group work and the quiz for that lesson. She wrote on the whiteboard, "Why does Richard Preston call Ebola-Reston 'the most dangerous strain ever' even though it didn't make any humans sick?" This was their reading quiz question. Some students asked, "Only one? Only one question?" The teacher smiled and replied, "Mm-hmm, and that means you want to have a really good answer."

The students got into groups for a ten-minute discussion on this issue before the quiz. The talk was animated, in English, and on task. The teacher answered some students' questions, clarifying the chronology of events in the book. She got them to think about why the author called this particular strain the most dangerous. She then listened to another group and she said, "That's a good part of the answer." She urged them to think more deeply. After checking on each group, the teacher said to the class as a whole, "So do you think you have the answer in your head?" Some students said yes, while others said no. Then she added, "And if you do have the answer in your head, do you think you can express that answer clearly?"

When the quiz started, there was an air of intense concentration in the room. The only audible noises were the quiet sound of pens and pencils on paper, and the hum of the air conditioner. After a while the teacher said, "You can write for about one more minute." She told the students, "Ask yourself, 'Is it complete and is it clear?'"

When the quiz was finished, the teacher told the class, "Okay. Study questions. Get in the same groups please." The students turned toward their neighbors and began to talk. They were all speaking quietly in English, some reading aloud from their papers.

After a while the teacher asked, "Everybody, what's the hardest question?" Some students said, "Number five." The teacher responded, "It's going to be hard to answer number five if you don't know this word." On the board she wrote, *pave (v)* and *paving*. She asked a student that she called "Mr. Engineer" to explain *paving*. She recapped his answer, adding that in Houston paving can be *asphalt* or *concrete*. Then she asked, "Why did paving that road, that road that was just dirt before, make such a difference?" As a student read aloud, he said the word *insulation* and the teacher elicited the difference between *insulation* and *isolation* from the group. Next someone else said *insulation* when the word was actually *isolation*. The teacher asked, "Insulation?" and several students responded, "Isolation!" The teacher said, "In English those two words are quite distinct."

The teacher asked, "Do you all know what bird flu is?" She added, "There's a lot of news about it right now." This comment prompted a discussion about viral mutation. The teacher gave the examples of HIV and AIDS. A student commented that one particular virus "has a long latency period." The class then discussed the practice of isolating people who were contagious, but also noted the issue of health officials getting careless with isolation—a problem that had occurred in the book they had read.

At the teacher's request, a student read aloud a paragraph about paving the highway from Kinshasa. The author had asserted that this was a very important event, and the teacher asked the students why it was. One student said that all the people were affected. The teacher gently pressed her for a more explicit answer by commenting, "I still don't see the connection." She then gave the class a hint, saying, "They paved it from coast to coast." Then a student commented about the truck drivers returning home and having sexual relations with their wives. Another student talked about increased traveling and the teacher confirmed that there was increased trade. Thus the truck drivers had been influenced by the paving of the road. To conclude this discussion, the teacher said, "So Richard Preston believes," and summarized the author's point of view.

The teacher reminded the students about their main writing assignment on the global consequences of AIDS, and connected it to Preston's ideas. After a discussion of the Ebola-Reston virus, the teacher elicited students' ideas about other viruses that had recently been in the news. A woman from Taiwan immediately raised the topic of SARS.

In sum, this lesson was based on the culminating discussion of *The Hot Zone*, which the students had read in its entirety. The teacher had the students prepare for the quiz in groups, write their quizzes independently, and then rejoin their groups to discuss their study questions before sharing their ideas in a whole-group discussion dealing with complex concepts and contextualized vocabulary. In the process, they engaged with significant social issues—situated in Africa in the lengthy book they had read, but brought home to them in Houston by the teacher's skillful management of the lesson.

## Patterns Observed across CBI Classes

These six brief snapshots highlight the complex, textured nature of the interactions that take place in community college content-oriented ESL classrooms. Four strong patterns emerged that show how these teachers address language issues when the focus is on content learning. These patterns are summarized and exemplified in Table 1.1.

First, each of these lessons involved a strong group or pair work component, which provided the students with opportunities to talk and listen. In subsequent steps, the students' own opinions were shared with the entire class. During the group work, the students clarified their understanding of texts, articulated their opinions, and sought help from the teacher as needed in a semi-private forum before the whole-group discussion.

Second, in each lesson the teacher elicited the students' own ideas. In these six content-based lessons, there was no lecturing per se (though the teachers did provide brief, contextualized explanations of concepts, grammar points, and vocabulary). Instead, the students' own papers and spoken ideas generated the basis of discussion.

Third, all these teachers found ways to relate the content issues to the students' lives. For instance, in the course based on *The Hot Zone*, the teacher led the students to connect the threat of viral diseases to their own lives (e.g., the Taiwanese woman's discussion of SARS). This process, called *personalization,* has been shown to correlate with language teacher effectiveness ratings (Omaggio, 1982). In these lessons, personalization was accomplished partly through choice. For instance, the Biology and the Environment students had chosen which conservation organizations to investigate; the Biology and Ethics students had selected their articles; the poetry students chose the poems to analyze. My consistent impression was that these students seemed to have made conscientious choices and were deeply invested in the topics they were studying.

Fourth, the language issues addressed were always approached in a highly contextualized way. The highlighted vocabulary items all arose from the content-based materials and discussions in class or from homework. The grammar and pronunciation points in these lessons all came out of the content discussions (i.e., I

**Table 1.1**

Four Patterns of Teaching Actions and Examples that Illustrate a Focus
on Language in Six CBI Lessons

| Course | Teacher Uses Group Work to Scaffold Discussions | Teacher Elicits Students' Own Ideas | Teacher Personalizes Lessons | Teacher Highlights Language in Context |
|---|---|---|---|---|
| Poetry | Groups analyze "The Letter"; groups debate which poem to choose for their presentation | T elicits Ss' reactions to "The Letter"; gets Ss to engage in literary analysis; asks them re: the poet's life | T integrates rap music lyric; reminds Ss they *quibbled;* has Ss choose poems for presentations | T explains words found in poem (e.g. *hinder, coquette*) & supports meanings with gestures |
| Biology & Ethics | Groups discuss articles selected by individual Ss & choose one | Ts have Ss choose their articles & articulate their own selection criteria | T connects selection criteria to the Ss' own writing issues | All discourse issues arose directly from articles Ss selected |
| American Education | Groups discuss Fred's options & generate advice for him about his term paper issue | T elicits Ss' advice for Fred & ideas about plagiarism, grammar, & vocabulary | T creates a dilemma for Fred, a Truman College student much like her Ss | All vocabulary & grammar issues arose from the tasks & the groups' own texts |
| Biology & the Environment | Pairs of student authors conduct research & co-author their papers re: conservation groups | Authors' classmates analyze the papers & ask questions; authors respond to questions from classmates | T reminds Ss that their college signed the Tovar Declaration; connects issues to the Everglades | All language issues discussed arose from the Ss' own compositions re: conservation groups |
| Civil Rights | Ss agree/disagree with statements, & then discuss scenarios | T elicits Ss' opinions re: controversial statements & local civil rights scenarios | T gives example of slogan about Japanese women; beggars in Honolulu | All vocabulary arose from the topics in the group work & reports |
| *The Hot Zone* | Ss prepare for quiz in groups & later address study questions in groups before plenary discussion of issues | T elicits Ss' ideas re: & understanding of author's claims & of concepts in the book; elicits their awareness of viral diseases | T relates concept of paving to Houston; connects book's issues to viral diseases they know about (e.g., SARS) | All vocabulary arose from the topics & tasks of group work & from the Ss' ideas about the reading they had done |

saw no separate, pre-planned grammar lessons in these observations). The explicit focus on language issues was sometimes pre-determined by the teacher (e.g., the poetry teacher's list of lexical items from the poem). However, it was more often triggered by the students' questions or utterances (as when "not very sociable" led the poetry teacher to offer *reclusive*). Teachers regularly elicited what the students did know, and then built on that knowledge (as in the lesson on paraphrasing), rather than simply providing definitions or corrections. Likewise, the academic discourse conventions that they had been studying were utilized by the students themselves as they did various tasks. For instance, in the Biology and the Environment course, it was the students who identified the thesis statement and supporting evidence in their classmates' papers. In the Biology and Ethics lesson, the students gave as their article selection criteria concepts such as "clear statements" and "major and minor supporting details"—the very elements they had been learning to incorporate in their own writing. In many cases, the teachers' gestures and facial expressions further supported students' interpretation and learning of unfamiliar terms.

By identifying these patterns I do not mean to suggest that the use of CBI provides a panacea for simultaneously promoting language learning and conceptual development (though CBI contexts do provide highly contextualized opportunities for vocabulary learning). Rather, it is the teachers' expertise and pedagogical skills that provide the needed scaffolding for community college ESL students to grapple with sophisticated concepts and authentic materials such as those discussed in this chapter.

## Implications

A concern that is frequently raised about ESL teachers working with CBI (sometimes by the teachers themselves) is that they do not have the subject matter knowledge to teach the content in content-based curricula. In these six observations, that concern did not arise. In one case (the Biology and Ethics course), the ESL specialist and the discipline specialist were team teachers. In another (the Biology and the Environment course), the ESL course was linked to a biology course (i.e., the students were enrolled in both classes and the two professors coordinated their efforts). But in all six lessons, the teachers demonstrated deep personal interest and investment in the topics. In each case, the ESL teachers seemed confident and sufficiently knowledgeable at the level needed for these lessons. They were quite capable of explaining the needed vocabulary and/or dealing with the discourse conventions of the genre and the discipline.

The research question posed at the beginning of this chapter asked how community college ESL teachers in CBI courses address language issues when the focus is on content learning. The vignettes reported here provide brief descriptions of how six teachers managed the interplay of language and content. As noted, they used diverse strategies to help the students master both the language and the topical concepts, but the patterns summarized in Table 1.1 are those that predominated.

In each of these lessons, I came away from the observation with the strong sense that the students had learned about both the language and the subject matter, and that they had also gained in confidence as learners of content, not just learners of English. The teachers' focus on language always arose from the texts the students were using and the tasks they were doing, but the language emphasis did not dominate the lessons. Instead, the focus shifted briefly but carefully to comments about grammar, discourse, or vocabulary (and in one case, pronunciation, and in another, spelling), and then back to the content topic and how language forms were used to convey content.

I no longer think of the "balance" between content and language with the image of a pendulum or a balancing scale. Instead, having carefully and respectfully watched these students and teachers in action, I see the intermittent but purposeful focusing on language elements in these content-based lessons as a skillful weaving or braiding of concepts, intertwining ideas and the language with which to express and understand them. The interplay of language and content in CBI is fluid, richly textured, and interwoven. My focus has shifted. I have abandoned the two-dimensional model of a pendulum or balancing scale for the more flexible image of CBI lessons as sewing or quilting, in which language issues permeate the conceptual issues, and bind together a complex fabric of learning opportunities. And, as with quilting, the result can be a unified artistic whole, made up of many different and originally disparate pieces.

# Chapter 2

# Content Teacher Perceptions of Content-Based Assignments in Writing Courses

■ Lara Ravitch

NUMEROUS RECENT REVIEWS OF LITERATURE IN THE FIELD OF TESOL SUGGEST THAT a content-based or topic-based curriculum is one of the most effective approaches to second-language teaching (Grabe & Stoller, 1997; Jourdenais & Shaw, 2005; Brinton, Snow, & Wesche, 1989). In brief, in an academic writing class, such a curriculum aims to provide students with assignments in which they use language to explore and learn a meaningful body of knowledge. Thus, rather than writing about what they already know, learners in a content-based class read about a topic (or topics) of interest to them (individually or as a class) and use the knowledge gained in that research to write a paper. This approach, then, uses writing in the same way that it is used in a science or history class: Students write in order to learn, rather than simply learning to write.

In higher education, both applied linguistics research and basic composition research suggest that the types of papers that students write in their language and composition classes ought to reflect the types of papers that they are required to write in content courses (Ferris & Hedgcock, 1998; Stoller & Grabe, 1997). This suggestion reflects the rejection of the traditional hierarchical model of learning, in which students must learn certain basic forms (e.g., the word, the sentence, the paragraph, the five-paragraph essay) in a certain order before attempting more advanced analytical writing. Instead, the new model suggests that students should holistically learn skills for the disciplines, contextualized within the genera expected in content courses. Thus, for example, rather than writing descriptive essays in composition courses, students would write lab reports or ethnographic studies, as they eventually will need to do in mainstream biology or anthropology classes.

Clearly there are many benefits of interdisciplinary writing, and CBI has been used to varying degrees, and in varying formats, depending on the needs of the context (see Bailey, this volume). This chapter examines the application of a content-based approach to community college writing instruction as a means to preparing students for writing in the disciplines.

## Context of the Research

The context for this study is Truman College, a large, urban community college based in Chicago, Illinois, with an extremely diverse student body. Like many community colleges across the country, much of its diversity comes from its substantial immigrant population, most representatives of which are English language learners (ELLs). Many of these students are refugees or have experienced interrupted schooling. While this diversity is enriching and exciting, both for faculty and students, it consistently presents difficulties for classroom instruction and challenges for building effective learning environments. Even trained ESL teachers find the diversity of linguistic and educational background challenging, while content teachers in the disciplines sometimes resort to simplified multiple choice tests to minimize the demands of English use.

## Issues that Motivated the Research

Due to the challenges of this context, Truman has struggled to find the best way to use ESL classes to prepare ELLs for writing in the disciplines. Instructors are increasingly turning to CBI to improve instruction and help students make the gains in critical thinking and the ability to decode and construct texts that are necessary for them to succeed in writing in their content classes. There seem to be two persistent areas of struggle. First, there is the work of designing assignments that the students enjoy, that help them improve their English, that can be accomplished in the time allotted, and that place appropriate linguistic demands on learners. This part of the design process can be characterized as internal—that is, concerned primarily with the problems that occur within a single classroom, group of learners, and semester. The second concern is external—that is, concerned with how the learner who graduates from an ESL content-based course may perform in his or her future content classes in other disciplines. Although the focus of this paper is primarily on the latter question, and specifically on investigating how teachers of those future classes perceive these assignments, the internal questions must be answered before progressing to the external. Since these issues have already been the focus of a great deal of research and discussion (cf. Brinton & Holten, 2001; Swain, 1996; Wesche & Skehan, 2002; Grabe & Stoller, 1997), certain suggested methodologies and approaches have already come to be defined as best practices.

There are many approaches to CBI that are currently in popular use, and they have been categorized in a variety of ways. The type of CBI commonly in use at Truman is what Babbitt, Mlynarczyk, Murie, and Wald (2004) call theme-based instruction. This approach is ideal for stand-alone ESL classes with diverse students because it strives to cover general topics of interest to all students.

Babbitt et al. (2004) distinguish among three types of theme-based instruction: sustained content, short-term content, and umbrella content. According to these authors, in *sustained content,* the entire class studies one content area (e.g., psychology) for a semester, with all students doing the same assignments. A class might spend three weeks on a paper about B. F. Skinner, three weeks on Ivan Pavlov, and three weeks on Sigmund Freud. This type of content is often most associated with English for Specific Purposes (ESP), but has also been used in English for Academic Purposes (EAP) with students from varied backgrounds. However, there are concerns that lengthy focus on a specific area that is not inherently interesting to all students might not be effective (Valentine & Repath-Martos, 1997). *Short-term content approach* avoids this problem by using various, unrelated topics, each studied by all students for a short period. For example, a class taught with the short-term content approach to curriculum development might cover three weeks on biodiversity in the Amazon, three weeks on the civil rights movement, and three weeks on gender-based differences in communication styles. In this manner, students with varied interests should each come into contact with something that engages them. However, there is some concern that such short-term, surface-level engagement with content is not enough to realize the benefits associated with sustained-content instruction (Murphy & Stoller, 2001). Finally, the *umbrella content approach* is designed to offer opportunities for every learner to examine one content area from separate perspectives that are interesting to each of them. Thus, the umbrella content approach avoids the pitfalls of sustained content, as well as those associated with short-term content. For example, all learners may study about psychology, but the class may spend a few weeks on social psychology, then psychiatric nursing, then the influence of technology on brain chemistry in an effort to make the topic relevant for students majoring in a variety of disciplines. Alternatively, students may study some basic principles of psychology as a group and then determine individual focus areas, so that students interested in chemistry, for example, might look at brain chemistry, while those hoping to become nurses could research issues in psychiatric nursing.

Another instructional approach that can be integrated with CBI is problem-based learning (PBL), an approach used in various disciplines (e.g., medical education, legal studies), which has as its underlying rationale the fairly intuitive belief that the skills one is taught in school are of little interest or use unless they are applied to the solution of authentic problems (Hmelo & Evenson, 2000). For student writers who often see writing as merely a requirement to prove to a teacher that they can meet her expectations (Elbow, 1981), a problem-based approach can be enlightening and empowering. Indeed, advocates of critical applied linguistics see problem posing as an essential element in students' assumption of agency and power (Benesch, 2001). Students in a problem-based classroom would thus have assignments such as researching an issue of social injustice and writing a paper in which they suggest a solution to this problem. In order to solve the problem, they would engage in rhetorical processes such as description, explanation, analysis, and argumentation, addressing their paper to a clear audience (perhaps fellow citizens, a governing body, or an academic organization). This approach organically provides them with a clear purpose—coming up with solutions to the problem. Because this process makes the *description* of the problem necessary to the *solution* of the problem, learners begin to see writing skills not merely as something they must do in order to pass a course, but as tools for making a change, pursuing understanding, and claiming a powerful role in the community.

Literature in CBI indicates that PBL is quite compatible with the approaches to CBI that seem appropriate to the community college EAP context, and indeed it is easier to integrate these two approaches than to attempt separate course designs. Stryker and Leaver (1997) note that higher-order thinking skills should be a central element of content-based courses. Stoller and Grabe (1997) suggest that learning tasks should increase in complexity, so that content is recycled and used for more and more complicated purposes. Certainly, problem-solving at different levels of complexity accomplishes this goal. Finally, Stoller (2002) suggests problem-solving sequences that require learners to synthesize information for multi-step projects.

In ESL, problem-based learning is often a part of project-based learning, which stems from a similar rationale: Language is learned best when it is put to use for a particular purpose. Donnelly and Fitzmaurice (2005) note that the two approaches are much alike, and are often used in combination. They suggest that in project-based work, learning is driven by the production of a final end product, whereas in problem-based work, learning is driven by the process of solving a problem. For example, in project-based learning, the focus may be on creating a poster, a film, or a website, while in problem-based learning, the focus might be on learning to identify a problem, understanding how to describe it clearly, and examining others' perspectives on the problem. Although this distinction has merit, the rationale for integrating the two approaches comes from the overlap that Donnelly and Fitzmaurice describe: Finding a solution, after all, can be considered a project, while creating projects typically involves at least one problem that needs to be solved.

## Research Questions Addressed

Following the recommendations and guidelines developed in the literature cited above, then, ESL teachers can design content-based assignments that address the internal concerns of the ESL class. The next step is to determine whether they are externally viable. That is, ESL teachers designing content-based lessons must ask whether the courses they have designed are in fact related to the work their students will actually do in their future content courses in their respective disciplines.

To pursue this line of inquiry, the present study focused primarily on these questions and sub-questions:

1. Which writing-related objectives in ESL content-based courses do content teachers in the disciplines see as important?

2. What perceptions of those assignments do content teachers in the disciplines have, specifically:

   a. Do they view the assignments as likely to develop reading, writing, and thinking skills that will be important in their own classes?

   b. Do they view the content of the assignments as appropriate to their disciplines?

   c. Do they view the structure of the assignments as similar to what students will be expected to face in content classes in their disciplines?

   d. Do they find certain types of assignments or course designs more effective than others?

## Data Collection and Analysis Procedures

In order to address these questions, I undertook a process of teacher inquiry, which was informal and exploratory at first but became more formalized and systematic as time went by. The data collection involved several steps. When I began to teach at Truman College, I collected data on content teachers' objectives through an email survey and a follow-up meeting. Then, I created several assignments based on these objectives (along with other criteria) that would use project- and problem-based learning to contextualize the content for the students in my ESL 100 (Advanced ESL Reading and Writing) and English 101 (College Composition) classes. In some instances, the regularly administered end-of-course student surveys contributed pertinent information. Finally, I investigated content teachers' perceptions of these assignments and how they might help students succeed in content classes.

I followed a series of steps in order to produce syllabi, activities, and assignments that use the suggestions and guidelines from ESL research for building appropriate content-based tasks and activities. First, following Stryker and Leaver's (1997) recommendations for building content-based curricula, I performed a needs analysis involving students, content teachers, and English teachers. I spoke to English teachers at a variety of levels and used department course guidelines to determine the objectives that were relevant for each level. From the students, I determined which subjects they were studying and where their career goals lay. Using that information, I selected teachers to interview in order to determine what types of writing—and what types of problem-solving—are done through writing in their respective disciplines and professions. Finally, I asked for recommendations of samples of the writing in those fields. After reading several such samples, I triangulated my analysis of the students and genera with the recommendations of the teachers.

The most widely represented professional interests of my ESL 100 and English 101 students were nursing and business. However, all Truman College students take a wide range of general education classes in areas such as math, humanities, and social science that do not have an English pre-requisite. Interviews with faculty in other disciplines determined that there were instructors in different areas who had a wide range of overlapping objectives, as well as some specific discipline-based objectives. After examining writing samples from different disciplines, I found that many of the professed goals of the instructors were related to the skills required by the writing assignments. The most prevalent among these were (1) summary, analysis (especially using the strategies of compare/contrast and cause/effect), (2) description (especially in lab reports and nursing charts), and (3) argumentation.

As I performed this iterative investigation over several semesters, I created and piloted a variety of problem-solving assignments using cross-disciplinary content that involved the same processes and requirements described above. I piloted these assignments in my ESL 100 and English 101 courses and then distributed materials to content instructors of my acquaintance using opportunistic sampling. The materials included assignment descriptions, supporting documents, and a Likert-scale survey with space for open-ended responses (see the Appendix, p. 36). The ten faculty members who agreed to participate in this more detailed part of the study were in the following disciplines: biology (3 participants), literature (2), social science (4), and business (1).

Eight participants returned in-depth responses to written surveys and, in some cases, in interviews either in person or by email. Participants were aware that their responses were not anonymous—indeed, some elected to complete even the initial survey by email.

## Findings

I will discuss the results of my investigation in terms of four courses that were influenced by this process. Three sections of ESL 100 (the Advanced ESL Reading and Writing course) and one section of English 101 (the College Composition course) figured in this process. Two offerings of the ESL 100 course centered around project-based learning. These were the International Problem Projects class and the Election Issue Projects class. Another version of ESL 100 was built around what I call discipline-based papers—those sorts of assignments students would encounter in their future (i.e., non-ESL) coursework. The English 101 class discussed involved students writing papers on Science & Society Problems.

## International Problem Projects (ESL 100)

This writing task in ESL 100 was a sustained-content assignment, in which each student was allowed to choose his or her semester-long content focus. Students chose an international issue to research (for example, government corruption in Bangladesh or human trafficking in Eastern Europe) and write about over the course of the semester. However, while all students chose different issues, the process that they used for writing (summarizing sources, writing an introduction to explain their issue, writing a body that explained the viewpoints of stakeholders in the issue, and writing an analytical conclusion that suggested a solution for the issue) was the same for each student. Because they completed the project in phases, they were able to handle the difficult task of a semester-long research paper. Additionally, because each student studied one topic all semester, they were able to derive the benefits associated with sustained content. They also avoided the pitfalls of traditional sustained-content courses (getting bored or feeling overly directed) since each student had chosen the content him/herself and therefore found it intrinsically motivating.

The social science teacher who specialized in teaching international relations strongly agreed that this assignment would help students acquire thinking skills, engage with reading, and learn to write appropriately. In a follow-up discussion, he also commented that his classes do not allow for writing multiple drafts and a peer feedback process, and that he believed students' experiences using these strategies in ESL classes would transfer easily to his classes because of the similarity in content.

## Science & Society Problem Papers (English 101)

In my English 101 course the following semester, I designed short-term content assignments, but in order to avoid the drawbacks associated with short-term content, I followed Stoller and Grabe's (1997) recommendations for using threads and transitions to link the separate topics. That is, our assignments highlighted common elements (threads) among the different topics. As we moved from one topic to another, we explicitly discussed the relationship between the topics (transitions). I used the textbook *Writing in the Disciplines: A Reader for Writers* (Kennedy, Kennedy, & Smith, 2003) and had the class vote on which issues they wanted to study. One class chose cloning, technology, families, and education, while the other chose cloning, families, race and class, and technology. The class read the articles about one issue in jigsaw format, sharing, discussing, summarizing, and responding to their readings. Then, I made prompts that integrated the readings into a real world scenario. In groups, students analyzed the scenarios, debated possible solutions to the problems posed, and researched the issue in greater depth. Then, individually, students wrote papers describing the scenario to a specific audience, outlining the various solutions, and finally recommending one alternative. After each paper, we moved on to the next issue, covering a total of four issues by the end of the semester.

The responses of instructors to these assignments were varied. A biology instructor strongly agreed that they would help prepare students for thinking, reading, writing, and understanding of content appropriate to his discipline. In response to the survey, he wrote that he was pleased that students would "write a proposal where terminology and writing style in biology are used." He also indicated that "the topics for the assignment are of great relevance to biology." Another biology teacher noted that, while the social issues in the articles we read would not be the focus of a biology class, the information was still relevant and the processes used, such as group discussions in support of competing hypotheses, were similar to those used in biology classes.

On the other hand, a professor from social sciences—while agreeing or strongly agreeing that the assignments would develop appropriate thinking, reading, and writing skills—was concerned that the content was too advanced for students and that they would have difficulty thinking critically about the topics at hand. However, in my experience using these materials, students were challenged, but by the end of the extensive research and analysis process, were able to think outside of their preconceptions and write intelligent problem-solving proposals. In a post-survey discussion with the social science professor, I explained the lead-up to the assignment that the students undergo, and the professor immediately recognized that this process would alleviate the concerns he had initially expressed. Another social science professor pointed out that his assignments typically expected students in his classes to be competent researchers and writers already, and thus he would not think to include the steps of the research writing process in his assignments. However, in looking at the ESL assignments I had developed, the professor said that he thought that assignments were similar to those he assigned in his classes and, in fact, that he would like to adapt and incorporate some of the ESL assignments into his classes.

## Election Issue Projects (ESL 100)

The Election Issue Projects in ESL 100 was an "umbrella content" assignment, in which the whole class centered around a discussion of values and the presidential election of 2004 in the United States. However, students chose specific election topics to focus on for the semester. Their final product was a paper that analyzed the voting patterns of the American people from the perspective of American values. First, students explored the concept of values and wrote papers about values that were important to them. Then, they read *Newsweek* articles about the upcoming election and identified election issues. Next, the students explored issue-related websites and chose an election issue to research. They then wrote the introduction to their final paper, explaining what the issue was and what positions the Democratic candidate, John Kerry, and the opposing Republican candidate, George W. Bush, took on the issue. After this, they wrote a paper explaining two values that were important to them and how those values would influence their vote on a particular issue. Next, as a class, the students and I read parts of the Constitution, the students interviewed U.S. citizens, and we extracted a list of American values that seemed evident both in the Constitution and in the interviewees' responses (e.g., equality). Finally, each student wrote a paper analyzing an issue he or she had chosen according to two American values he or she chose (e.g., freedom of speech and equality) from a list of many that had been identified by the class as a whole. In their papers, the students were asked to predict the way the American public would likely vote, according to the given set of values.

This series of assignments was evaluated by the various faculty members as building thinking, writing, and reading skills that would help a student in the social sciences. One informant expressed concerns about the wording of a sample topic sentence within the response ("Stem cell research uses embryonic cells to study diseases") because it did not discuss the difference between adult stem cells and embryonic stem cells. As I noted in the earlier discussion of the Science & Society assignment, this instructor expressed a similar fear that the students would not be able to handle the content knowledge involved in the assignment. Interestingly, he suggested that, rather than helping students complete a complex analytical assignment by modeling a sample topic, it would be better if they did an easier assignment. However, in a separate survey of student response to these assignments, only two out of approximately 25 students found this complicated assignment to be "confusing," and most students said they learned analytical writing skills that they were then able to parlay into success on the exit exam, and presumably in future courses where writing is not supported.

## Discipline-Based Papers (ESL 100)

This was an umbrella content course that sought to expose students to more of the types of papers they might write in a variety of courses. For this reason, the umbrella content was education, and each unit focused on different elements or disciplines of education (technology, health, humanities, and business). Informants from the various disciplines were generally positive. The two literature professors "strongly agreed" or "agreed" that the assignment would build thinking, writing, and reading skills, as well as acquisition of content knowledge, that would be helpful in future literature classes. One professor cited the "analysis, creative responses, independent thinking, and ability to make connections" as being particularly helpful skills. For the biology assignment, the informants "strongly agreed" that the assignment would develop thinking, reading, and writing skills, in addition to acquisition of content knowledge that was appropriate for the discipline. One participant noted that the genre of "report" was one that students needed to know and that this preparation would help them for future reports. The business professor "strongly agreed" that the writing skills developed in the assignment would be appropriate preparation for an introductory course, although the readings were not specialized enough. Similarly, she stated that the content knowledge and structure of the assignment might be appropriate for an introductory business course but not for a more specialized class.

## Implications

The perceptions of these assignments from the content teachers in the disciplines were overwhelmingly favorable. Not only did almost all teachers "agree" or "strongly agree" that the assignments would prepare students for the skills and knowledge they would need, but many teachers also noted that their own classes were not able to support students' writing development to a great degree. These findings strongly support the use of well-designed content-based assignments in ESL classes; after all, if students are not going to learn to write a biology paper in biology class, then such instruction lies with ESL and English faculty.

The subject teachers in this study seemed to believe that students' writing was at a fixed point when the students came to their classes. The most common perspective on this belief was idealistic, with faculty members expecting students to have developed strong writing skills and to need little or no assistance with their writing. A different perspective, voiced by only one of the participants, is that students have poor writing skills and that any writing assigned in his classes must fit within their existing abilities. The comments made by this participant raise questions about where the responsibility lies for addressing the writing needs of ELLs. One interpretation of these remarks underscores the necessity for doing complex content-based assignments in English and ESL classes, because those may be the only places where students will encounter instructors who will teach them how to increase the complexity of their writing through modeling. Another interpretation might point to a need for increased training in and emphasis on writing instruction for teachers in the discipline.

This study, of course, is very small, with limited applicability to other contexts. However, the near uniformity of the responses from the content teachers in the disciplines is encouraging. It indicates that further research in this area is likely to support the idea that content-based assignments that follow the recommendations of TESOL literature and are attentive to the stated goals of content classes will be well perceived by content course instructors in the disciplines.

Learning about these reactions and perceptions should not be the end of the collaboration, however. Rather, ESL instructors should continue to redesign assignments to fit the expectations of teachers in the disciplines and to offer their own content-based assignments for adaptation by content instructors. Through increased collaboration, not only may ESL teachers improve their assignments, but they may also encourage content teachers to re-examine the ways their classes approach reading and writing.

# Appendix

**Content Teacher Survey on Effectiveness of Content- and Problem-Based Writing Assignments**

Directions: Please indicate your level of agreement with the statements below, and write specific comments to explain your choice.

1. This assignment will help develop thinking skills that are appropriate to my discipline.

   Strongly Agree          Agree          Disagree          Strongly Disagree

   Comments:

2. This assignment will help develop writing skills that are appropriate to my discipline.

   Strongly Agree          Agree          Disagree          Strongly Disagree

   Comments:

3. This assignment will help develop reading skills that are appropriate to my discipline.

   Strongly Agree          Agree          Disagree          Strongly Disagree

   Comments:

4. This assignment is similar to an assignment that a student in my discipline might be asked to do.

   Strongly Agree          Agree          Disagree          Strongly Disagree

   Comments:

5. This assignment involves acquisition of content knowledge that a student in my discipline might be expected to know.

   Strongly Agree          Agree          Disagree          Strongly Disagree

   Comments:

# Chapter 3

# "A Long Little Story": Exploring the Experiences of Nursing Students as English Language Learners

■ JoAnn Mulready-Shick

Y EARS AGO AS A YOUNG COLLEGE NURSING STUDENT, I RECALL PROVIDING HOME CARE for a family who predominantly spoke Spanish, yet the family's first grader was attending an English-only elementary school. She brought home a school informational sheet for her parents, who expressed frustration at being unable to read it. As I loosely translated the sheet for her parents, attempting to provide some language assistance by taking on the role of a go-between, I began to think about how educational systems did not reach out to non-native English–speaking students and families, expecting them to change and adapt to an unfamiliar educational environment.

## Context of the Research

Throughout the past twenty years, I have often wrestled with concerns related to learning, language, identity, and borderlands. *Borderlands* have been described as being "physically present wherever two or more cultures edge each other, where people of different races occupy the same territory, where under, lower, middle, and upper classes touch, where the space between two cultures shrinks with intimacy" (Anzaldúa, 1999, p. 19). As a nursing professor and researcher, my interest in a deeper understanding of how students experience possibly similar concerns in the nursing classroom has steadily grown.

I have instructed predominantly immigrant community college students who are learning nursing in an English-speaking classroom and are preparing to work primarily in predominantly English-speaking environments. Although many have spoken some English for a number of years, their formal study of the language has often been well in the past. I have witnessed students with limited academic language proficiency experience ongoing, numerous, persistent learning challenges, despite fairly well developed interpersonal communicative skills. I have provided students with support, encouragement, and grammatical and contextual language assistance that I often take for granted as a native English speaker. Simultaneously, I have observed students working with diligence to achieve their academic goals, some academically succeeding while others struggle and depart from the academic setting.

In community colleges today, students often choose nursing or other health career options as career choices and planned courses of study, a good sign given that the current workforce shortage is predicted to worsen over the next twenty years as the majority of practicing nurses retire. Yet large numbers of qualified applicants are either turned away from community college nursing programs or waitlisted, due primarily to acute faculty shortages. Given this reality, it is especially relevant to focus on the academic success of students currently enrolled in nursing education programs. Nurses educated in community colleges play an essential role in meeting the public's need for nurses as more than 60 percent of all U.S. nurses and allied health professionals are educated in this higher education sector (American Association of Community Colleges, 2007).

Nursing students educated in community colleges mirror the general community college student population; many are older, have important family and financial commitments, and come from increasingly diverse ethnic and linguistic backgrounds. Students with limited English language proficiency face major challenges in attaining academic success in nursing programs (Abriam-Yago, Yoder, & Kataoka-Yahiro, 1999; Guhde, 2003). Students with limited English proficiency, or more accurately, English language learners (ELLs), are individuals who have limited ability in speaking, reading, writing, or understanding the English language, speak a native language other than English, or live in a family or community environment in which a language other than English is the dominant language (U.S. Department of Education, 1998). The need for graduates to possess both greater English proficiency and multilingualism in health care careers, such as nursing, is growing in importance in an expanding multicultural, global society.

Hence, I was drawn to study the lived experiences of nursing students as ELLs. The philosophical perspective I brought to this study mattered because "everywhere, wherever, and however we are related to beings of every kind, we find identity making its claim on us" (Heidegger, 1969, p. 26). As an upper–middle class, white, monolingual woman with limited conversational Spanish abilities, my identity resembles that of many nursing educators. But seeing many sides and living between different worlds, including thinking about and responding to learning and academic issues, is part of my daily experience as an educator and nursing program director.

A recent interaction with a student further illustrates why this study became increasingly meaningful to me. Most of the students with whom I have interacted can be identified as multicultural and multilingual, with backgrounds that are different from mine. Yet we share common goals: learning and success. During my office hours one day, a student came by for extra help in understanding her multiple choice exam results. As she sat down, she remarked in a matter-of-fact way, "Well, you know, I *am* ESL." Although I told her that I had not known her language background until that moment, I didn't ask her what she meant by "I am ESL." I hadn't heard much of an accent or noticed much non-standard variation in her writing.

Later, I thought about her statement "I am ESL," considering it as something so obvious but which strikes me as something very profound. I thought of all of the students I had taught and how I had not thought seriously about the experiences of ESL students, or students who are not only working hard to learn nursing, but who also are working hard to learn, write, and speak more English. Upon reflecting on the student's statement, a quotation by Heidegger (1968/1993) came to mind: "What gives us this gift, the gift of what must properly be thought about, is what we call most thought provoking" (p. 381).

Therefore I was drawn to designing this study from an interpretive phenomenological, or hermeneutic, perspective. I was also drawn to studying the phenomenon—the lived experiences of nursing students as ELLs—from a critical perspective. Hermeneutics "[allows] oneself to be drawn into the complexity of the simple and overlooked" (Diekelmann & Magnussen-Ironside, 1998, p. 244); in other words, this approach brings out and makes manifest what is normally hidden in human experience and human relations by looking for meanings embedded in participants' narratives, both commonalities and differences. Hermeneutics "deconstructs the corresponding relationship between theory and practice and reveals the practical knowledge and expertise that evolves over time" (Magnussen-Ironside, 1998, p. 245). The goal of a critical hermeneutic inquiry, furthermore, is to make known the voices of persons who may not be considered members of privileged groups and who are often discounted (Lopez & Willis, 2004). Given my age, manner of speaking, and educational preparation, I needed to reflect on any inadvertent acts of oppression, which my position afforded me particularly during the study's data collection and analysis phases.

I approached this study from a constructivist perspective, that is, one in which participants create knowledge, understanding, and meaning acting in concert with one another in a particular time and place (Lave & Wenger, 1991). I sought and valued differing perspectives on the nursing students' experiences. Within this constructivist framework, learning is inextricably interconnected to previous schooling, within its specific historical context, and to current teaching practices. Consequently, I viewed students and faculty as learning together within socioculturally situated and pedagogically oriented environments.

To place oneself in a state of resonance with the other's situation and to give the other an opportunity to express her or his point of view is an awareness and connection described as *conocimiento* by the Mexican poet and feminist theorist Gloria Anzaldúa (2002). It is in the sharing, in the in-between world, in the seeing of many perspectives that the possibility for new learning, emancipation, and transformation takes place. There is much to learn from the stories of our students as lived in the classrooms we inhabit together.

## Issues that Motivated the Research

Even though English language acquisition and proficiency are widely viewed as vital components of educational attainment, many community college students, including nursing students, demonstrate limited English skills (Jackson & Sandiford, 2003; Szelenyi & Chang, 2002). Specifically, limited English language proficiency has been associated with higher attrition, lower nursing program completion rates, and lower scores on the national nursing licensure exam, thus impacting graduation and career attainment (Klisch, 2000; Malu & Figlear, 1998). Students *and* faculty are often unaware of the extent to which English language proficiency impacts student success (Abriam-Yago et al., 1999). Students acquiring English skills may benefit from supplemental instruction and innovative teaching strategies for ongoing language development including development of cognitive academic language proficiency. Yet programmatic attention to identifying students' needs and changing pedagogical practices for outcome improvement in community college nursing programs remains largely ignored.

Language proficiency is basic to the development of new knowledge, skills, values, and ways of thinking, which are essential elements of learning and success in education environments for all students. What is distinctive about nursing and other health education programs is that students find themselves engaged in multiple forms of communication and associated languages and literacies that are commonly practiced in written and spoken modes, across all settings in nursing academia and health care. For example, on a daily basis in the clinical setting, nurses are expected to provide accurate and concise written documentation about patients' conditions in the computerized medical record, as well as to communicate verbally, succinctly, and precisely via the phone to a variety of health care personnel. At the same time, they must provide easy-to-understand instructions to patients about to be discharged.

Furthermore, academic activities within college nursing programs are considered cognitively demanding, requiring conscious focus on understanding language and concepts. Nursing students often learn in "context-reduced" communicative situations, such as attending large lecture classes and reading complex texts, which present few contextual clues and are linguistically demanding (Abriam-Yago et al., 1999). For example, nursing books contain voluminous amounts of written text with little associated visual imagery, in which reading levels exceed high school expectations. Comprehension and application of such information, nonetheless, are necessary for nursing practice. Interpretation of context-reduced communicative situations depends on the student's knowledge of the language (Cummins & Schecter, 2003; Fillmore & Snow, 2000; Santos, 2004). Given these conditions, ELLs may face greater challenges than their native English–speaking classmates.

To address these learning needs, varied teaching strategies have been recommended, including use of note-taking guides and academic language fluency handouts for new or difficult vocabulary, using consistent outlines, speaking at a slower pace in lectures, examining reading levels of recommended textbooks, and providing additional time on exams (Flinn, 2004; Guhde, 2003; Klisch, 2000). Although some nursing faculty members possess an understanding of strategies helpful in teaching culturally diverse students (including ELL students), many have yet to employ such strategies (Flinn, 2004). Consequently, the majority of learning environments reflect neither heightened faculty awareness nor innovative teaching practices.

A desire to implement innovative teaching techniques in the linguistically diverse classroom is seldom identified as a main interest within health care academe. Correspondingly, faculty indifference and resistance are often viewed as obstacles to changing pedagogical practice (Bok, 2006; Pardue, Tagliareni, Valiga, Davison-Price, & Orehowsky, 2005). Moreover, most educators have yet to acquire an expertise in multilingualism (Cummins & Schecter, 2003). Compounding these concerns are nurse educators, who, like other higher education faculty, hold advanced degrees in disciplinary work but rarely in education or linguistic studies. Given academic and disciplinary priorities, the needs of ELLs in nursing programs have yet to rise to the top.

## Sociocultural Context of Learning and Success

A closer examination of faculty practices shifts the dialogue from the needs of particular students to more complex issues, including the interaction of faculty and students in the educational environment and the social and cultural contexts of learning (Braxton, 2000; Shaw, Valadez, & Rhoads, 1999). In this context, *culture* is defined as "the shared values and beliefs that serve four purposes: to convey a sense of identity, to facilitate commitment to an entity other than self such as a college, to enhance the stability of a group's social system, and to provide a sense-making device that guides and shapes behavior" (Rendón, Jalomo, & Nora, 2002, p. 136). Culture plays a central role in the classroom, but an increasing number of nursing students enrolled in community colleges come from cultural backgrounds different from the majority of faculty. Ninety percent of nursing faculty are characterized as white, middle class, English-only speakers who are 50 years of age or older and have received little or no preparation in teaching students with cultural backgrounds different from their own (Branch, 2001).

Nursing faculty often lack an awareness that the educational setting itself can disadvantage those from cultural backgrounds different from their own (Trueba & Bartolomé, 2000). Monocultural practices can minimize or ignore students' heritage and abilities and directly impede student success (Rendón, 1999). Both the lack of faculty understanding of cultural differences, along with student perceptions of hostility, prejudice, and racism, may account for significant barriers to student achievement (Campinha-Bacote, 1998; Hassouneh-Phillips, 2003).

A handful of nurse educators, however, have focused their research interests on faculty awareness and concerns about success for students from multicultural, multilingual backgrounds. Their work highlights faculty members, known as "bridging" or "bicultural" faculty, who do exemplify greater awareness of differing worldviews, are cognizant of their power dynamics in the classroom, and implement a variety of instructional strategies conducive to learning for students from diverse backgrounds (Kelley & Fitzsimons, 2000; Yoder, 1997). Additional findings highlight teachers who are implementing newer pedagogical practices, including narrative and critical pedagogies, that draw on student knowledge and shared experience to equalize power relationships in the classroom and enhance learning (Diekelmann & Lampe, 2004; Ironside, 2004; Mikol, 2005). These practices are currently carried out by a small, but reportedly increasing, number of innovative educators.

## Research Questions Addressed

Seeking a deeper understanding of educators' and students' experience in the community college nursing classroom brings forth many questions: *Do students see themselves as both nursing students and ELLs, and if so, what is the experience like to be both? Does it make sense to connect these two phenomena? Do the perceptions of a predominantly monolingual educator have any connection to what students themselves are experiencing?*

This study specifically focused on the experiences of six nursing students who were learning in an urban community college setting. Although teaching and learning occur across many sites in nursing, classrooms, labs, and clinical areas, and involve a broad host of participants, the classroom environment represents a common learning environment shared by large numbers of students. Centering on the phenomenon of the lived experience of students as ELLs and the concerns that shape their everyday realities in the nursing classroom, the research question posed was, "What does it mean to be a student learning nursing and English in the classroom?" Since ELLs have been reported to be a distinct group with specific concerns (National Clearinghouse for English Language Acquisition and Language Instruction Educational Programs, 2006; Szelenyi & Chang 2002), this inquiry focused exclusively on the perspectives of this particular group of nursing students in order to shed light on the phenomenon of the ELL experience and related concerns about student experience, learning environments, and academic success.

## Data Collection and Analysis Procedures

The object of inquiry for the human sciences, such as nursing and education, is the reality of human experience, both that which is present and that which is hidden from awareness. Ontologically, the most critical order of reality is in its meaning. In the human sciences, "understanding is considered more powerful than explanation and prediction because it stands more fully in the human world of self-understandings, meanings, skills, and traditions" (Dreyfus, 1994, p. xv). The focus on experience and meaning, or what it means *to be*, describes phenomenological inquiry both philosophically and methodologically.

This investigation elicited students' stories or narratives of everyday experiences through audiotaped one-hour interviews. I adapted the phases of text analysis described in Crist and Tanner (2003). I transcribed each audiotape verbatim and thus remained close to the oral rendering. Next, I read the interview transcripts in their entireties, and I wrote interpretive summaries following every two interviews. I named portions of the text for central concerns in order to portray examples of patterns of meaning and context. I identified themes, or broad sweeping descriptions of what stands out to the interpreter, within each text as well as across texts. I also wrote a summary or a written interpretation of the themes with supporting exemplars from each interview. This process continued until no new themes emerged from the data.

The heart of hermeneutics is the interpretation of the text. The hermeneutic circle, with its non-linear and continuous nature, involves writing, thinking, reading, and dialogue. During this period, further reading of relevant works and dialogue with others research team members were sought to extend understandings. Texts were further interpreted from a critical hermeneutic perspective, by probing beneath the surface of narratives and considering embedded issues of power and struggle.

In my study, the participants were community college students enrolled in an urban nursing program in New England who had completed foundational courses in college-level English, arts, and sciences. Participants had been selectively admitted to a nursing program and had successfully completed at least one foundational nursing course, equivalent to completion of one year of study. Volunteers self-identified as ELLs. To address the research question, "What does it mean to be a student learning nursing and English in the classroom?" during the face-to-face interviews, participants were asked to share a story that reminded them of what it meant to be learning English and nursing at the same time. To stay true to the narrative interpretive interviewing process, I aimed to remain focused on the students' experiences and steered clear of directing the interview as much as possible. I took brief notes before each interview and wrote up my reflections after each one to foster self-awareness (Smith, B.A., 1999).

## Findings

At the time of this writing, the analysis is still underway, so in this section, I will present some preliminary answers to my research questions (see Mulready-Shick, 2008, for complete study). These initial findings suggest that nursing students as ELLs share common everyday concerns. These concerns include recognizing the need to alter their study skills by increasing academic learning time to accommodate both their ongoing English language development and the voluminous amount of nursing disciplinary content. All students raised concerns about classroom and testing practices and about not having the time needed to digest the volume of assigned nursing readings. Working for economic survival and its impact on academic achievement weighed more heavily on some participants than others. Language concerns varied too, depending on the extent of cognitive academic language competency acquired.

Learning new terminology was but an early building block in comprehension and development of conceptual wholeness, and participants created highly individualized approaches to enhance knowledge and understanding. To develop academic and health care language proficiency, participants reported numerous innovative strategies. Strategies varied among the individual participants. Strategies familiar to all included looking up new words, underlining key concepts in readings, and reading many times. They also remarked that pictures, audiovisuals, videos, and audio helped in learning the language of nursing and health care.

The following exemplars illustrate the innovative strategies developed. One 30-year-old second-year nursing student, who came to the United States in her teens with very little formal study of the English language, detailed various inventive ways that aided her language development and learning. Strategies ranged from using an online dictionary, learning from the Internet and television, and creating mnemonics, pictures, and stories to construct visual representations. This participant relates many of the strategies that characterize essential knowledge gained along the way.

> Because my language comes from the Latin, somehow, it helps just knowing the Latin prefix, then I can look at the word, and go, Oh that has something to do with . . . , you know? That's where medical terminology comes in handy because I try to look at the Latin because that is how each word is made up. So then I can put it together. I make up little things. Like say for example, "parasympathetic."

Parasympathetic makes everything slower, right? So "para," P A R A [*spells out the letters*] in my language it means "stop." So when I am thinking of the signs and symptoms of parasympathetic, I remember, "slowing down, stopping." That's how I bring my language into it, you know.

I do go on Wikipedia.org and sometimes that helps with pictures and the meanings of the words, you click on it and the meanings of the words comes up so along with the pictures, Internet sites help a lot. You know I am just trying to make sense out of simple words. Not elaborate, you know, vocabulary, what the pathophysiology is of a certain disease—simple words. It can be a story, you can just make up a little story. I made up one for the thyroid. But it was a long little story. At the time I made up a bunch of little stories that I studied making those little connections, but then I don't go back and look at it. I just think it just helps me learn, to connect the stuff and it just helps me to process.

I also use the Discovery Health Channel . . . I was just looking at "Mystery Diagnosis." They don't tell you the diagnosis right at the beginning. They were talking about . . . describing [all the symptoms] . . . And I said, . . . "that has to do with the adrenal glands." And it was funny because I picked up even before they said. But that is the visual part. The visual part that I am trying to connect—the visual, the language and I am able to process the information I learned. Now I can see it because I have gone through it . . . you know. Now it is easy if I have a mental picture of the brain, the body, then I can see where it affects, you know, so I can pinpoint. So it's almost imaginary, the visual.

For nursing interventions, you know, it's funny when they [the faculty] are talking in class and you don't see a real person. . . . But when you *see* it and you are looking at a real human being, then the words become clear on your mind what it is. Maybe it has something to do with the English, maybe it doesn't. But I think it does. You have now *seen* the words. . . .

Not only did participants learn new methods while studying, but they also created adjustments during class time, such as taking notes sparingly and taping lectures. Just the process of writing in class and figuring out new words often proves daunting. The adjustments made by this participant to meet her language challenges were expressed in her decision to tape all classes. To have time during class to listen, to jot down only a few notes, and to have the time to think, comprehend, and pull it all together, worked well for her.

That's why I tape. The reason is because I have to think about the writing when I am writing it, the words. Sometimes I forget the spelling of words. And I don't know if it has to do with the English or, you know, or just part of who I am. And so when they [the faculty lecturing] are saying and I have to write I have to process what they are saying so either I have to pay attention to what [I am] saying or I have to pay attention to what I am writing. . . .

Thank goodness nothing goes wrong with the tape [laughs] because I don't take notes [laughs]. That's how I do it. I just listen and don't write. Sometimes I just write letters, [motions as if writing a letter of the alphabet] like, things so I can remember, just say—Oh this is important so I write a letter. Like words to remind me so when I go transcribe the tape, word by word [laughs]. Yeah, I do. It takes up a long time. I just don't listen. I go through the tape and I have like, this semester I have a whole bunch of stuff, like I have this much [creates a motion for a large amount] of everything.

Transcribing five hours of lecture per week, likely fifteen hours or more, significantly extended her learning time. Yet the combination of these strategies was yielding positive results. Although this portrayal demonstrated the unique style of one participant, increasing study time and making numerous adjustments in study habits was a familiar theme for all participants who were making academic progress as nursing students and ELLs. Yet at the same time, participants remarked that those who did not increase their study time were often less successful.

What is also revealed in these narratives are classroom practices impeding learning. Participants recounted how faculty lectured non-stop, plowing ahead with more and more content. Often lecture slides contained few visual clues. Time was not spent on assessing learning, gathering feedback, or asking questions. Within these narratives were student voices highlighting exemplars of classroom practices that minimized learning opportunities and thwarted academic progress.

Students revealed themselves as powerful knowers. The negative impact of lecturing and the positive impact of media, technology, visual imagery, and stories on learning give faculty much to consider in altering teaching methods. Students implored faculty to move beyond traditional means and provide greater innovation, suggesting greater use of visualization and multiple means of representation.

These exemplars offer a glimpse into the heuristic knowledge that participants developed over the course of time in the nursing program. My preliminary analysis suggests that by listening to students, faculty members have much to learn about teaching, learning, and student success. Faculty awareness is generally limited to how actively or passively students participate and how well they perform on writing assignments and exams (Stasinopoulos, 2006). By exploring students' experiences, however, faculty can learn much more about the common concerns that shape their everyday lives.

Finding the time to ask students, "What does it mean *to be* a nursing student and an ELL?" reveals unexpected insights into how students learn best. Creating the space to invite students into this type of dialogue allows for that which is most meaningful to come forth.

## Implications for Policy and Practice

A study like this one, focusing on student learning in the classroom, prompts deliberation of several policy implications. Policymakers claim interest in retaining and graduating greater numbers of students from diverse backgrounds. Yet the American Council on Education's (ACE) Center for Advancement of Racial and Ethnic Equity 2004 Report, reflecting on the minority experience in higher education over the past twenty years, concluded that the country's future competitiveness is likely to falter if students with English language needs under-perform in college and graduation rates show little improvement (American Council on Education, 2004).

Moreover, in an increasingly competitive enrollment environment, current nursing school admission practices jeopardize the selection of students from racially, ethnically, and linguistically diverse backgrounds (Belack, 2005; Mulready-Shick, 2005, National Advisory Council on Nurse Education and Practice, 2000). In an era of growing regulation from multiple stakeholders, state boards of higher education, state boards of nursing, and national accrediting bodies expect schools to demonstrate and quantify higher levels of performance and quality. Schools respond accordingly to external pressure and tighter controls by altering practices. For example, schools may raise admissions criteria and choose applicants based solely on quantifiable data, such as those with the highest grade point averages and nursing admission exam scores—in other words, by selecting only those who perform best on standardized English, reading, math, and science exams.

Therefore, ELLs are further jeopardized as such policies act as barriers for those without the highest grades and most well developed test-taking skills. Consequently, students from under-represented backgrounds as well as those considered educationally disadvantaged are and will continue to be placed at an even greater disadvantage (Belack, 2005). Similarly, successful program completion for enrolled students from under-represented backgrounds or who are educationally disadvantaged is increasingly threatened. As schools are mandated to conform to predetermined outcome measures, such as higher nursing licensure exam pass rates, stricter standards are often enacted in course and graduation requirements, such as requiring higher passing grades or high-stakes course and program exit exams. As administering greater numbers of multiple choice exams becomes the standard for measuring learning and defining academic progression, completion and graduation rates for students with continuing English language developmental needs are further impacted. At the same time, a handful of nursing education experts continues to raise questions about the problematic practice of high-stakes multiple choice testing and its relationship to thinking, learning, caring, and performing safely in practice (del Bueno, 2005; Ironside, 2004).

Assisting students from culturally and linguistically diverse backgrounds to successfully complete educational programs in order to enter nursing practice remains a continuing challenge for the majority of nurse educators (Fletcher, Beacham, Elliott, Northington, Calvin, Hill, et al., 2003; Newman & Williams, 2003). There is good reason for concern about nursing students' experiences in educational settings, classroom practices, and academic achievement, particularly for ELLs, both now and for the foreseeable future. Hence, studying the lived experiences of students in the nursing education setting is germane for the many reasons enumerated in this chapter. The perspectives of students as ELLs is a particular area of research cited by the literature in need of greater attention. Additional research exploring the everyday lives of ELLs in the classroom may reveal new understandings about student experience, learning, and college success.

The ability to significantly change classroom practices lies within our horizons. In this study—even in the midst of their busy lives—participants eagerly shared their daily concerns along with their desire to become more active participants in enhancing learning environments. Students' narratives bring to our awareness concerns that may be invisible to the educator teaching from a monocultural or monolingual perspective. The power faculty hold in influencing the direction of learning in the classroom is revealed in these narratives. Faculty practicing from English-only perspectives are likely unknowingly limiting learning in the classroom by not employing a wider range of alternative pedagogical practices. The students' stories enable English-only educators to cross boundaries and experience the classroom from fresh perspectives. I firmly believe that it is our moral imperative as faculty members to bring to light practices that possibly advantage certain groups over others. From listening to narratives of nursing students as ELLs, possibilities emerge for innovative practices and opportunities for faculty and students to become co-creators in designing and enhancing learning experiences for all.

# Part 2
## Technology in Community College ESL Programs

# Chapter 4

# Community College ESL Learners' Access to and Perspectives on Technology

■ Cristie Roe

T HE INCREDIBLE PACE OF TECHNOLOGICAL INNOVATION IN THE AMERICAN EDUCATIONAL system has a major impact on students and educators at all levels, but most notably in community colleges (cf. Levin, 2000; Rhoades, 1998). While we, as educators, are adapting our curricula and teaching methods to these continuously changing technologies, we must make an effort to reflect on and investigate the effects of these innovations on our students. Nowhere is this effort more important than in the teaching of ESL, since methods of instruction can seriously impact second language learners' affective responses to the language, and their progress in mastering it (Kumaravadivelu, 2006). As Barakzai and Fraser (2005) note, "It is imperative that no group be disadvantaged by a particular curricular delivery method" (p. 373). And students learning English as a second language, particularly those students who come from less technologically advanced societies, may find the dual tasks of learning English and mastering computer technology overwhelming. Therefore, this study seeks to provide insights into ESL learners' interactions with technology in community college courses, and how they feel about the requirement that they develop both language and technology competencies simultaneously.

## Context of the Research

M any students in First World nations "now inhabit classrooms that are equipped with computers, Internet connections, desktop publishing capabilities, interactive multimedia learning resources, and Computing and Communication Technologies (CCT) that include new e-tools and genres" (Labbo, 2006, p. 204).

However, students in less developed countries often have relatively little or no access to up-to-date computer technology, especially if they come from working-class or impoverished neighborhoods. For example, Aduwa-Ogiegbaen and Iyamu (2006) maintain that Nigerian high school students are at a severe disadvantage when they attempt to study English at the post-secondary level because they lack exposure to, and experience with, computers in the classroom. In addition, "older non-traditional students have often completed their prior education before the common use of computers and may find the technology . . . daunting" (Barakzai & Fraser, 2005, p. 375). It is precisely these students, the less affluent, less edu-cated, non-traditional students, who make up the bulk of community college ESL enrollment in Phoenix. Unlike universities, whose foreign student bodies tend to be dominated by youth from middle- to upper-class families with at least K–12 schooling experience, community colleges in many parts of the United States gener-ally draw most of their non–native English speaking students from lower-income immigrant populations who either cannot afford university tuition or cannot pass the entrance requirements of a university due to a lack of preparatory schooling in their native countries (Levin, 2000).

Yet community college students must be able to adapt to computer-enhanced learning since community colleges are in the vanguard of technological cur-ricular innovation (Levin, 2000). Indeed, "there is an expectation that computers are superior cognitive tools and that employing them will improve instruction" (Menager-Beeley, 2001, paragraph 1), an expectation that those of us who teach in community colleges find especially prevalent.

Among the benefits that faculty and administrators believe students will gain from computer use are (a) development of "technological skills that will be required of literate, globally active citizens of the future" (Labbo, 2006, p. 206); (b) access to limitless amounts of online materials and information (Skehan, 2003); (c) the ability to "gather information to produce creative work" (Calderon-Young, 1999, p. 168) that can be shared easily with classmates; (d) increased confidence and self-esteem (Lai & Kritsonis, 2006); and (e) efficient and successful mastery of the English language (Al-Jarf, 2002). The latter is attributed to several reasons. Com-puter use is believed to "support students' development of . . . core literacy skills" (Labbo, 2006, p. 202), develop students' ability "to analyze and interpret complex information that is presented in an ever-changing series of linked modalities" (Labbo, 2006, p. 205), and increase problem-solving ability (Wetzel & Chisolm, 1998). Furthermore, language education research suggests that students of foreign languages learn best when they are focused on a task that uses the target language, rather than on the language itself, and computer-assisted instruction has been shown to facilitate task-based learning in second-language classes (Kumaravadivelu, 2006; Skehan, 2003; Warschauer, 2005).

Despite the promise and some evidence of enhanced academic and social achievement associated with computers in the classroom, there are reasons for concern that perhaps colleges are innovating too rapidly, without taking adequate time for evaluation of new technologies' effects on student learning. For instance, one drawback to computer-enhanced instruction is the increased cost it generates in higher education (Lai & Kritsonis, 2006). This expense is particularly problematic in community colleges where so many of the students are working adults, often struggling to obtain basic necessities while paying for tuition, fees, and books. As a result, community colleges are generally under more pressure than universities to keep tuition and fees low, and this affects the amount and types of advanced technology that colleges can afford to purchase.

Another problem, especially for older students and those from less developed countries, is the difficulty of mastering even rudimentary computer use, such as word processing, while managing the subject matter in their courses. On this issue, Barakzai and Fraser (2005) observe that "at the same time [students] are trying to assimilate new terms and cope with a large amount of information, [they also] are expected to . . . analyze, synthesize, and evaluate" technology and online materials that "often contain words and phrases that are not commonly used in conversation" (p. 374).

In the same vein, Chisholm (1995/96) points out that "although computers and software convey a sense of objectivity and neutrality, they essentially are not culture-free" (Assertions and Questions, paragraph 1). That is, these tools are created, for the most part, by highly educated individuals in technologically advanced countries, and thus tend to reflect the values of the most powerful and privileged strata of those countries. Furthermore, while students do have individual learning styles, some cultures "exhibit learning style preferences" that tend to influence the group members' "preference for specific learning and cognitive styles" (Chisholm, 1995/96, paragraph 1).

Finally, Lai and Kritsonis (2006) contend that "computers cannot handle unexpected situations," because they process finite bits of data in formulaic ways (paragraph 4). Conversely, "second language learners' learning situations are various and ever changing" (Lai & Kritsonis, 2006, paragraph 4). Thus, the computer is unable to adapt itself to the student's needs, but rather requires the student to adapt to the technology. This situation places the burden entirely on the student to simultaneously learn about the demands of the technology and develop proficiency in both a foreign language and a new culture, which may be more than many students can handle. In contrast, however, Chapelle (2005) observes that technology may facilitate language learning with the introduction of hypermedia input modifications (e.g., use of visuals, hyperlinked definitions, or L1 translations) which help the learner to comprehend text. Clearly more research is needed to clarify the effects of these modifications.

For all of these reasons, it is necessary that we investigate ESL students' perceptions of computer use in their community college curricula. I have observed in my own ESL classes, which include immigrant students from every part of the world, that older students and students from less technologically developed areas struggle a great deal to master computer use while they are learning English. Many of these students have never even used a typewriter, and thus have never learned basic keyboarding. This gap makes the challenge of developing word processing skills while they are slowly acquiring fluency in English monumental indeed.

## Issues that Motivated the Research

In order to determine how ESL students feel about the challenge of using computers in their ESL classes, I conducted this study at Phoenix College in Phoenix, Arizona, during the Fall 2006 semester. Phoenix College is one of ten campuses that make up the Maricopa Community College District, which is now one of the largest community college systems in the United States. Phoenix College, the oldest of the ten campuses, has an annual enrollment of about 25,000 students, some 18 percent of which come from other countries (Phoenix College, 2007). Furthermore, as is the case in most community colleges across the country, Phoenix College is rapidly expanding the use of computer technology throughout all of its departments and courses. As a result, ESL students on this campus increasingly cannot avoid computer use of various types in their college coursework, including email messaging, basic word processing, and language exercises via software such as Rosetta Stone®. Students often need to read their instructors' PowerPoint presentations instead of handwritten notes on a chalk board, which likely would have been the typical mode of presentation in their native countries.

## Research Questions Addressed

The purpose of this study was to determine how the students felt about using computers in their community college ESL coursework. The specific questions that this study sought to address were:

1. What level of access and experience with computers did the ESL students have before coming to the United States?

2. How do most ESL students perceive the requirement that they use computers in their ESL grammar and writing courses? (Oral proficiency courses were not included in the study because, at the time of the study, only grammar and writing courses were using computers regularly in the classroom.)

Before answering these questions, some background information about the respondents is summarized.

## Data Collection and Analysis Procedures

During the Fall 2006 semester, a survey (see Appendix, page 61) was administered to the 654 students that were enrolled in ESL grammar or writing courses. It was distributed to the instructors of eleven courses, who administered the questionnaires during a class period and who then collected and sent them to the Office of Institutional Research (OIR). A total of 178 surveys (27 percent) were returned. The survey asked questions about the students' background and their experience with computers in their home countries. The students' responses to the surveys were completely anonymous. The survey data were analyzed by examining reported frequencies in response to the questions about computer use.

## Findings

The first and second items on the questionnaire asked the students about their country of birth and how long they had lived in the United States. The results are reported in Table 4.1. Nearly half the respondents were from Mexico. Approximately 30 percent came from Sudan, Russia, Vietnam, Ethiopia, Cuba, Iran, Iraq, Columbia, El Salvador, and the Philippines combined. Approximately 20 percent

**Table 4.1.**
Students' Country of Birth and Average Length of Residence (LOR)
in the United States (n = 176)

| Country | Frequency | Percent of Sample | Average LOR in U.S. (years) |
|---|---|---|---|
| Colombia | 4 | 2.25 | 2.6 |
| Cuba | 12 | 6.74 | 3.2 |
| El Salvador | 2 | 1.12 | 5.3 |
| Ethiopia | 7 | 3.93 | 2.6 |
| Iran | 3 | 1.69 | 3.5 |
| Iraq | 8 | 4.49 | 5.0 |
| Mexico | 87 | 48.88 | 4.6 |
| Philippines | 2 | 1.12 | 5.3 |
| Russia | 3 | 1.69 | 2.8 |
| Sudan | 7 | 3.93 | 3.1 |
| Vietnam | 2 | 1.12 | 3.5 |
| Other | 39 | 21.91 | 3.1 |

came from other countries. The sample also included fourteen students (seven from Sudan, seven from Ethiopia) from sub-Saharan East African countries, which reflects a recent area of growth in Maricopa's immigrant population.

As shown in Table 4.1, although there were few students from El Salvador and the Philippines, they, along with the Iraqi students, had been in the United States the longest, with an average of five years or more in this country. The students from Mexico were not far behind, with an average of about 4 ½ years in the United States. All other nationalities averaged 3 ½ years or less. However, only about 15 percent of the survey respondents had been in the United States a year or less, so that, in general, the average range of residency was 2 ½–5 years for all participants.

How long the respondents had been in the United States can also be discussed in terms of the entire the sample, as shown in Table 4.2. Approximately one-fourth of the students had been in the Unites States for two to three years. Nearly 40 percent had resided in the United States for more than five years.

The survey requested that the students indicate their gender. Slightly fewer men responded than women. Data were collected from 103 women (57.87 percent of the sample) and 74 men (41.57 percent of the sample). (One respondent did not indicate his or her gender.)

The questionnaire also asked the students to indicate their age range. These data are provided in Table 4.3 on page 56. Almost exactly half the respondents were younger than 30 years of age.

In order to address the first research question, the survey asked whether the students had had experience with computers in their home countries. Three options were given and the responses were divided almost evenly across the three: (a) "I never used a computer" (n = 60; 33.71 percent of the sample); (b) "I used a computer a few times" (n = 60; 33.71 percent); and (c) "I used a computer many times" (n = 58; 32.58 percent).

The information about previous computer use is particularly interesting when we focus on those students who had never used a computer before. In Table 4.4 on page 57 these data are shown by country of origin.

The highest percentage of students with no previous computer experience came from Iraq, Vietnam, Mexico, and Cuba. These four countries yielded percentages

**Table 4.2.**

Length of Residence in the United States (n = 170)

| Length of Residence | Frequency | Percent of Sample |
|---|---|---|
| Less than a year | 7 | 3.93 |
| 1 year | 23 | 12.92 |
| 2–3 years | 43 | 24.16 |
| 4–5 years | 26 | 14.61 |
| More than 5 years | 27 | 39.89 |

*Table 4.3.*
Summary of Age of Student Sample (n = 177)

| Age Range | Frequency | Percent of Sample |
|-----------|-----------|-------------------|
| 14–17     | 4         | 2.25              |
| 18–22     | 50        | 28.09             |
| 23–29     | 35        | 19.66             |
| 30–39     | 46        | 25.84             |
| 40–49     | 30        | 16.85             |
| 50–59     | 11        | 6.18              |
| 60+       | 1         | 0.56              |

higher than the average for all participants combined (33.71 percent with no prior computer usage). It is especially important that such a high percentage of the Mexican students had never used a computer before, since this is the nationality that makes up the majority of ESL students at Phoenix College. Thus, while students with no prior computer usage are the minority, they are a very large minority—more than one-third of the respondents—and they include close to half of the students from our largest ESL nationality. However, the number of students in some segments of the sample (e.g., those from Vietnam, El Salvador, the Philippines, etc.) is very small, so these results must be interpreted with caution.

A similar analysis was done using categories based on the ages of the respondents who had never used a computer before. These data are shown in Table 4.5 on page 58. Not surprisingly, the highest percentage of students with no previous computer experience came from the older age ranges (40 to 60+). However, it is also notable that for all of the age ranges, at least a quarter of the respondents had never used a computer before coming to the United States.

Whether or not students have had prior access to computers is in part a function of personal history and circumstance, but it is also a matter of whether or not such technology is available in the society. For this reason, another item asked the respondents about access to computers in their home environment more broadly. These data are reported in Table 4.6 on page 58, which shows that only about 20 percent of the respondents came from countries or villages in which the residents did not have access to computers outside of offices.

The second research question in this study asked how the students feel about the experience of using computers in their community college ESL coursework. For this reason, three Likert scale items were included in the questionnaire to elicit their perspectives. These items are reproduced in Table 4.7 on page 59.

**Table 4.4.**

Percentage of Students Who Had Never Used a Computer, by Nationality

| Country | Frequency | Percent of Sample | No. Who Had Never Used a Computer before Coming to U.S. | Percentage of Total Who Had Never Used a Computer Before | Percentage of That Nationality |
|---|---|---|---|---|---|
| Colombia | 4 | 2.25 | 0 | 0 | 0 |
| Cuba | 12 | 6.74 | 5 | 9 | 42 |
| El Salvador | 2 | 1.12 | 0 | 0 | 0 |
| Ethiopia | 7 | 3.93 | 1 | 0.2 | 14 |
| Iran | 3 | 1.69 | 1 | 0.2 | 33 |
| Iraq | 8 | 4.49 | 4 | 7 | 50 |
| Mexico | 87 | 48.88 | 37 | 67 | 43 |
| Philippines | 2 | 1.12 | 0 | 0 | 0 |
| Russia | 3 | 1.69 | 0 | 0 | 0 |
| Sudan | 7 | 3.93 | 1 | 0.2 | 14 |
| Vietnam | 2 | 1.12 | 1 | 0.2 | 50 |
| Other | 39 | 21.91 | 5 | 9 | 13 |

As shown in Table 4.7, the following results emerged from the three items that explored the students' reactions to computer use in the classroom.

1. About 70 percent "felt good" ("strongly agree" and "agree") about their first experience using a computer in an ESL class.
2. A slightly higher percentage (74 percent) felt good about their subsequent use of computers.
3. More than four-fifths (82 percent) believed the use of computers in ESL classes to be helpful.

Therefore, it can be seen that the ESL students that participated in this study were quite positive in their reactions to computer use. This pattern held true for their confidence in learning computer skills as well as for their belief that the use of computers would be beneficial to them.

Thus, despite my concern that the use of computers in ESL classes might be too burdensome for many ESL students, the students themselves seem to be over-whelmingly positive in their responses. While one might expect older students and students from less developed countries to express more negative reactions to computer use, that was not the case in this study. (However, there were too few negative responses for a demographic breakdown. That is, there were not enough

**Table 4.5.**

Percentage of Students Who Had Never Used a Computer, by Age

| Age Range | Frequency | Percent of Sample | No. Who Had Never Used a Computer before Coming to U.S. | Percentage of Total Who Had Never Used a Computer Before | Percentage of That Age Range |
|---|---|---|---|---|---|
| 14–17 | 4 | 2.25 | 1 | 0.2 | 25 |
| 18–22 | 50 | 28.09 | 12 | 22 | 24 |
| 23–29 | 35 | 19.66 | 9 | 16 | 26 |
| 30–39 | 46 | 25.84 | 14 | 2.5 | 30 |
| 40–49 | 30 | 16.85 | 17 | 31 | 57 |
| 50–59 | 11 | 6.18 | 5 | 9 | 45 |
| 60+ | 1 | 0.56 | 1 | 0.2 | 100 |

members of most of the demographic sub-groups, such as 40–60 year olds, or students with no prior computer experience, to compute the needed statistics to address this issue.) In short, the students who participated in this study were almost uniformly pleased to be using computers in their classes, even though the primary purpose of the course, at least as far as the students were concerned, was to learn English rather than to master computer use. These results concur with those of Alghazo (2006) and Barakzai and Fraser (2005), whose studies also demonstrated positive outcomes and responses to computer use by ESL learners.

However, some possible problems must be taken into consideration in interpreting these data. First, less than a third of the surveys I distributed were returned, and it is not known whether the missing surveys were never filled out by the students or were filled out and turned in to faculty who failed to return them to the OIR. It is therefore possible that the results might have been different if more students had

**Table 4.6.**

Computer Access in Students' Native Towns, Villages, or Reservations (n = 169)

| Level of Computer Access | Frequency | Percent of Sample |
|---|---|---|
| Nobody has a computer. | 11 | 6.18 |
| Only businesses and government offices have a computer. | 26 | 14.61 |
| A few people have computers in their homes. | 80 | 44.94 |
| Most people have computers in their homes. | 52 | 29.21 |

### Table 4.7.
Students' Responses to Likert Scale Items

|  | Item 5. The first time I used a computer in ESL class at Phoenix College, I felt good about my ability to use a computer. | Item 6. Now, at the present time I feel good about my ability to use a computer. | Item 7. Use of computers in ESL classes is very helpful. |
|---|---|---|---|
| **Strongly Agree** | | | |
| Frequency | 57 | 69 | 97 |
| Percent | 32.02 | 38.76 | 54.49 |
| **Agree** | | | |
| Frequency | 68 | 63 | 49 |
| Percent | 38.20 | 35.39 | 27.53 |
| **Neutral** | | | |
| Frequency | 24 | 30 | 15 |
| Percent | 13.48 | 16.85 | 8.43 |
| **Disagree** | | | |
| Frequency | 11 | 5 | 1 |
| Percent | 6.18 | 2.81 | 0.56 |
| **Strongly Disagree** | | | |
| Frequency | 9 | 4 | 8 |
| Percent | 5.06 | 2.25 | 4.49 |

returned their surveys. Second, even though the surveys were anonymous, they were distributed and collected by faculty members during class time. As a result, there is a possibility that some students may have felt obligated to choose responses that they believed would please their instructors.

## Implications

The results of this study seem to indicate that, in general, ESL students at Phoenix College embrace and appreciate the opportunity to work with computers regardless of their prior experience, or lack thereof, with technology. In my own experience, even the students who struggle a great deal and appear the most flustered as they painstakingly learn to type, edit, save, and print their papers using computers often tell me at the end of the semester how glad they were to be able to use the computers, and how much they believe that doing so will benefit them in their lives and future coursework. While the small size of this study as well as possible confounding variables preclude any definitive conclusions about ESL students' perceptions of computer use, it is clear that this study raises the possibility that

ESL students in general desire and appreciate the opportunity to use computers in their grammar and writing courses.

There are probably very few faculty left in academe who do not believe that computer literacy is as vital to students today as reading and writing proficiency are, and it is for this reason that so many of us want our students to learn computer use as well as the English language in our classes. However, we must be cautious to temper our enthusiasm and optimism about new technologies with careful research and evaluation of their effects on student learning. Therefore, larger scale studies of this type should be done, and more detailed questions should be asked, to determine whether these results do indeed apply to the vast majority of ESL students, or whether a significant percentage may be disadvantaged by the need to gain computer skills at the same time that they are improving their ability to communicate in English. As educators, we must be vigilant to continually examine the methods and materials we use in order to ensure that all of our students receive the type of instruction they will benefit from the most.

# Appendix

## ESL Student Survey[1]
## Fall 2006

Please take a few minutes to complete this survey. As a student your feedback is important in order that we may improve our services. All responses will be kept confidential. Information is reported as group data only.

**Please fill in the bubbles like this:** ●    Not like this: ⊘ ⊗ ⊘

**1**    **I was born in (select only one response)**

- ○ Mexico
- ○ Sudan
- ○ Russia
- ○ Vietnam
- ○ Ethiopia
- ○ Cuba
- ○ Bosnia/Hercegovina

- ○ Guatemala
- ○ Iran
- ○ Iraq
- ○ Colombia
- ○ the Philippines
- ○ El Salvador
- ○ Other _____

**2**    **I came to the United States**

- ○ less than a year ago
- ○ 1 year ago
- ○ 2–3 years ago
- ○ 4–5 years ago
- ○ more than 5 years ago

**3**    **Before I came to the United States**

- ○ I never used a computer
- ○ I used a computer a few times
- ○ I used a computer many times

**4**    **In my native town, village, or reservation**

- ○ nobody has a computer
- ○ only businesses and government offices have computers
- ○ a few people have computers in their homes
- ○ most people have computers in their homes

Strongly Agree / Agree / Neutral / Disagree / Strongly Disagree

**Fill in only one response circle for each statement below.**

○ ○ ○ ○ ○   **5**   The first time I used a computer in an ESL class, I felt good about my ability to use a computer.

○ ○ ○ ○ ○   **6**   Now, at the present time I feel good about my ability to use a computer.

○ ○ ○ ○ ○   **7**   Use of computer in ESL classes is very helpful.

**8**   **Gender**   ○ Male    ○ Female

**9**   **My age is**
- ○ 14–17
- ○ 18–22
- ○ 23–29
- ○ 30–39
- ○ 40–49
- ○ 50–59
- ○ 60+

---

1. In order to comply with the college's policy on human subjects research, it was necessary to have the surveys formatted and the data tabulated by the OIR.

# Chapter 5

# ESL Teacher and Student Perspectives on Technology in the Community College Classroom

■ Marit ter Mate-Martinsen

THIS CHAPTER REPORTS ON RESEARCH-BASED SURVEYS AT SANTA BARBARA CITY College in California, which were conducted to document the use of technology in community college ESL classes and to determine ESL students' and teachers' attitudes toward the use of technology. Like the study by Roe (this volume), this study aims to document the impact of technology in the community college ESL context and the various ways that the tools of technology can be evaluated with the needs of community college ESL learners in mind.

## Issues that Motivated the Research

Computer-assisted language learning (CALL) has been a well-researched field for years, but relatively few studies have been conducted on technology in the community college ESL classroom. While Warschauer (1999) argued that CALL, with the reference to computer-*assisted* language learning, is no longer useful since CALL should be viewed as a natural "part of the ecology of language use" (para. 4), not merely an accessory to language learning, this shift in thinking about the integration of technology is easier said than done. The reality is that many immigrant students—perhaps especially those from low socioeconomic backgrounds—may have never touched a mouse or keyboard until their first ESL class at the community college. Many of them have limited access to computers at home or in the community, a difference in access that Allison (2006) viewed as contributing to the "digital divide" among ESL community college students (p. 54).

## Context of the Research

Clearly English language development should be at the heart of any ESL program, but what place does technology have in the community college classroom? As the ESL computer lab coordinator at Santa Barbara City College (SBCC), a community college in California, I embarked on this study to document the range of ways that technology is integrated into community college ESL classrooms and to gain a wider perspective on ESL teachers' and students' views of technology.

SBCC educates approximately 1,365 ESL students a semester, of which 80 percent are Mexican immigrants, 10 percent are immigrants from other countries, and 10 percent are international students, primarily from Asia or South America. While it is common knowledge that some teachers use a substantial amount of technology, other teachers limit the use of technology or avoid it all together. Although it is assumed that students practice basic word processing skills to type their paragraphs and essays for their writing classes, currently there are no technology objectives integrated into the three-course ESL core curriculum of (a) reading, speaking and listening, (b) grammar, and (c) writing. Thus, the choice of whether or not to use *technology,* a term widely used at SBCC, is left to each instructor. In other words, some students are exposed to a wide range of technology-based activities while others are not.

## Research Questions Addressed

The purpose of this study is to explore teacher and student perspectives on technology. Four specific research questions were addressed:

1. What access to technology do SBCC ESL students have at home?
2. Do the ESL students prefer classes where teachers use technology?
3. How and why do the students' ESL teachers use or avoid technology?
4. What are student and teacher perceptions about the impact of technology on student success in their ESL studies, content courses, and in the workforce?

## Data Collection Procedures

In this section I will discuss the data collection procedures used in this study, by first describing the participants who contributed information and then explaining the materials used to elicit the data. Finally, I will explain the procedures involved in gathering and analyzing the data.

In this study, 168 ESL students participated, which equals approximately 12 percent of the ESL student body. In an effort to obtain a representative sample of the diverse ESL student population at SBCC, students were included from level 1 (beginning-level ESL) through level 5 (advanced ESL), daytime and nighttime students as well as immigrant and international students. In addition, 24 ESL instructors, who account for 67 percent of the ESL faculty, took part in the study. This group consisted of both part-time and full-time, daytime and nighttime ESL instructors. Finally, two English Skills[1] faculty members and a career counselor participated as well.

Answers to the research questions were sought using a number of different procedures:

1. ESL students completed a questionnaire (see Appendix, p. 79).
2. ESL faculty answered a survey (see Appendix, p. 80).
3. I conducted follow-up interviews with ESL faculty members (see Appendix, p. 81).
4. English Skills faculty responded to a survey.
5. I interviewed a career counselor.

The questionnaires consisted of both open and closed questions and ranged from five to twenty questions in length. The surveys and interviews included questions that were directly related to this study, but as the ESL computer lab coordinator, I also incorporated questions that would be beneficial only to the ESL program at SBCC.

On the student survey, Question 3 focused on Research Question 1:

QUESTION 3: Do you have a computer at home?

          Yes              No

---

1. After students finish ESL, they move to English Skills, a basic skills program. English Skills prepares native and non-native English students for English Composition.

Questions 16, 17, and 18 were related to Research Question 2: Do ESL students prefer teachers who use technology?

**QUESTION** 16: What do you like better, an ESL class where the teacher uses technology or an ESL class where the teacher does not use technology?

Class uses technology　　　Class doesn't use technology

**QUESTION** 17: Do you want all your ESL teachers to use technology in your ESL classes? Yes or No. Why or why not?

**QUESTION** 18: Do you want all your ESL teachers to teach you technology skills in your ESL classes? Yes or No. Why or why not?

Questions 6, 7, and 8 in the ESL teacher survey centered on Research Question 3: How and why do ESL teachers use or avoid technology?

**QUESTION** 6: How often do you use technology with your students in class?

Never　　　　Sometimes　　　　Regularly

**QUESTION** 7: If you use technology, what activities, tasks, and projects do your students complete on the computer? Check all that apply.

Use Rosetta Stone®　　　　Use grammar CD-Roms

Use Microsoft® Word　　　　Use Pipeline emails

Use Pipeline online　　　　Use ESL/publisher

　message board[2]　　　　　websites[3]

Use website created by teacher　　Use non-ESL websites

Use Smarthinking for tutoring[4]　　Conduct research on Internet

Create PowerPoint　　　　Other

---

2. Pipeline is the online campus portal used at SBCC. It provides many online services, including email and message board, which is an online bulletin board.
3. Textbooks are often linked to publisher companion websites, where students can do further practice.
4. Smarthinking is an online tutoring service.

Question 4 in the follow-up interview elaborated on this question with "in what ways?" Furthermore, in the student survey, Questions 9 and 12 addressed the issue of use as well.

**QUESTION** 9: Do all your teachers use computers in your ESL classes?

**QUESTION** 12: What computer skills do you practice in your classes?

| | |
|---|---|
| Use Rosetta Stone ® | Use grammar CD Roms |
| Use Microsoft® Word | Use Pipeline emails |
| Use Pipeline online message board | Use ESL/publisher websites |
| Use website created by teacher | Use non-ESL websites |
| Use Smarthinking for tutoring | Conduct research on Internet |
| Create PowerPoint | Other |

In the ESL faculty interview, the purpose of Question 9 was to answer Research Question 4: What are student and teacher perceptions about the impact of technology on student success in their ESL studies, content courses, and in the workforce?

**QUESTION** 9: What technology skills would be beneficial for our ESL students to develop to succeed in their ESL classes, content courses, and jobs?

The student survey provided open-ended questions related to this issue as well:

**QUESTION** 19: Do computers help you with your job, or to get a better job?

**QUESTION** 20: What computer skills can help you find a better job?

I also focused the survey of English Skills faculty and the interview with a career counselor on this research question about the impact of technology.

All the ESL faculty members were provided with hard copies of the student questionnaire and were asked to distribute and collect them in their classes. Thereafter, 168 student questionnaires (12 percent) were returned.

The ESL teacher questionnaire was emailed to both full- and part-time ESL faculty and copies were also placed in faculty mailboxes. The faculty survey also included the option to leave contact information for a follow-up interview, and such interviews were subsequently held with ten ESL faculty members. Four English

Skills instructors were contacted by email, and two faculty members responded to eleven questions via email. Finally, a telephone interview took place with a career counselor, who had extensive experience working with both the ESL and regular student population at SBCC.

## Data Analysis Procedures

To analyze the data, I tabulated the frequency and range of the faculty and student responses to the survey and interviews. I also examined the frequency and range of responses based on student background variables, including full-time versus part-time students, daytime versus nighttime students, and students who own a computer versus students those who do not.

## Findings

With respect to the first research question, "What access to technology do SBCC ESL students have at home?" the data indicate that nearly half (46 percent) of the SBCC ESL students surveyed do not own a computer at home (see Table 5.1). As shown in Table 5.2 on page 68, especially high percentages of evening students (71 percent) report not having access to a computer at home, and 80 percent of evening students also indicated that they attend classes part-time. These percentages stand in sharp contrast to those of daytime students, only 32 percent of whom do not have their own computer, and only 30 percent of whom attend classes part-time. In other words, lower-level, part-time evening students are less likely to have access to computers outside school than advanced, daytime students.

With respect to the second research question, "Do students prefer classes where teachers use technology?" 163 students (97 percent) indicated that they like to use

### Table 5.1.
Characteristics of Students Who Own and Do Not Own Computers

|  | R1* n=21 | G2* n=20 | G3* n=20 | W2 n=43 | W3 n=19 | R4 n=26 | R5 n=20 | Total n=168 | % of Students |
|---|---|---|---|---|---|---|---|---|---|
| Ss own computers | 3 | 5 | 10 | 20 | 15 | 19 | 19 | 91 | 54 |
|  | (14%) | (26%) | (50%) | (47%) | (79%) | (73%) | (95%) |  |  |
|  | 3 | 4 | 5 | 23 | 15 | 23 | 14 | 87 | 52 |
| % of FT students | (14%) | (21%) | (26%) | (53%) | (79%) | (88%) | (70%) |  |  |

Note: In the column headings for Table 5.1, G stands for grammar, W for writing, and R for reading, speaking, and listening classes. The numerals 1, 2, 3, 4, and 5 indicate student levels, while an asterisk (*) denotes an evening class and Ss stands for students.

***Table 5.2.***

Demographic Information about the Student Respondents

|                     | Daytime Students<br>n=107 | Evening Students<br>n=61 | Total<br>n=168 |
|---------------------|:-------------------------:|:------------------------:|:--------------:|
| Full-time status    | 75 (70.1%)                | 12 (19.7%)               | 87 (51.8%)     |
| Part-time status    | 32 (29.9%)                | 49 (80.3%)               | 81 (48.2%)     |
| FT with computer    | 49 (45.8%)                | 4 (6.6%)                 | 53 (31.6%)     |
| PT with computer    | 24 (22.4%)                | 14 (23%)                 | 38 (22.6%)     |
| Total with computer | 73 (68.2 %)               | 18 (29.5%)               | 91 (54.2%)     |

computers in their classes and 166 students (99 percent) prefer classes that use computers over classes that do not. The following comments are representative of the most commonly found responses:

Reasons Students Give for Using Technology in Class

- "It's helpful and important."
- "I practice while I am learning English."
- "help for my future and work."
- "I like because make more easier learn English."
- "I can learn more English."
- "it help to support our English."
- "more joy to learn English."
- "we do our homework faster and more professional."
- "in the future we expect more technology."

Reasons Students Give for Not Using Technology in Class

- "They don't have to, only if needed."
- "Some teachers can't use computer."
- "My teacher doesn't use computer but we need computer, so the teacher should learn how."
- "Sometimes it's very confusing."
- "It's a little inconvenient. Sometimes the laboratory is full."

As these student comments illustrate, many of the students in the study indicated that they enjoy the use of computers in their classes since it helps them with their English skills: It makes language learning easier, faster, more enjoyable, and more professional compared to handwritten assignments. The one percent of daytime students who prefer teachers who do not use computers in their classes gave as reasons that using technology is sometimes confusing or inconvenient since the campus lab might be full or their schedules are tight. Some students remarked that it enables them to do additional English practice outside of class such as during their required lab assignments. The apparent strong enthusiasm for technology in class may be due to the fact that many have limited access to computers at home, a point I will return to later in the discussion section of this chapter.

The third research question, "How and why do teachers use technology?" revealed that 100 percent of the ESL instructors surveyed reported using computers in their classes in a variety of ways. Table 5.3 shows the results for full- and part-time teachers. The results are based on data collected from ESL instructors.

Table 5.3 shows that the majority of ESL teachers use Microsoft® Word in their classes (96 percent), followed by the use of Internet activities and research (63 percent), ESL websites (58 percent), grammar CD-ROMs (54 percent), and Pipeline email (50 percent). Publisher websites (42 percent) and Pipeline message board (38 percent) are less frequently applied to ESL courses, and Smarthinking, teacher-created websites, PowerPoint, Rosetta Stone®, and Inspiration Software® are rarely used. Table 5.3 also indicates that both full-time and part-time faculty make use of this wide array of technology software tools, and among those part-time faculty who are using technology tools, they are making use of a similar range

**Table 5.3.**

Numbers and Percentages of Full-Time and Part-Time Teachers
Using Various Software Options

| | PT Teachers n=16 | % of PT Teachers | FT Teachers n=8 | % of FT Teachers | PT and FT Teachers | % of PT and FT Teachers |
|---|---|---|---|---|---|---|
| Microsoft® Word | 15 | 94 | 8 | 100 | 23 | 96 |
| ESL websites | 8 | 50 | 6 | 75 | 14 | 58 |
| Internet activities/research | 9 | 56 | 6 | 75 | 15 | 63 |
| Grammar CD-ROM | 6 | 38 | 7 | 88 | 13 | 54 |
| Pipeline email | 6 | 38 | 6 | 75 | 12 | 50 |
| Publisher websites | 7 | 44 | 3 | 38 | 10 | 42 |
| Pipeline message board | 5 | 31 | 4 | 50 | 9 | 38 |
| Smarthinking | 3 | 19 | 1 | 13 | 4 | 17 |
| Teacher website | 1 | 6 | 3 | 38 | 4 | 17 |
| Microsoft® PowerPoint | 2 | 13 | 1 | 13 | 3 | 13 |
| Rosetta Stone® | 0 | 0 | 1 | 13 | 1 | 4 |
| Inspiration Software® | 0 | 0 | 1 | 13 | 1 | 4 |

Note: PT=part-time and FT=full-time.

***Table 5.4.***

Computer Skills that Students Report Practicing in Their ESL Classes
at SBCC

| | R1* n=21 | G2* n=20 | G3* n=20 | W2 n=43 | W3 n=19 | R4 n=26 | R5 n=20 | Total n=168 | % of students |
|---|---|---|---|---|---|---|---|---|---|
| Microsoft® Word | 5 | 11 | 9 | 32 | 15 | 16 | 12 | 100 | 60 |
| Pipeline email | 3 | 13 | 10 | 29 | 12 | 16 | 15 | 98 | 58 |
| Internet activities/research | 5 | 16 | 7 | 22 | 12 | 18 | 8 | 88 | 52 |
| Grammar CD-ROM | 5 | 2 | 14 | 21 | 10 | 19 | 14 | 85 | 51 |
| Teacher website | 3 | 3 | 2 | 7 | 2 | 5 | 1 | 23 | 14 |
| Rosetta Stone® | 4 | 7 | 4 | 3 | 5 | 1 | 0 | 24 | 14 |
| Publisher websites | 1 | 10 | 1 | 2 | 2 | 3 | 0 | 19 | 11 |
| Smarthinking | 0 | 0 | 0 | 0 | 0 | 1 | 10 | 11 | 7 |
| Microsoft® PowerPoint | 0 | 0 | 1 | 0 | 3 | 0 | 1 | 5 | 3 |

Note: G stands for grammar, W for writing, and R for reading, speaking, and listening classes. The numerals 1, 2, 3, 4, and 5 indicate student levels, while an asterisk (*) denotes an evening class and Ss stands for students.

of technology tools as full-time faculty. However, a greater proportion of full-time faculty use many of these software tools more frequently than part-time faculty. All percentages are higher in the full-time faculty column except for the use of publisher websites and Smarthinking. Both full-time and part-time teachers rarely use Microsoft® PowerPoint.

To gain additional insight into the ways teachers use technology in the classroom, the student questionnaire asked the ESL students about the range of computer skills they practice in their ESL classes. Table 5.4 summarizes the students' responses.

Table 5.4 indicates that students most frequently report practicing computer skills related to Microsoft® Word (60 percent), Pipeline (58 percent), the Internet (52 percent), and grammar CD-ROMs (51 percent). In addition, these data also indicate that a greater proportion of students in daytime classes report practicing computer skills related to Microsoft® Word, the Internet, and Pipeline than students in evening classes. Finally, the data also highlight some variation across class levels with a similar instructional focus: for example, students in the evening Level 2 Grammar class reported very little practice with grammar CD-ROM software but more frequent practice with grammar exercises on the Internet, including publisher websites, compared to students in the evening Level 3 Grammar class.

A representative sample of the open-ended responses teachers gave as to why they use technology in their classes follows.

- "It's an effective tool that reflects real-world skills most people need once they start working."
- "I use it because it's required for some courses . . . it's an excellent source of enrichment for students."
- "Because I love it! And because it offers so many possibilities for learning."
- "To give students access to technology they might not have at home."

The reasons given as to why teachers tend to limit the use of technology were:

- "I'm limited to how often I can reserve a lab. We don't have enough lab space on this campus to accommodate our program."
- "The equipment didn't work . . . I wasted lots of time. When SBCC gives us technology that works, I'll use it. Until then, forget it. Waste of time."
- "I've never had much success in the lab. I just can't figure out what to do."

These teacher responses illustrate that while teachers in the study seem to share a similar hope that technology use will enrich their students' learning, the teachers also experience limitations around the logistics of use (e.g., inadequate lab space, equipment failures) and their own competence with technological resources.

Research Question 4 focused on student and teacher perceptions about the impact of technology on student success in their ESL studies, content courses, and in the workforce. The data reveal that there were important areas of overlap in the responses given by students, teachers, and the career counselor I interviewed. For instance, many students commented that technology has helped them to "learn English faster," because of the language tools available to them on computers. As a result, they feel they have increased their success as language learners. Some students pointed out that they can do their homework more effectively on the computer than on paper, because they can use many different programs. Also, a number of students explained how computers have helped them with their spelling and vocabulary, especially by using spell check and the thesaurus features in Microsoft® Word. Some students noted that computer use contributes to their academic success because computers expand their access to peers and teachers outside of their classes. For example, when they have a question, they can email their teacher or classmate and receive a prompt response. Many lower-level students commented how important it is to develop computer skills in their ESL classes because it will help them in the future, particularly with respect to work opportunities. One student noted, "it's helpful for my future and work," and another wrote, "in the future we

*Table 5.5.*

Range of Technology Skills that SBCC Faculty and Staff Feel Is Beneficial
for ESL Students to Develop to Succeed in Their ESL Classes,
Content Courses, and Jobs

| ESL Faculty | English Skills Faculty & Career Counselor |
|---|---|
| Keyboarding | Keyboarding |
| Microsoft® Word | Microsoft® Word |
| (Pipeline) email | (Pipeline) email |
| Internet research skills | Internet research skills |
| Microsoft® PowerPoint | Microsoft® PowerPoint |
| Publisher websites | Publisher sites (English Skills only) |
| ESL software | |

expect more technology." A number of students also shared how the use of computers in their classes has helped them with their current jobs or to find a better job.
One student remarked, "I work the cashier and it helps use computers. I am now
faster cashier" due to practicing computer skills in ESL classes.

The ESL teachers mentioned that it would be especially useful for ESL students
to develop keyboarding, word processing, email, Internet research, and PowerPoint
presentation skills, which are also important tools to develop for English Skills and
content courses (see Table 5.5). As shown in Table 5.5, similar responses about
the impact of technology were given by English Skills teachers as well as by the
career counselor. In addition, ESL and English Skills faculty indicated that they
often referred students to publishers' companion websites, because these sites
enable students to further practice concepts and skills presented in their textbooks.
ESL faculty specifically mentioned the value of ESL software for English language
development. The career counselor maintained that many of the computer skills
addressed in the ESL and English Skills classes are desirable qualifications in the
job market as well. Together, the interview data from the teachers and counselor
seem to point to a cluster of essential technology skills that are relevant to success
in ESL, English Skills, content courses, and the workforce.

## Discussion

The discussion of these findings is organized around four main subheadings.
First I will discuss the ESL students' perspectives on technology and then the
teachers' perspectives, before turning to the technology skills students need to
participate effectively in ESL courses and content courses at SBCC, and eventually the workforce.

## ESL Students' Access to Computers

Brutza and Hayes (2006) pointed out that access to technology remains a persistent issue for many community college ESL students; their work has found that a majority of ESL students rely on open computer labs on campus to be able to use computers and complete course assignments. Similar to their findings, my study points to the important role that technology resources at SBCC play in providing ESL students—particularly those who attend in the evening or on a part-time basis—with access to computers and various software applications. In this study, students in the high-level classes—whether daytime or evening—were more likely to have a computer at home (Research Question 1), possibly because international students make up a larger percentage of high-level classes at SBCC and these students tend to be from a higher socioeconomic class. In contrast, many students—particularly evening and part-time students—report limited to no access to computers outside school and thus are only able to practice and develop their technology skills at school. In fact, this "digital divide" (Allison, 2006, p. 54) holds true for many community college programs that serve large second-language immigrant populations (p. 54). In other words, many immigrant students are able to overcome the digital divide by enrolling in community college ESL courses.

## Student Perspectives on Technology

For the second research question, a student preference (99 percent) for teachers who use technology in their ESL classes was observed. Clearly students want their teachers to utilize computers: "I need computers for my studies and job," one student remarked. Interestingly, more than a decade ago, Bradin (1996 as cited in Hanson-Smith, 1997) stated, "In time, computers will permeate all aspects of teaching and learning" (p. 14). Furthermore, Clifford (1998) noted, "computers will not replace teachers, but teachers who use computers will replace teachers who do not" (p. 5). Thus, to borrow Clifford's language, if the tables were turned and students were in charge of hiring teachers, they would clearly prefer teachers who use technology. Students are well aware that it is crucial for them to hone their technology skills to stay current in academia and to be competitive in the job market, and that the community college provides a valuable gateway.

## ESL Teachers' Perspectives on Technology

All surveyed ESL faculty utilize computers in their classes to some extent. However, student surveys revealed that some teachers never use computers in their classroom—a discrepancy that may be due to a number of the faculty members (33 percent) not completing the survey. The majority of the surveyed faculty members employ Microsoft® Word in their writing classes, and most of them have used Pipeline email at some point in time, but occasionally with "frustration," as one faculty member phrased it. A few low-level reading teachers have used Rosetta Stone®. Most grammar teachers use grammar CD-ROMs, and some advanced reading or writing instructors have used Smarthinking, Pipeline Message Board, the Internet for basic research, and/or PowerPoint. Overall, these results indicate that there is a wide range in faculty use of technology in their classes. In addition, full-time teachers tend to integrate technology skills more frequently than part-time teachers. In other words, depending on each individual instructor, students may be exposed to widely varying degrees of technology in their ESL classes. Thus, more technology training may be necessary for part-time teachers, so there can be more consistency in the use of technology among full-time and part-time and daytime versus nighttime teachers. Also, by developing technology training workshops for ESL faculty, teachers can become aware of the multitude of technology tools available to them and their students as well as the range of approaches for using technology effectively in the classroom.

The teachers who use technology do so because they feel it provides richness, real-world skills, and countless possibilities for learning and presentation styles. These views echo Lam's (2000) findings that teachers use technology because it motivates students, provides them with further practice as well as a real-life context, and adds an array of presentation styles to instruction. On the other hand, SBCC teachers who under-utilize technology explained that this pattern is due to limited access to the computer lab, a problem that has been addressed by programs like the one at Truman College in Chicago, where mobile computer labs have been put in classrooms. Some SBCC faculty explained that they often do not know what to do when they are in the computer lab, a finding that was also identified by Lam (2000). The SBCC ESL student surveys also indicated that students responded negatively when teachers could not effectively use computer lab resources (e.g., one ESL student wrote, "Some teachers can't use computer"). Several ESL students suggested that their teachers should learn how to use computers better because the students also need to acquire computer skills.

Whether teachers use or avoid technology to improve language learning, pedagogy plays a key role. Draud and Brace (1999) surveyed 1,900 students taught in technology-equipped classrooms. They found that 95 percent of students prefer teachers who use technology. However, Draud and Brace found that many students made the argument that the effectiveness depends on the instructor. In other words, technology does not replace good teaching, but as Zhao (2003) pointed out, it is difficult to evaluate the effectiveness of technology as an isolated item due to many factors, such as what counts as technology and how it is applied and assessed. Kern (2006) wrote, "It is not the technology per se that is effective or ineffective but the particular ways in which the technology is used" (p. 189). Thus, the findings of the present study have much larger implications for the ESL program at SBCC. Technology should not only be further integrated into the ESL curriculum, but this transition needs to go hand in hand with pre-service and in-service teacher training on the best practices of technology use in the ESL classroom—an assertion that might hold true for many community college ESL programs. Interestingly, part-time evening instructors at SBCC tend to use technology less than their full-time counterparts who teach mostly daytime classes. This difference might be due to their varying degrees of technology expertise. Considering that part-time evening students have the least access to technology but show a preference for teachers who use computers (100 percent), there seems to be a mismatch between student needs and institutional resources.

## Technology Skills for ESL, Content Courses, and the Workforce

Research Question 4 highlighted the impact of technology on student success in their ESL studies, content courses, and in the workforce, and demonstrated how there are important technology skills that overlap within these three areas. Thus, the integration of technology skills early on in the ESL curriculum may increase students' preparation for content courses and the workforce.

In addition to learning new concepts, students are also expected to quickly develop their technology skills to take part in the academic community beyond the ESL classroom. It is well known that it can be challenging for ESL students to transition into academic community college classes due to overwhelming amounts of new information, concepts, and vocabulary. Buttaro (2001) alluded to this problem when making a case for content-based ESL classes:

> Many ESL students feel overwhelmed and frustrated in college classes because they are learning a new language along with new and complex concepts. They are expected to perform at the level of native speakers even though their proficiency in the English language is quite often inadequate for the task. (p. 81)

In other words, since ESL students often continue to struggle with their English language skills in content courses, ESL teachers would do well to incorporate technology skills early, so their students can master the specific technology skills required of them in content courses. This way, students can focus entirely on the content, and not also "feel overwhelmed and frustrated" by the technology skills that are also required of them in their content courses.

While English language instruction should remain at the heart of any ESL program, technology use can be a supplemental skill that will greatly benefit students in both their second language development and academic content courses. This way, when students move beyond ESL and English Skills courses, they will be able to focus primarily on grasping content and not be faced with learning new technology skills as well. Furthermore, if teachers carefully integrate core technology skills into the ESL program, students that are not retained in ESL will be able to benefit from their improved English language skills along with their enhanced technology knowledge because of their increased marketability in the workforce.

## Implications

This study suggests that ESL students require technology skills to enhance success in their language and academic studies. Furthermore, students perceive such skills as a means to remain competitive in the job market. Therefore, it is essential to weave technology objectives into community college ESL curricula, but in such a way that language learning is not compromised. Instead language learning should be amplified with technology. Also, any inclusion of technology must be paired with professional development for pre-service and in-service ESL teachers that focuses on best practices of technology, because effective pedagogy is critical.

To ease ESL students and faculty into using various forms of technology, it is useful to conceptualize technology on a continuum. Figure 5.1 (adapted from Gebhard, 2006, p. 109) puts technology on a low to high technology continuum, for example, by considering the use of sticks as low technology and cell phones as high technology.

Although Gebhard may have expanded the definition of technology farther than is necessary for community college instruction, the idea of a technology continuum is valuable for ESL programs because it can ease both students and teachers into using technology effectively. For instance, instead of introducing PowerPoint to ESL students and teachers with limited technology skills, it might be beneficial

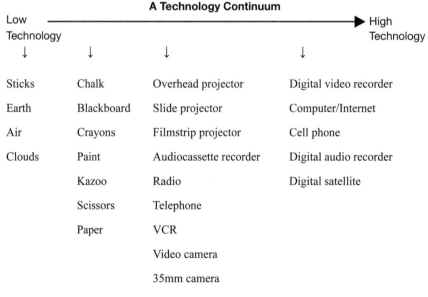

**A Technology Continuum**

Low ⟶ High
Technology                                                                    Technology
↓          ↓          ↓                        ↓

| Sticks | Chalk | Overhead projector | Digital video recorder |
|--------|-------|--------------------|-----------------------|
| Earth | Blackboard | Slide projector | Computer/Internet |
| Air | Crayons | Filmstrip projector | Cell phone |
| Clouds | Paint | Audiocassette recorder | Digital audio recorder |
| | Kazoo | Radio | Digital satellite |
| | Scissors | Telephone | |
| | Paper | VCR | |
| | | Video camera | |
| | | 35mm camera | |

***Figure 5.1.*** A Technology Continuum

to do a poster project on butcher paper first. For teachers with a limited CALL background, a poster project is a less intimidating place to start, and the teacher is able to practice pedagogical strategies such as a step-by-step approach that are necessary for teaching with tools higher on the technology continuum. For students, a poster project provides them with skills that are readily transferable to higher technology tools such as PowerPoint. For instance, students can develop layout techniques and presentation skills with a poster project, thereby building their confidence before making a digital presentation. Thus, moving from low tech to high tech on the continuum can be good training ground for both the teacher and the student.

Based on the results of this study, I propose the technology continuum depicted in Figure 5.2, in which various technological options are ranked in terms of ease of technology skills. Thus, the technology skills gradually become harder (from lower to higher technology). For instance, in a Level 2 grammar course, students might do exercises on grammar CD-ROMs outside of class. In the next level, students might also practice grammar on the Internet.

Please note that these are minimum technology requirements that should be gradually integrated or scaffolded into ESL programs in community colleges. Also, the continuum should be dynamic, as technology keeps advancing and soon additional technology skills will be required or desired in content courses and the job market. In discussing the integration of technology with sustained

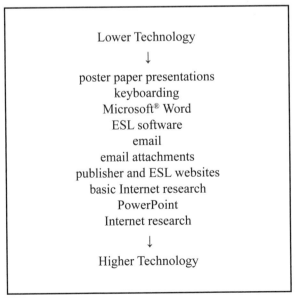

Lower Technology

↓

poster paper presentations
keyboarding
Microsoft® Word
ESL software
email
email attachments
publisher and ESL websites
basic Internet research
PowerPoint
Internet research

↓

Higher Technology

***Figure 5.2.*** Lower to Higher Technology Continuum

content-based ESL coursework at community colleges, Kasper (2002) eloquently
stated,

> To be most effective, technology must be used to support well-
> planned curricular goals and should involve carefully designed activi-
> ties that provide students with meaningful educational experiences.
> Used appropriately, technology can be a valuable tool in building the
> skills students need to succeed in college and the workforce. (p. 141)

Thus, by carefully scaffolding core technology skills into the ESL community college curriculum, ESL students' success can be fostered in their academic coursework, and ultimately make them more marketable in the workforce.

# Appendix

## ESL Student Survey

Directions: Please answer the questions in English. Thank you!

**1. Are you a full-time or part-time student?** *(Full time= 12/more units; part-time= 1-11 units)*
❑  Part-time ❑  Full-time

**2. Are you a daytime student, nighttime student or both?**
❑  Daytime ❑  Nighttime ❑  Both

**3. Do you have a computer at home?**
❑  Yes ❑  No

**4. Have you taken any computer classes at SBCC?**
❑  Yes ❑  No

**5. If yes, what computer classes have you taken/ are you taking at SBCC?**
❑   ESL 29 ❑   COMAP 140 ❑   COMAP 141 ❑   COMAP 142

**6. What classes are you taking this semester?** *(put an X in all the correct boxes)*

|  | Level 1 | Level 2 | Level 3 | Level 4 | Level 5 |
|---|---|---|---|---|---|
| Grammar | ❑ | ❑ | ❑ | ❑ | ❑ |
| Writing | ❑ | ❑ | ❑ | ❑ | ❑ |
| Reading | ❑ | ❑ | ❑ | ❑ | ❑ |
| Conversation | ❑ |  |  |  |  |

ESL 29 | COMAP 140 | COMAP 141 | COMAP 142

**7. Do you use computers in your ESL classes this semester?**
❑  Yes ❑  No

**8. Do you like to use computers for your classes?**
❑  Yes ❑  No
Why or why not? _____

**9. Do all your teachers use computers in your ESL classes?**
❑  Yes ❑  No

**10. Do you use Pipeline in your ESL classes?**
❑  Never ❑  Sometimes ❑  Often

**11. Do you use Microsoft Word in your classes (i.e., type a paragraph for class)?**
❑  Never ❑  Sometimes ❑  Often

**12. What computer skills do you practice in your classes?** *(You can choose more than 1).*
❑  Rosetta Stone CD-ROM ❑  Use grammar CD-ROMs
❑  Use Microsoft Word for typing ❑  Use Pipeline email
❑  Use Pipeline message board ❑  Use ESL/Publisher websites
❑  Use website created by teacher ❑  Use non-ESL websites
❑  Use Smarthinking for tutoring ❑  Conduct research on the Internet
❑  Other_____

**13. Do computer activities help you with your English?**
❑  Yes ❑  A little ❑  No

**14. What English skills do you practice on the computer?** *(you can choose more than 1)*
❑  Speaking ❑  Listening ❑  Reading ❑  Writing ❑  Grammar

**15. Do your teachers use English when they explain computer activities to you?**
❑  Always ❑  Sometimes ❑  Never

**16. What do you like better, an ESL class where the teacher uses technology or an ESL class where the teacher does not use technology?**
❑  Class uses technology ❑  Class doesn't use technology

**17. Do you want ALL your teachers to use technology in your ESL classes?**
❑  Yes ❑  No
Why or why not? _____

**18. Do you want ALL your teachers to teach you technology skills in your ESL classes?**
❑  Yes ❑  No
Why or why not? _____

**19. Do computers help you with your job, or to get a better job?**
❑  Yes ❑  No ❑  Maybe

**20. What computer skills can help you find a better job? _____**

*Thank you very much for answering the questions* ☺

## ESL Faculty Survey

Directions: Please take a few minutes to answer the survey. The purpose of this survey is to learn more about the use of technology in our ESL program at SBCC. Thank you SO MUCH in advance for taking the time to complete the survey.

1. Are you a full-time or part-time instructor?
- ❑ Part-time                                              ❑ Full-time

2. Are you a daytime or nighttime instructor?
- ❑ Daytime                                               ❑ Nighttime

3. What classes are you teaching this semester? Please check all that apply.

|              | Level 1 | Level 2 | Level 3 | Level 4 | Level 5 |
|--------------|---------|---------|---------|---------|---------|
| Grammar      | ❑       | ❑       | ❑       | ❑       | ❑       |
| Writing      | ❑       | ❑       | ❑       | ❑       | ❑       |
| Reading      | ❑       | ❑       | ❑       | ❑       | ❑       |
| Conversation | ❑       |         |         |         |         |
| ESL 29       | ❑       |         |         |         |         |

4. Do your students use Pipeline email or message board as a part of your classes?
- ❑ Never                   ❑ Sometimes                   ❑ Regularly

5. Do your students use Microsoft Word as part of your classes (i.e., type a paragraph to turn in to you)?
- ❑ Never                   ❑ Sometimes                   ❑ Regularly

6. How often do you use technology with your students in class?
- ❑ Never                   ❑ Sometimes                   ❑ Regularly

7. If you use technology, what activities, tasks or projects do your students complete on the computer? Check all that apply.

- ❑ Rosetta Stone CD-ROM
- ❑ Use Microsoft Word for typing
- ❑ Use Pipeline message board
- ❑ Use website created by teacher
- ❑ Use Smarthinking for tutoring
- ❑ Use grammar CD-ROMs
- ❑ Use Pipeline email
- ❑ Use ESL/Publisher websites
- ❑ Use non-ESL websites
- ❑ Conduct research on the Internet
- ❑ Other_____

8. Why do you or do you not use technology in your classroom?

_____

_____

9. If you use technology, when do you use it?
- ❑ As a lab assignment only          ❑ In class only          ❑ As class and lab assignments

10 a. If the department were to offer more technology-based workshops for flex credit, what would you be interested in learning how to use? Check all that apply.

- ❑ Rosetta Stone
- ❑ Grammar CD-ROMs
- ❑ Microsoft Word for typing
- ❑ Pipeline emails
- ❑ Pipeline message board
- ❑ Activities on ESL websites
- ❑ PowerPoint
- ❑ Internet activities
- ❑ Smarthinking
- ❑ Internet websites for research
- ❑ Dreamweaver to create a website
- ❑ Other: _____

10 b. What would be the best time for you to attend a flex credit workshop on technology?

- ❑ M-Th between 2-3 pm
- ❑ Friday morning
- ❑ Saturday morning
- ❑ M-Th between 4:45 and 5:45 pm
- ❑ Friday afternoon
- ❑ Other _____

11. Do you think that the department should have technology objectives for each course?
- ❑ Yes                          ❑ No                          ❑ I don't know

12. If yes, what technology objectives would you recommend for the courses you are teaching or are familiar with? For example:

| Course | Possible Technology Objectives |
|--------|--------------------------------|
| ESL 51 (Writing 2) | • Learn how to type a basic Word document<br>• Learn how to write and answer a Pipeline email message |
| ESL 130 (Reading 5) | • Learn how to use Pipeline message board<br>• Learn how to create a PowerPoint presentation |
| Course | Possible Technology Objective/s |
|        |                                 |

*Thank you kindly in advance for taking the time to respond to this survey!*

Optional: Would you be willing to elaborate on your survey feedback? If so, please leave your name and phone #:
Name: _____          Phone: _____

---

**ESL Teacher Follow-Up Interview: Technology Use in the ESL Classroom[5]**

Name: _____

1.  On a scale of 1-5 (1=most comfortable and 5=least comfortable), how comfortable do you feel with technology?
    *MOST      1      2      3      4      5      LEAST COMFORTABLE*
2.  How do you feel a second language should be taught? How would you describe the way you teach a second language?
3.  What does the term computer-assisted language learning mean to you? Can you give me examples?
4.  Have you ever used technology in your language teaching? In what ways?
5.  Why did you use/didn't use technology in your language teaching? If no: If circumstances were different/more favorable, would you use technology in your classroom?
6.  Have you experienced any difficulties using technology in language teaching? Has that affected your use of technology in any way?
7.  Has using technology influenced your teaching in any way?
8.  How important do you feel it is to use technology in language teaching? What role do you think technology plays in language teaching?
9.  What technology skills would be beneficial for our ESL students to develop to succeed in their ESL classes, content courses and jobs?
10. Is there enough support for teachers wishing to use technology in language teaching in the ESL department at SBCC? What type of support would you like to see made available?
11. How did you start using technology in your language teaching? Has anyone ever talked to you about it or have you read something about it?
12. As a teacher, do you feel threatened by advancements in educational technology, or do you welcome it?

Extra: Picture your ideal computer assisted language classroom. What technology would you envision using and what computer skills would you be teaching to your students? What could the department do to help you achieve this?

---

5. Questions are based on Lam's (2000) questionnaire.

# Part 3
## Retention and Persistence Issues in Community College ESL Programs

## Chapter 6

# Differences in Academic Vocabulary Knowledge among Language-Minority Community College Students: Implications for Transition

■ Maricel G. Santos

"BEFORE MY READING WAS NOT VERY HARD. . . . NOW THERE ARE A LOT OF NEW words . . . if I just knew the meanings [it] will be easier. If I read a newspaper, it don't give me too much work [because] it's made for general populations, but I read a special book in psychology, biology, it has a specific topic, it could be more difficult . . . if I don't know the meaning of one word in a sentence . . . sometimes I just can't figure out what it's talking about."

These are the words of Isabel (a pseudonym), a 30-year-old single mother from El Salvador, describing her frustrations with the vocabulary used in her content-area textbooks. Enrolled at Bunker Hill Community College in New England, Isabel aspires to get a nursing degree, but she worries about "being able to make it." Previously Isabel had taken ESL courses in both non-academic and academic settings, but she admits that nothing had prepared her for the academic vocabulary demands at the community college.

Students like Isabel were at the forefront of my mind when I designed the study described in this chapter (see Santos, 2003, for full study). In my interactions with language-minority[1] community college students, it was clear that their concerns about English vocabulary were a persistent source of anxiety and frustration. We

---

1. The term *language-minority students* refers to students enrolled in U.S. schools who speak another language besides English at home, including foreign-born students and those born in the U.S. (Crawford, 1997). In the analysis, *language minority* is abbreviated LM for editorial convenience when referencing the various student groups.

know little about the instructional needs of language minority community college students, like Isabel, who are making the transition out of predominantly English-focused instruction and entering academic content instruction (Alamprese, 2004; Rance-Roney, 1995; Wrigley, 2007; Zafft, Kallenbach, & Spohn, 2006). Expanding this research base would help to identify community college students who would benefit from additional vocabulary instruction that would better prepare them for the vocabulary demands of their academic coursework.

## Context of the Research

Developing a solid vocabulary base is best viewed as an ongoing process in which language-minority students will encounter new challenges as they learn to read in various academic disciplines. For students who are new to a particular discipline, such as psychology, many technical words (e.g., *dissociation, photosynthesis*) may be unfamiliar. For academically underprepared students, however, the academic words may also be unfamiliar. These include non-technical items, such as *proceeds, basis, accomplishes,* and *however,* that occur with relatively high frequency across a range of academic disciplines (Coxhead, 2000; Nation, 2001; Schleppegrell, 2001; Yang, 1986).

While the meanings of technical words usually are reinforced through class discussion or lecture (Wallace, 1982, as cited in Farrell, 1990), the learner is expected to know meanings for the *non-technical* or *academic words* in the text. In this sentence from an introductory psychology textbook—"The transfer of material from short- to long-term memory proceeds largely on the basis of **rehearsal**" (Feldman, 2000, p. 209, emphasis in original)—important clues about how *rehearsal* relates to *transfer* and *memory* are found in the meanings of academic words (*proceeds, basis*). This examples illustrates the way academic words provide a "frame" in which to understand the information in a text (see Higgins, 1966). In this way, a working knowledge of academic words may be essential to a student's ability to learn content from texts (Scarcella & Rumberger, 2000; Scarcella, 2003; Zamel & Spack, 1998).

## Issues that Motivated the Research

Previous studies have identified the difficulties with academic vocabulary experienced by college ESL students (e.g., Cohen, Glasman, Rosenbaum-Cohen, Ferrara, & Fine, 1988; Marshall & Gilmour, 1993). With the exception of work by Kuehn (1996), research has not focused on language-minority community college students. ESL/EFL studies at four-year colleges and universities may not generalize to the language-minority community college population, which tends to differ from the general college student population in important ways: Community college students are older, more likely to attend school part-time, and more often manage family and work responsibilities while taking classes (Grubb, 1999; Reder, 2000).

*Academic integration*—the level of engagement in the academic life of the college—represents an important factor in students' persistence and academic achievement in college (Baker & Velèz, 1996; Chae, 2000; Pascarella & Terenzini, 1991; Tinto, 1993). The positive effects of academic integration on academic achievement are found to be particularly strong for minority and underprepared students (Moss & Young, 1995; Stovall, 2000). While there are varying perspectives on the measurement of academic integration (Braxton, 2000), there is consensus that academic integration develops through formal interactions around academic or career development tasks with peers, teachers, or academic support staff. Examples of these interactions include the extent to which students meet with teachers or peers to discuss course content, or the extent to which students make use of academic support services.

Is there a relationship between academic vocabulary knowledge and academic integration for language-minority community college students? Answers to this question will shed light on potentially important ways that community colleges could support language-minority students' language and literacy development as well as their sense of connection to the academic life of the community college. Tinto (1996), a prominent scholar on college student persistence, viewed academic skills as central to a student's ability to participate in the academic community and ultimate degree attainment, emphasizing that "persistence in college requires at least a minimum level of competent membership in . . . the academic [community]—thus, the importance of the acquisition of academic skills and the meeting of minimum standards of academic performance to the process of persistence in college" (p.106).

Academic integration activities may provide language minority students with valuable opportunities to demonstrate their sense of connection to academic life at the community college. With respect to language acquisition, these activities may serve as an important source of interaction with "expert users" of the language (see Ellis, 2000; Wong-Fillmore & Snow, 2000; Pica, 1994). Scarcella (2001) contended that interaction with standard English speakers "provides [English language learners] with exposure to standard English and provides them with the practice and feedback required to develop phonology, lexicon, morphology, syntax, and pragmatics" (p. 216). Interaction exposes students to comprehensible input and feedback (Gass, 1997; Long, 1996); also through interaction, students are able to monitor their own linguistic output (Swain, 1995). As such, language minority students with high levels of academic integration may exhibit strong academic skills because they have increased opportunities to be exposed to academic words through interactions with competent users of academic language.

The link between academic vocabulary knowledge and academic integration is also grounded in sociocultural perspectives on the role of academic socialization through language (Corson, 1997; Greenleaf, Schoenbach, Cziko, & Mueller, 2001; Ochs, 1993; Schleppegrell & Christian, 1986). In this light, language-minority students are acquiring language skills at the same time they are acquiring knowledge about "the community college world." Academic integration activities may serve as important contexts where language-minority students are socialized into new ways of using English and learning in English. Peters (1986) emphasized the pervasive role of language in schools: "In the academic context, language both spoken and written typically has a constitutive rather than an ancillary role (see Hasan, 1980); that is, it constitutes the whole of the ongoing activity in the social situation rather than serves as an accompaniment to other activities" (p. 170). The value of academic interactions does not lie in the discussion of things in general, but in the "talk about text" (Olson, 1997), in other words, "a kind of discourse where learners can talk repeatedly about knowledge gained from texts, using an acquired metalanguage set against a meaningful system used to interpret and extend understanding" (Corson, 1997, p. 684). Thus, in participating in academic integration activities, language-minority students may grow more comfortable and confident with their academic language skills.

## Research Questions Addressed

This study aimed to address two specific research questions:

1. How do three groups of community college students—language-minority students in advanced ESL, language-minority students in regular introductory psychology, and native English–speaking students in regular introductory psychology (hereafter Intro Psych)—differ in their academic vocabulary knowledge, as measured by the University Word Level Test?

2. Is the variation in University Word Level Test scores a function of students' level of academic integration, and if so, does this effect differ for language minority students in advanced ESL, language minority students in Intro Psych, and native English speakers in Intro Psych?

This exploration seeks to raise awareness of differences in academic vocabulary knowledge among language-minority community college students. By including a comparison with native English–speaking students, this study also contributes to our understanding of the ways that *all* students—regardless of language background—require instructional support in this academic arena.

### Sample Description

The sample in this study consisted of 168 students enrolled in Fall 2001 at Bunker Hill Community College in Boston, Massachusetts, including 104 language-minority students and 64 native English–speaking students. The language-minority students were recruited in seven advanced ESL classes (n=73) and four introductory psychology classes (n=31). The native English–speaking students were also recruited in the same psychology classes. This cross-sectional data permitted the examination of academic vocabulary skills for language-minority students at two key points in the transitional process: (a) just prior to the completion of advanced ESL coursework and (b) in the beginning of regular content coursework. The following labels will be used to refer to the three groups of students:

LM-ESL = language-minority students in advanced ESL

LM-Psych = language-minority students in introductory psychology

NS-Psych = native English–speaking students in introductory psychology

These three groups comprised an independent variable referred to as *learner profile*.

Table 6.1 on page 88 provides demographic characteristics for the students in the sample. Women represented about 51 percent of the total sample. About two-thirds of the sample were 19 to 24 years old; the average age was 24.16 ($SD = 7.37$), somewhat lower than the schoolwide average in Fall 2001 (age 28) and the current national average (age 29) (American Association of Community Colleges, 2007). The students in advanced ESL tended to be slightly older ($M = 27.33$, $SD = 8.67$) than the language-minority students in Intro Psych ($M = 24.67$, $SD = 6.04$) and the native English–speaking students in Intro Psych ($M = 24.16$, $SD = 7.37$). Approximately 19 percent of the students were married, and about 22 percent had children. Of those students who were married or had children, most were language-minority advanced ESL (LM-ESL) students.

Asian students, followed by Afro-Caribbean and Hispanic students, represented the three largest non-white ethnic groups in the sample (Table 6.1). The race/ethnicity categories were based on the students' *self-reported responses* on a background questionnaire. While labels such as "Asian" and "African" run the risk of glossing over important sociocultural, linguistic, and geopolitical boundaries, I opted to use those labels that the participants themselves used to self-identify. This ethnic breakdown was generally reflective of the overall percentages at the community college: In Fall 2000, Hispanic and Asian students constituted the largest proportion of non-white ethnic groups, after African-American students, of the total enrollment. The sample also included fifteen language minority students from sub-Saharan countries, including Sudan, Eritrea, Ethiopia, Nigeria, Sierra Leone, and Somalia, a relatively understudied population in United States higher education research, despite their increasing numbers in metropolitan areas (Logan & Deane, 2003).

A relatively high percentage (63 percent) of the students aspired to an associate's degree, with an additional 4 percent intending to obtain an associate's degree and then transfer to four-year schools. Overall, these numbers suggest that a majority of the students in the sample aspired to some form of academic credentialing. This trend provides an important context for this study, in that the acquisition of aca-

*Table 6.1.*

Background Characteristics of Community College Student Sample, by "Learner Profile" (based on L1 and instructional program) (n=168)

| | Learner Profile | | | |
|---|---|---|---|---|
| | LM-ESL (n=73) | LM-Psych (n=31) | NS-Psych (n=64) | Total (n=168) |
| No. of females | 34 (47%) | 18 (58%) | 34 (53%) | 86 (51%) |
| No. of students by age group | | | | |
|    18 or younger | 3 (4%) | 2 (6.67%) | 18 (29%) | 23 (14%) |
|    19–24 | 35 (49%) | 18 (60%) | 39 (62%) | 92 (56%) |
|    25–39 | 27 (38%) | 9 (30%) | 6 (10%) | 42 (25%) |
|    40 or older | 7 (9.72%) | 1 (3%) | — | 8 (5%) |
| No. of married students | 24 (33%) | 6 (19%) | 1 (2%) | 31 (19%) |
| No. of students with children | 24 (33%) | 8 (26%) | 5 (8%) | 38 (22%) |
| Race/ethnicity[2] | | | | |
|    African American | — | — | 11 (19%) | 11 (7%) |
|    African | 6 (8%) | 9 (30%) | 2 (3%) | 17 (11%) |
|    Asian | 21 (29%) | 4 (13%) | 3 (5%) | 28 (17%) |
|    Afro-Caribbean | 17 (23%) | 5 (17%) | 4 (7%) | 26 (16%) |
|    Hispanic | 14 (19%) | 7 (23%) | 1 (2%) | 22 (14%) |
|    White | 15 (21%) | 5 (17%) | 36 (61%) | 56 (35%) |
| No. of students with jobs | 52 (71%) | 21 (68%) | 41 (64%) | 114 (68%) |
| No. of students enrolled FT | 49 (71%) | 27 (93%) | 53 (82%) | 129 (81%) |

2. Afro-Caribbean refers to Black non-Hispanic students, mostly from Jamaica or Haiti. For language minority students, White refers to non-Hispanic whites from countries where English is not the dominant language, whereas for native English–speaking students, White refers to non-Hispanic whites from countries where English is the dominant language.

demic vocabulary is essential if students are to excel academically and, ultimately, attain credentials.

## Data Collection and Analysis Procedures

Academic vocabulary knowledge was measured using the University Word Level Test (Beglar & Hunt, 1999), a multiple choice test based on Nation (1983, 1990) and designed to estimate the size of a student's academic word knowledge. As in the examples below, the student is presented with six words and three definitions. The student is required to match the three definitions with three of the six words (Beglar & Hunt, 1999).

| | | | | |
|---|---|---|---|---|
| 16. _d_ | depend on | | a. | Transfer |
| 17. _b_ | judge the worth of | | b. | Evaluate |
| 18. _e_ | succeed in gaining something | | c. | Sustain |
| | | | d. | Rely |
| | | | e. | Attain |
| | | | f. | Ignore |

The test contained a total of 54 definitions, so the total possible score was 54 points.[3] Raw scores were used in the analysis.

Students' academic integration was based on the reported frequency of several activities related to academic life—that is, how often students met with their professors to discuss coursework, or met with their advisor to discuss their academic plans; used academic support services; formed study groups; used the library; and attended career-related workshops (cf. Chae, 2000; Hagedorn, Chi, Cepeda, & McLain, 2007). Students indicated the frequency (0–5, never to very often) with which they engaged in each activity. To best capture the central tendency of these ordinal data, the mode of the students' responses was used in the analysis.

A two-way ANOVA design was used to examine differences in UWLT scores based on two independent variables: learner profile (i.e., LM-ESL, LM-Psych, or NS-Psych) and academic integration. Post-hoc comparisons using Tukey's HSD were conducted to gain insight into the exact nature of significant differences between levels of each independent variable. Effect sizes were calculated using omega-squared ($\omega^2$), which provides a standardized index for gauging the impact of the independent variables on the variation in UWLT scores. Self-report data were collected on the language minority students' L1 academic literacy and L1 oral proficiency, but these effects were not statistically significant, and thus are not discussed here.

## Findings

As shown in Table 6.2 on page 90, the mean UWLT score for the full sample was 42.86, with scores ranging from 14 to 54. On average, language-minority advanced ESL students (LM-ESL) scored lower than language-minority introductory psychology students (LM-Psych) who, in turn, scored lower than native English–speaking introductory psychology students (NS-Psych). The standard deviation

---

3. The UWLT consists of two forms, each with 27 items, designed for pre- and post-testing purposes. In this study, the two forms were combined to create a 54-item test, as advised by the test designers when using the test for norm-referenced purposes (see Beglar & Hunt, 1999).

*Table 6.2.*

Mean UWLT Scores and Standard Deviations as a Function of "Learner Profile"

| "Learner Profile" | Mean | s.d. | Min. | Max. |
|---|---|---|---|---|
| Language-minority students in ESL (LM-ESL) (n=73) | 36.38 | 9.28 | 14 | 52 |
| Language-minority students in Intro Psych (LM-Psych) (n=31) | 43.74 | 6.40 | 30 | 53 |
| Native English–speaking students in Intro Psych (NS-Psych) (n=64) | 47.80 | 4.65 | 36 | 54 |
| *All students* (n = 168) | 42.86 | 9.08 | 14 | 54 |

Note: Highest possible UWLT score = 54.

for the LM-ESL mean (*SD*=9.28) was about a third larger than that of the LM-Psych group (*SD*=6.40) and twice as large as that of the NS-Psych group (*SD*=4.65). This finding indicates greater variability in the LM-ESL scores. ANOVA results of these differences based on learner profile are significant ($F_{(2, 165)}$ = 42.65, $p < .05$) (see Table 6.3). In addition, the Tukey HSD procedure revealed that all pairwise differences among means were significant, $p < .05$. Greater variability in UWLT scores within the LM-ESL group seems reasonable as these students, presumably, were still developing their English skills, and we would expect the variation to reflect a myriad of factors—for example, years of exposure to English (Skehan, 1989). The difference in mean UWLT scores between LM-Psych students and NS-Psych students was not as large as the difference in means scores between LM-ESL and NS-Psych students. This narrower gap suggests that these language-minority students, who have "transitioned" beyond the need for ESL classes, appear to be closing the gap in their academic vocabulary knowledge relative to the native-speaking peers. Overall, these results confirm initial expectations that real differences in UWLT performance would occur based on differences in English proficiency level. However, as shown in the next section, it also appears that an

*Table 6.3.*

Analysis of Variance (ANOVA) Results for UWLT Scores as a Function of "Learner Profile"

| Source | df | MS | F | $\omega^2$ |
|---|---|---|---|---|
| "Learner profile" | 2 | 2273.05 | 42.65** | .33 |
| Residual (error) | 165 | 53.29 | | |

Note: $\omega^2$ = effect size. *$p < .05$. **$p < .01$.

additional source of variation may stem from differences in academic integration levels.

Table 6.4 reports mean UWLT and standard deviations for the three learner profile groups based on their self-reported levels of academic integration. As we look at the changes in mean UWLT scores across the various academic integration levels (Table 6.4), it appears that both groups of language minority students experience a slight boost in their average UWLT scores when they move from *no* academic integration activity (mode of 0) to *low* integration levels (mode of 1). From low-to-moderate (mode of 2) to moderate (mode of 3) levels, both language-minority student groups appear to experience a drop in average UWLT scores. For students who are native English speakers, mean UWLT scores appear to stay the same initially, but these students also seem to experience a drop in scores at higher integration levels. These trends are illustrated in Figure 6.1. (The lines in Figure 6.1 do not extend past Level 3 because the students' range of responses to the academic integration questions did not span the full range possible on the questionnaire [0-5].)

Although the UWLT scores based on integration levels do seem to differ for the two language-minority student groups compared to the NS-Psych group, there was no significant interaction ($F_{(11, 152)} = 1.64, p < .14$) between these two variables. As shown in Table 6.5, the main effects of learner profile and academic integration were found to be significant, suggesting that both variables contribute to the variation in UWLT scores in the sample. Although the significant main effects in Table 6.5 are sufficient to reject the null hypothesis of no significant differences between UWLT means based on learner profile and academic integration, post-hoc comparisons were performed to identify which academic integration levels were

**Table 6.4.**

Mean UWLT Scores and Standard Deviations (in parentheses) as a Function of "Learner Profile" and Academic Integration (n=164)

| "Learner Profile" | Academic Integration Levels (categories based on mode) | | | | |
|---|---|---|---|---|---|
| | None | Low | Low-to-Moderate | Moderate | Total |
| Language-minority students in ESL (LM-ESL) (n=71) | 36.38 (8.52) | 41.53 (6.26) | 32.89 (11.32) | 33.57 (10.08) | 36.45 (9.39) |
| Language-minority students in Intro Psych (LM-Psych) (n=31) | 42.40 (3.13) | 45.18 6.94 | 43.58 (7.30) | 41.33 (6.03) | 43.74 (6.40) |
| Native English–speaking students in Intro Psych (NS-Psych) (n=62) | 49.21 (2.84) | 48.12 (4.53) | 50.00 (1.69) | 43.67 (6.36) | 48.05 (4.49) |

Note: Highest possible UWLT score = 54.

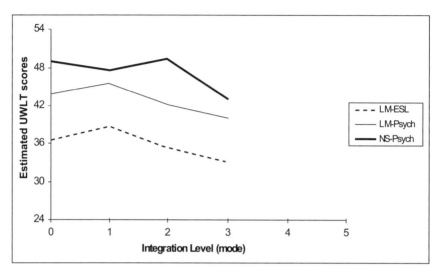

**Figure 6.1.**   Graph Illustrating Differences in Estimated UWLT Scores as a
Function of Academic Integration Level (mode) (n=168)

**Table 6.5.**
Analysis of Variance (ANOVA) Results for UWLT Scores as a Function
of "Learner Profile" and Academic Integration (n=164)

| Source | df | MS | F | $\omega^2$ |
|---|---|---|---|---|
| "Learner profile" | 2 | 4122.50 | 40.10** | .32 |
| Academic integration level | 3 | 509.43 | 3.30** | .04 |
| Residual (error) | 158 | 51.40 | | |
| Total | 163 | 13171.53 | 80.81 | |

Note: $\omega^2$ = effect size. *$p$ < .05. **$p$ < .01.

creating the most difference in scores. Results indicated that the mean UWLT scores
were significantly higher for students reporting *no integration* compared to students
reporting *low integration* ($F_{(1, 158)}$ = 4.64, $p$ = .0327), and also significantly higher
for students reporting *no integration* compared to students reporting *moderate
integration* ($F_{(1, 158)}$ = 8.09, $p$ = .005).

What does it mean that, at apparently more engaged levels of academic integration, students in this study appeared to experience slight declines in their mean
UWLT scores compared to students at less to no engagement? This pattern seems
to run counter to the hypothesis that academic integration efforts might in fact
provide a *facilitative* environment for the acquisition of academic vocabulary. One

interpretation is that the students who attempt to integrate academically and perform below average on the UWLT are engaged in help-seeking activities. In other words, the efforts to integrate academically for these students with lower UWLT scores may reveal *their academic struggle and need for academic support,* not their sense of connection to the academic environment of the community college, as academic integration has been conventionally defined in the literature.

We can also speculate that early attempts to academically integrate are not sufficient to have a positive impact on academic skill outcomes. If students have not developed effective "college survival skills" (e.g., how to seek help from your professor, or make optimal use of academic support services) (see Richardson & Skinner, 1992), their initial attempts to academically integrate themselves, however moderate, may not be sufficient to mitigate gaps in the area of academic vocabulary knowledge. In addition, we can speculate that it is yet too early in the students' academic careers to find evidence of the positive effects of academic integration activities on academic vocabulary knowledge.

These findings invite contemplation of future studies investigating how both language-minority and native English–speaking students may uniquely experience the "academic integration" phenomenon. The fact that students in each learner profile group posted average to above average UWLT scores at reported minimal to zero levels of academic integration suggests that there may be alternative routes to academic vocabulary development not revealed by their academic integration level. Indeed, Table 6.5 reports that the effect size for academic integration only accounted for 4 percent of the overall variance in UWLT score, even though it was highly significant in the ANOVA model. Furthermore, compared to the effect size for academic integration, the effect size for the main effect of learner profile is much larger (33 percent). We still have a large proportion of unexplained variance, 67 percent, to account for. It is reasonable to expect that the true effects of academic integration in conjunction with "learner profile" may remain hidden because ulterior interactions remain unexamined. As noted earlier, these integration data were collected over the course of the fall semester when students typically are still settling into their school routines. Longitudinal studies are needed to examine this possibility.

## Implications

For those language-minority students intent on earning college degrees, it is clear that general English proficiency is not sufficient; they also need to acquire the academic English skills that enable them to manage the complex and cognitively demanding task of learning academic content in English (see Carrasquillo & Rodriguez, 1996; Cummins, 2000; Jiang & Kuehn, 2001). This study provides a preliminary basis for directing academic vocabulary instruction to language-minority students at (at least) two critical points in their academic trajectory—while in ESL programs and during their early ventures into regular content coursework. Explicit attention to English vocabulary instruction is a logical emphasis in many academic ESL programs, but content-area teachers in other departments may not be aware of the need for vocabulary instruction in content courses. Most ESL teachers do not feel that they are content experts and thus may not be prepared to guide students' comprehension when they attempt to read authentic discipline-specific texts. Because of these respective needs for information, ESL and content-area faculty have much to gain by working together (see Ravitch, this volume). Inter-departmental collaborations are one way that community colleges can ensure that students have access to *ongoing* support that promotes their simultaneous acquisition of academic English and content knowledge.

The study findings around academic integration signal the need for increased dialogue about the nature of students' academic integration experiences. It is possible that the prevailing focus on the frequency of participation in academic integration activities may be masking important variation in our students' perceptions of academic integration and their reasons for participating in these activities (Moss & Young, 1995). In this study, the effect of academic integration did not significantly differ for language-minority students and native English–speaking students. This finding suggests that the responsibility to support students' academic integration is best viewed as a shared responsibility across academic departments. Finally, the findings from this study provide a basis for analyzing academic integration experiences as potentially "vocabulary-rich" learning contexts. In sum, increasing our knowledge of the academic vocabulary needs of our language-minority students and the vocabulary demands placed on them by their academic coursework will enable us to support their successful transition into content courses and, ultimately, their success in college.

# Chapter 7

# Transitioning from ESL and the GED to Post-Secondary Education: A Case Study of a College Transitions Program

■ Elizabeth M. Zachry and Emily Dibble

Enrolling in post-secondary education is particularly daunting for ELLs who do not possess high school credentials. While important alternative secondary credentialing programs have been put in place, such as the Spanish-language GED, most post-secondary institutions presume proficiency in English if learners are to succeed and obtain post-secondary credentials (Tyler, 2005). Because of the academic English demands of post-secondary education, the need for programs that enable adult English learners to transition from General Educational Development (GED) programs into community college becomes increasingly essential.

Research in post-secondary education has highlighted the dismal enrollment and success rates of students who enter college with a GED diploma. Research has shown that GED recipients are much less likely to continue into post-secondary education and have lower labor-market outcomes than traditional high school graduates (e.g., Boesel, Alsalam, & Smith, 1998; Boudett, Murnane, & Willett, 2000; Tyler, Murnane, & Willett, 2000; Cameron & Heckman, 1993; Smith, T.M., 2003). Policymakers have recently begun to fund and develop programs to aid GED recipients as they transition into post-secondary education (Office of Vocational and Adult Education [OVAE], 2007). Federal funding for Adult Basic Education (ABE)-to-college transitional programs only began to be systematically funded in the late 1990s and still comprises a small portion of the federal government's education budget (OVAE, 2005; U.S. Department of Education, 2004). Despite low funding, many types of transitions to college programs have cropped up, representing a diverse typology of program contexts. These programs range from "low-touch" supplementary advising programs (Advising Model), which aim to orient GED students to post-secondary education opportunities, to intensive college-preparatory programs (College Preparatory Model), which offer academic courses in reading, writing, and math (Zafft, Kallenbach, & Spohn, 2006, pp. 15, 28). Another model of particular relevance to adult ELL populations, the ESOL Model, focuses on building learners' English language skills with the goal of reducing the amount of time spent in ESL classes at the start of their college career (Zafft et al., 2006, p. 21). This model differs from intensive college-preparatory programs by focusing specifically on ELLs' academic language skills, with less attention to preparation in math (Zafft et al., 2006).

This chapter contributes to a growing body of knowledge about the design and success of transitions to college programs by examining the Transitions to College program (hereafter the Transitions program) at Bunker Hill Community College (BHCC). In this chapter, we highlight how an intensive college-preparatory transitions program sought to increase the post-secondary success of either GED recipients or high school graduates who graduated more than five years ago, most of whom were English language learners. Rather than being based on the ESOL Model, the transitions program highlighted here follows the College Preparatory Model, meaning that it provides intensive instruction in all subjects, including math. However, this program differs from many college preparatory transitions programs because it primarily serves an ELL population because of the high numbers of ELLs transitioning out of BHCC's adult basic education, ESOL, and GED programs. In fact, as we will discuss in greater detail below, nearly 90 percent of the students in the Transitions program were ELLs during the period we conducted this study (2006–2007). Therefore, this case study provides an interesting commentary on how college-preparatory transitions programs can work for adult learners of English.

## Context of the Research

The context for this study is Bunker Hill Community College (BHCC), a large urban college serving 11,673 credit and 3,295 non-credit students in an inner-city Boston neighborhood. Its service area consists of a large language-minority population, including primarily Latinos, but also substantial proportions of students of Asian and Eastern European descent. Its non-credit and credit ESL programs each serve approximately 1,200 students each year (2,400 students total). The Transitions to College program at BHCC is managed by a coordinator in the Adult Basic Education (ABE) division of the college, who reports to the Dean of Academic Support and College Pathways Programs. The authors of this report include an outside researcher (Elizabeth) and the Executive Dean of Institutional Effectiveness at BHCC (Emily).

The Transitions program differs from other college-preparatory transitions programs in that it also articulates with BHCC's adult basic education ESOL[1] and GED programs. In order to participate in BHCC's Transitions program, students must have been enrolled in an ESOL, ABE, or GED program and have a high school diploma or GED. Thus, students enrolled in Bunker Hill's ESOL, Spanish GED, or English GED courses are recommended to the Transitions program. From Spring 2000 to Spring 2006, approximately 6 percent of Bunker Hill's ESOL students[2] and 7 percent of the GED students enrolled in Bunker Hill's Transitions program.

The Transitions program was first developed in 2000 after the Massachusetts Department of Education sent out a request for proposals for the development of a transitional program that would better prepare GED recipients for entering college. BHCC's ABE department responded to this call by proposing a series of three academic classes, including reading, writing, and math courses, as well as a transitions seminar, which would assist students in learning how to navigate college successfully. Bunker Hill was one of eight community colleges in the state of Massachusetts that received funding for developing an ABE-to-college transitions program. It has been managed by the ABE department at BHCC since its inception and has remained relatively the same in structure since its development in 2000.

## Issues that Motivated the Research

Several studies have documented the urgent need for transitional programs that prepare GED recipients for the demands of college work (Hamilton, 1998; Kuehn, 1996; Rance-Roney, 1995; Reder, 2000; Wrigley, 2007). While relatively few GED recipients pursue post-secondary education compared to their peers with traditional high school diplomas, those who do are often poorly prepared for the college-level academics. For instance, a small study that analyzed the success rates of GED recipients in a two-year college from Fall 1991 through Fall 1996 found that 85 percent of these students needed developmental coursework before moving on to college-level courses (Hamilton, 1998). Other studies have confirmed this trend, with substantially more GED recipients enrolling in remedial courses than traditional high school graduates (Reder, 2000). However, there is a silver lining: GED recipients who enrolled in post-secondary institutions generally had course

---

1. Bunker Hill has several different ESOL/ESL programs, including an ESOL program run by the adult basic education department, a non-credit Basic English as a Second Language program, and a credit ESL program that offers college-level courses. "ESOL" will be used to describe Bunker Hill's adult basic education ESOL program.

2. These low enrollment numbers can be attributed to the fact that few of BHCC's ESOL students have a high school diploma or obtain a GED while in the ESOL program.

completion rates and GPAs similar to those of the average student at the college (Hamilton, 1998). These results indicate that GED recipients may be able to achieve at rates similar to traditional high school graduates when given proper remediation.

Little research exists that documents the structural attributes and effects of these programs. The Office of Vocational and Adult Education (OVAE), which oversees federally funded adult education programming, has documented the need for more research into these programs and has begun collecting baseline information on learners who transition from adult education programs to post-secondary education (OVAE, 2007). Additionally, some studies have discussed specific features of transitional program models (Brickman & Braun, 1999; Schwendeman, 1999; Zafft et al., 2006). However, because transitional programming is still a burgeoning field, few studies have discussed how these programs aid ELLs, in particular, and how they affect learner outcomes.

This study attempts to fill this gap by presenting research on a college-preparatory transitions to college program geared primarily toward an ELL/GED population. It begins with a discussion of how the program was structured and sought to meet the specific needs of GED recipients[3] from ELL backgrounds. It analyzes programmatic and learner outcomes to document how successful this program was in meeting its goals. It concludes by examining the importance of these results for broader adult ESL policy and education.

## Research Questions Addressed

The Transitions program at BHCC has several goals. Its primary focus is to increase the number of GED recipients and English language learners who enroll in college and post-secondary educational or vocational programs. As a corollary to this goal, it seeks to better prepare GED recipients and immigrant and refugee English language learners for college-level academic work and college responsibilities. Another function of the program, which will be described in more detail later, is to articulate service between the program and the college's credit-bearing developmental reading, writing, and math courses. To accomplish these goals, the Transitions program also seeks to develop a community of learners using the cohort model.

To examine the success of BHCC's Transitions program in meeting these goals, this case study addressed two primary research questions:

1. How is the Transitions program structured?
2. What is its impact on college readiness, enrollment rates, and success of ELL/GED students?

---

3. Some students in the program had high school diplomas from their native countries; however, most students had received a GED. Therefore, these references refer to an ELL/GED population.

# Data Collection and Analysis Procedures

To address these questions, we conducted an in-depth study of BHCC's Transitions program using a case study format. We began by reviewing informational materials on the program, including proposals, progress reports, course syllabi, and textbooks. Using these materials as a guide, we then developed an interview protocol in order to conduct semi-structured, in-person interviews with the faculty and staff who were responsible for developing and managing the program. Our interview protocol focused on specific programmatic aspects, including the types of students served, the program, course content design, the role of assessment, support services, financing, and technological support.

Throughout 2005–2006, we conducted interviews with instructors and administrative staff. In addition to interviews, we conducted classroom observations and conducted brief focus groups with students. While the scope of this chapter prevents us from presenting details from these interviews and observations, a descriptive report is available through TESOL (Zachry, 2008).

Our analysis in this case study highlights trends in student achievement and retention using two institutional data sources. First, we analyzed longitudinal data from BHCC's comprehensive student database, which contains information on student enrollment, grades, and demographic background. We also examined data from the Transitions program. Based on the National Reporting System (NRS)[4] methods required by the state, these data track the progress and learning gains of students in ABE programs.

We analyzed data from these two sources to track students' longitudinal progress at BHCC as well as their individual learning gains over an academic year. Using the BHCC student database, we tracked cohorts of students who participated in the Transitions program from Fall 2000 through Spring 2006. We analyzed how many students were retained within the program as well as how many transitioned into higher level developmental and credit-bearing courses at BHCC. These results were also compared with longitudinal data on BHCC students who had received a GED but not participated in the Transitions program. Using the NRS student achievement data from the Transitions program, we analyzed students' learning gains using the method prescribed by the Massachusetts Department of Education. In this method, learning gains are quantified by comparing students' assessment scores on the Test of Adult Basic Education (TABE)[5] before entering the Transitions program with a quarterly reassessment of their learning gains while enrolled in the program. According to Massachusetts DOE regulations, students' skills must

---

4. The National Reporting System (NRS) is an outcome-based reporting system for state-administered, federally funded adult education programs in the United States.
5. Starting in fiscal year 2007, the TABE has been replaced by the new Massachusetts Adult Proficiency Test (MAPT).

increase by 0.4 grade equivalent, or a 27-point increase in their TABE scores, to show significant learning gain.

In the Transitions program, findings for ELL students are not disaggregated from findings on native English–speaking students, but rather by ABE literacy level. Therefore, the findings on ELL learning gains should be interpreted cautiously as the sample of Transitions students includes native English–speaking students, although this latter group is relatively small in comparison to the number of ELLs.

# Findings

The first section of our findings describes how programmatic elements of BHCC's Transitions program sought to develop students' academic skills and further prepare them for college. We begin with a discussion of the target student population, their skills, and their needs. We then examine how different aspects of the Transitions program sought to increase their college readiness. In the second section, we discuss several programmatic and student outcomes. We examine the program's success at articulating with BHCC's developmental courses and its ability to expand BHCC's pre-college-level instruction. Our analyses of student outcomes center upon the program's success in retaining students, improving their learning, and helping them transition into credit-bearing courses. We conclude by discussing the importance of this program and its successes for ELL programming and policy.

## Program Structure

This section explains the design and structure of BHCC's Transitions program. More specifically, we analyze the target student population, the program's design and content, the role of assessment, and its use of technology.

### Student Population

The Transitions program at BHCC is kept intentionally small in order to allow students to have maximum contact with their instructors and advisors, with the program enrolling about fifteen new students each semester.[6] In the 2004–2005 academic year, the program enrolled a total of 52 students.[7] While designed for fifteen new students each semester, students from previous semesters may continue to enroll if they have not completed the course series or raised their skills to the

---

6. This enrollment level represents the target enrollment number for the 2005–2006 school year, a reduction compared to previous years when there were twenty slots available for students.

7. By NRS definitions, which count only students who received at least twelve hours of instruction, only 50 students enrolled in the program.

level needed for entry into college. In 2004–2005, the majority of students in the Transitions program were English language learners: Most students spoke Spanish (62 percent) or a language other than English (27 percent). In other words, nearly 90 percent of the students in the Transitions program were ELLs. With respect to ethnicity, the majority of these learners were of Latino descent, followed by white (13 percent) and African American (10 percent). Approximately two-thirds of the Transitions students were female.

Transitions students are recruited from other Bunker Hill ABE programs, including the ABE ESOL, Spanish GED, and English GED programs, and from other ABE programs throughout the Boston area. Students enter the program typically at the intermediate to advanced levels of literacy (based on NRS definitions). Most students have reading, writing, and math skills between the sixth and tenth grade level. Students with skills higher than the tenth grade are considered college-ready and are encouraged to enroll in the higher-level developmental courses or college-level courses.

We should note that the students in the Transitions program differ from the "typical" learners who enroll in BHCC's non-credit adult ESOL programs in three primary ways. First, these students tended to enter community college with higher level English skills than many students in BHCC's ABE ESOL program. Additionally, unlike many ESOL students, all of these students had a high school diploma or GED. Finally, as dictated by the Transitions program entry requirements, all those in this program were seeking to enter college-level courses.

## Design and Content

Unlike the ESOL Model for ABE-to-college transitions programs, which focuses solely on students' language skills, BHCC's Transitions program is based on a College Preparatory Model (Zaftt et al., 2006). The program focuses on developing students' academic and non-academic skills (e.g., time management and study skills) through a three-course series. Two different academic courses are taught, including a combined Transitional Reading and Writing course, Transitional Pathways to College Math course, and a Transitional Pathways to College Transitions (Student Success) seminar. The courses are taught on three different nights of the week for three hours each for a full semester, thus making it a fairly intensive ABE-to-college transitions program. Students may enroll in one to three courses per semester. Additionally, students may opt out of taking one of the academic classes (either math or reading/writing) if their assessments reveal their skills to be college-level. However, all students are required to take the Transitions (Student Success) seminar.

To enroll in the program, students must demonstrate that they are able to do five hours of homework a week for each of the Transitions courses in which they enroll. This requirement keeps most students from enrolling in more than two courses in one semester. For instance, in 2004–2005, most students took one (27 students) or two classes (42 students), while only eleven students took three or four classes.[8] Interestingly, nearly as many students enrolled in the math course (36 enrollments) as in the English courses (39 enrollments) and the reading courses (42 enrollments) in the 2004–2005 school year. No matter how many courses students take initially, participants generally complete the Transitions program within two semesters.

In order to support students' ability to learn at their own pace, the program allows students to repeat an academic course if they have not mastered the skills needed for entry into the college's upper-level developmental reading, writing, or math courses. This design presents an interesting contrast to BHCC's traditional developmental courses, whereby students who pay for the course but fail it are required to re-enroll and pay to take the lower-level developmental course again. In contrast, in the Transitions courses, students are not penalized with a failing grade at the end of the semester nor do they pay to repeat the class. Instead, if one of the assessments reveals that the student's skills are not high enough to enter the upper-level course, the student may re-enroll in the Transitions course for another semester free of charge. Despite this policy, BHCC data reveal that few students have repeated a course: only thirteen students repeated a course in the 2004–2005 school year.

With respect to curricular content, BHCC's Transitions program is similar to other college preparatory ABE-to-college transitions programs in that it articulates with BHCC's developmental courses (Zafft et al., 2006). The reading/writing and math courses mirror the college's lower-level developmental reading, writing, and math courses. By using the same curricula and textbooks, the Transitions reading/writing courses are designed so that students who complete the Transitions program can bypass the lower-level developmental classes and move directly into upper-level developmental courses. For the most part, Transitions courses are taught by instructors with experience working with non-native speakers, which provides important support to the ELLs' ongoing academic literacy development in both reading/writing and math courses.

The Transitions reading/writing course generally emphasizes the development of critical reading and writing skills. Specific goals include developing the ability to distinguish between the main idea and details, identify facts and sequencing, summarize longer passages, recognize and use appropriate academic English in paper development, and understand writing as a step-by-step process. While this course uses different textbooks than the developmental courses, it focuses on the same skills.

In addition, the Transitions reading/writing course supplements these texts with novels (e.g., Ernest Hemingway's *The Old Man and the Sea*), reading and writing rubrics (e.g., Arlington Education and Empowerment Program (REEP) writing assessment), and other instructor-assigned materials.

---

8. In 2004–2005, the Transitions program offered four courses, with reading and writing as two separate courses. Because of funding cuts in 2005–2006, the program now combines reading and writing into one course and now only offers three courses.

The Transitions math course uses the same textbook as the developmental math course offered in the college (*Basic College Mathematics, 6th ed.*). However, the Transitions math course predominantly focuses on less material than the lower-level developmental math course. The Transitions math course develops students' foundational mathematical skills (e.g., addition, subtraction, multiplication, and division) while the lower-level developmental math courses include an additional focus on elementary algebra, geometry, and trigonometry. These differences exist because Transitions math teachers often tailor the curriculum to the students' skill levels while instructors in the developmental math courses tend to adhere to the set curriculum regardless of students' learning needs. As a result, Transitions math teachers are able to attend to those areas of mathematics learning when linguistic difficulties (e.g., comprehension of word problems) may be the source of students' struggle rather than insufficient mathematical knowledge (see Spanos, Rhodes, Dale, & Crandall, 1988; Gutierrez, 2002).

In addition to these academic courses, BHCC's Transitions program offers a Transitional Pathways to College Transitions (Student Success) seminar to introduce students to college life and expectations, an innovative course not offered in the college's developmental program. All Transitions students are required to take this seminar upon entry into the program. In this seminar, students often work together on group projects, share ideas about their future goals, and assist each other with assignments. Additionally, students are encouraged to assist one another outside of class by gathering homework for absent students and creating cooperative networks for sharing information about assignments and class discussions. In addition to building these social networks, the Transitions seminar seeks to teach students about important aspects of college life, including the selection of a major, course requirements for various academic tracks, time management skills, effective note-taking skills, and test-taking strategies.

### Role of Assessment

While the academic course work in Transitions and developmental courses is similar, there are differences in the way that Transitional students and developmental students place into their respective programs and advance to the next course. The Accuplacer® Computerized Placement Test (CPT) is used in both programs to assess students' skills (see Schuemann, this volume). Students who score a 60 or below can enroll in either the lower developmental courses or the Transitions program. Students who score above 60 are encouraged to enroll directly into BHCC's higher level developmental or college-level courses.

BHCC's Transitions program also uses the TABE to assess and place students in classes. Students must score a minimum of a 6.0 on the English TABE reading, writing, and math tests in order to enroll in Transitions classes. This requirement helps ensure that non-native English speakers have the appropriate English proficiency to succeed in the Transitions program. If students do not score a 6.0 or higher on the TABE, then they may be referred to the ABE ESOL or GED programs (depending on their credentialing and needs). The TABE is not used in programs outside of the ABE department (where the Transitions program is housed), as it is used primarily to document the skills and learning progress of students in ABE programs.

Differences also exist in how students advance from these courses. While the developmental students are graded and advance to the upper-level developmental course if they receive a passing grade, grades are not used in the Transitions program. Instead, Transitions students must re-take the TABE and the CPT Accuplacer® test in order to show progress. Additionally, Transitions students must re-take the CPT Accuplacer® test at Bunker Hill's assessment center in order to place into higher-level developmental reading, writing, or math courses. As with other students enrolling in these courses, exiting Transitions students must score between 60 and 90 on the corresponding CPT Accuplacer® test in order to advance into the higher-level developmental reading, writing, or math course. If students score higher, then they are placed in regular college-level courses. While these assessments are not designed for ELL populations, their use in the Transitions program provides important documentation of the ELLs' mastery of English as well as their ability to perform on par with native English–speaking peers.

### Use of Technology

In addition to the regular use of word processing and Internet programs, the academic software program Passkey plays an essential role in the preparation of prospective Transitions students. The Passkey program consists of lessons in three academic subject areas (reading, writing, and math), which students may use outside of class to further their skills. Students are encouraged to use the Passkey program for one semester or summer before entry in the Transitions program in order to further prepare them for taking the TABE assessment. While students are waiting for entry into the program, they are assigned lessons on the Passkey program to develop their reading, writing, and math skills. The Passkey program is keyed individually for each student's skill level, and students are generally assigned a group of 24 lessons, with eight lessons each in math, reading, and writing. Passkey is used to track students' skills and progress as it records their mistakes, challenges, and successes. The Transitions program's academic advisor monitors each student's progress and gives weekly advising to students as they progress through their assignments.

## Meeting Students' Needs

When analyzing the successes and challenges of BHCC's Transitions program, we found that the program has met many of its goals. Both the programmatic and student outcomes are discussed to evaluate whether the program met its goals of helping ELL/GED students enroll and succeed in college.

### Articulation with Bunker Hill's Developmental Courses

One of the primary goals of BHCC's Transitions program was to provide an alternative to the college's fee-based developmental courses, which would aid ELL/GED students to enter college with higher academic skills. While the program clearly achieved the goal of articulating with BHCC's developmental courses by using the same assessments and curricula as the lower-level developmental courses, did it help students move into college? It appears that the answer is yes. Longitudinal data from Fall 2000 to Spring 2006 indicate 20.8 percent of Transitions students (71 out of 342) enrolled in upper-level developmental reading, writing, and math courses. This rate is much higher than the enrollment rates of GED students who did not participate in the Transitions program: only 1.5 percent of GED students (8 out of 522) enrolled in upper-level developmental reading, writing, or math courses from 2000 to 2006. This differential suggests that the Transitions program provides an effective means for helping GED and ABE students to enter post-secondary education. Additionally, the Transitions program has achieved its goal of increasing the percentage of ELL and GED students who receive developmental support in reading, writing, and math. Interest in the program is demonstrated by the full roster of students each semester and the long waiting list for entry into the program.

### Retention

The Transitions program has demonstrated a high retention rate (see Lewis, this volume). From Fall 2004 to Spring 2005, 33 percent (15 out of 45) of Transitions students were retained within the program. The overall retention rate across six years—from Fall 2000 to Spring 2006—was 28 percent (95 out of 227). Students also demonstrated high levels of attendance, with Transitions students attending 85 percent of the time during the 2004–2005 school year.

An important caveat is that retention does not carry the same significance in the Transitions program compared to the developmental programs. In developmental programs, students who are retained may still advance to the next level in the multilevel sequence of courses. In contrast, the Transitions program has only one level of courses, and students are expected to graduate out of the program as soon as possible. Being retained in the Transitions program is not necessarily a positive event (as it generally is other programs) because the program is designed to have students graduate and move into college-level courses. Thus, measuring retention may not be the best measure of the Transitions program's success.

### Development of a Student Cohort

With the Student Success seminar, the Transitions program hopes to create cohorts of students who will identify with and help one another as they move into college life, which may in turn help to heighten students' sense of connection to the academic and social life at BHCC (see Tinto, 1996). In a separate study conducted at BHCC,

Helsing, Broderick, and Hammerman (2001) found that ESL students valued the cohort (termed "peer group") for diverse reasons: Some ESL students relied on the peer group to make new friends, while others viewed the peer group as a safe place to try out new ways of thinking and communicating. Similarly, in our study, Transitions students commented in interviews that their relationships with peers helped them build confidence in their skills (an affective outcome) and supported their success in the Transitions program (an academic outcome). Additionally, Transitions program staff reported that students regularly gathered homework for absent students, carpooled to class, and called each other about assignments (signs of key social outcomes). Thus, the cohort model provides a clear example of the way that the Transitions program is able to be accommodating and responsive to the needs of ELLs.

### Learning Gains

The Transitions program has also been successful in boosting learning gains. During the 2004–2005 school year, a total of 29 students, or 55.8 percent of all Transitions students and 58 percent of NRS students (those who received more than 12 hours of instruction), completed an NRS level. In addition, 28 students, or 53.8 percent of all Transitions students (56 percent of NRS students), completed a level and also advanced a level. These learning gains compare favorably to the proportion of developmental reading, writing, and math students who were eligible to advance to the higher-level developmental courses at Bunker Hill. For instance, during the 2004–2005 school year, 47–70 percent of students in the lower-level developmental reading, writing, and math courses received a passing grade and were thus eligible to enter the higher-level developmental courses.

Unfortunately, these comparisons of learning gains are somewhat limited. First, the developmental program and the Transitions program measure learning gains in different ways. Learning gains in the Transitions program are based on students' performance on the TABE test. In Bunker Hill's developmental courses, learning gains are assessed either by students' performance on the CPT or by students' grades in lower-level developmental courses. Thus, learning gains are based on different assessments and different mechanisms for advancement.

Second, the developmental course program and the Transitions program have different mechanisms for entry into higher-level developmental courses. Although new Bunker Hill students may enter into higher-level developmental courses based on their performance on the CPT (like Transitions students), students who are already enrolled in lower-level developmental courses may enter into higher-level developmental courses by receiving a grade of C− or better in the lower-level developmental course. These grades are determined by individual teachers and, thus, are not a standardized measure of students' learning gains. For these reasons, the skills of lower-level developmental students and the skills of Transitions students entering higher-level developmental courses are not necessarily equivalent. Thus, the best that can be said from these data is that substantial proportions of Transitions and lower-level developmental students experience learning gains in any one year, as determined by their different assessments.

### Transitions to Academic Programs

The Transitions program also appears to increase the chances that students will eventually enroll in college-level academic and vocational courses. Longitudinal data from Fall 2000 to Spring 2006 indicate that 25 percent of Transitions students (87 of 342 students) enrolled in credit-bearing courses at BHCC as compared with 2.5 percent of GED students who did not participate in the Transitions program (13 out of 522 students). Thus, approximately 10 times as many Transitions students enroll in college courses as GED students who do not participate in the Transitions program. This finding reveals that the Transitions program is having an enormous impact in helping ELL and GED graduates to enroll in post-secondary education.

## Implications

The BHCC Transitions to College program highlighted in this chapter demonstrates that a grant-funded ABE program can successfully prepare ESOL, ABE, and GED students for college. Additionally, the Transitions program substantially increases these students' enrollment in post-secondary education. The need for college pathway programs such as the Transitions program is clearly shown by ABE and GED students' extremely low levels of post-secondary enrollment and their even lower rates of post-secondary success. The Transitions program reveals that intensive academic courses and supports can substantially increase ABE, ESOL, and GED students' enrollment and success in college.

The Transitions program is also important because it provides a free alternative to the college's developmental course track. As at most schools, BHCC's developmental education classes are a part of the college's standard curriculum courses, which are supported by student tuition fees. However, the Transitions program is offered through BHCC's adult basic education program, which is funded in full through a grant from the Massachusetts Department of Education. Thus, while students in traditional developmental education classes must pay tuition, students may enroll in the Transitions program tuition-free. The Transitions program thus provides a free alternative for students with lower skills to prepare for college-level work.

Providing a less costly, less time-consuming path through developmental education is an important consideration given the number of students who fail to advance out of developmental education. As recent research has shown, many students fail their developmental education courses and never progress into college-level courses (Attewell, Lavin, Domina, & Levey, 2006). While this situation is troubling on a number of fronts, it is particularly concerning because students who fail to show academic progress endanger their financial aid eligibility, making it nearly impossible for them to continue in college. The Transitions program provides an important alternative to this dilemma. Students in the Transitions program may take courses over multiple semesters and develop their skills without being penalized by failing grades. Additionally, because the Transitions program is tuition-free, struggling students are not burdened by the cost of preparing for college entry. For these reasons, BHCC's Transitions program provides an ideal mechanism by which students may intensively prepare for college-level work while also preserving their financial aid eligibility for future college enrollment. Both of these are crucial considerations given the innumerable difficulties developmental education students have in advancing into degree programs at community colleges.

The program's primary strengths are its articulation with Bunker Hill's lower-level developmental course track as well as the flexible nature of the program's intensity. Another strength is its development of a Transitions seminar, which introduces students to the challenges of college life, and its development of a student cohort, which encourages students' support of one another as they enter college. Finally, the Transitions program creates substantial learning gains for its students and aids them in successfully transitioning into college-level work. While these factors are not uniquely relevant to the needs of English language learners, providing a high-quality transitions program is one way a community college can signal its commitment and willingness to make the success of English language learners a priority.

# Chapter 8

# Unlocking the Door: ESL Instructors' Diaries Examining Retention of Migrant Hispanic Students

■ Bengt Skillen and Julie Vorholt-Alcorn

J ORGE SUDDENLY KNOCKS AND ENTERS THE ROOM. "HI TEACHER, CAN I COME IN?" I look over at him. All the students stop what they're doing and look at him. Still at the doorway he stands and waits with an expectant smile on his face. "Yes, Jorge, that is fine," I utter. Silently I say to myself, "There's fifteen minutes left in the three-hour class and now he chooses to come." I try to gather my thoughts and create a transition back into the lesson after the interruption. But I find myself thinking: "Jorge hasn't been to class in weeks and out of the blue he's back—and with a grand entrance. Why can't he just come to class every day and when he's late, slip in quietly and sit down? And what am I going to do with him when I give the quiz in two minutes? How can I teach him all of the information he's missed?"

This summer session experience, recorded by Bengt Skillen, is typical at this community college satellite campus. As a new teacher preparing to teach in the summer session, Julie Vorholt-Alcorn observed three classes near the end of the spring quarter. All three instructors she observed described situations similar to Bengt's. In Julie's first observation, only one student out of the usual fifteen was present when class began. The instructors advised Julie that "things operate at a different pace here" and that teaching requires "flexibility." For each class session during these observations, any number of students (from none to more than those currently enrolled) showed up at any time. Students might stay for the entire session or only for that one class.

This variability in attendance makes student retention an ongoing and enormous challenge. The fluctuating yet steadily declining enrollment was a concern shared by administrators and instructors alike and this particular satellite campus was in jeopardy of being closed down as the dropping attendance had become alarming. Coupled with the attrition problem during the term, the number of enrolled students had been steadily decreasing over the years. This pattern has led to some discussion about closing the satellite campus. The urgency of the situation led us, two ESL instructors, to examine techniques for improving student retention during the summer session in 2006 through keeping diaries about our own teaching in this situation.

# Context of the Research

## The Instructors

Both of us are Caucasian native speakers of English in our 30s. We both hold master's degrees in TESOL and both have more than five years of ESL teaching experience. Bengt has only taught ESL in the community college setting. Most of his students have been immigrants from Mexico and Central American countries, and have had little formal schooling. At the time the data were collected, Julie was teaching ESL in the community college setting for the first time, having worked primarily in university settings.

## The Community and the School

Canby Extension, the satellite campus discussed in this chapter, is located in a rural Oregon community about twenty miles from the suburban main campus. The community where Canby Extension is located has a large Spanish-speaking population with many bilingual and even monolingual Spanish services and businesses. In this setting, the need to learn to use English might be diminished because residents do not use English much in the community and often have access to English-speaking relatives who can provide interpretation and translation as needed. The satellite campus is located in a town that relies heavily on income from agricultural businesses, such as plant nurseries.

Satellite campuses of community colleges provide ways to reach students who might not normally be able to afford the time to travel the distances to main campuses. For members of immigrant communities who work long hours and in disparate locations, often employed in manual labor requiring travel, the convenience and ease of access of satellite campuses are essential and are becoming increasingly important.

During the regular academic year, the Canby Extension facility is used by the neighboring Canby High School during the daytime and by extension and outreach programs in the evening. When we collected our data, the facility was relatively new. It had an excellent infrastructure, including a computer lab and air conditioning.

## The Classes and the Learners

Bengt taught an entry-level English class (SPL 0-2) entitled Life Skills that presented topics for communicating basic needs and interacting in everyday contexts. These topics included giving information at a clinic or to an employer, asking the time and date, and describing family relations. The class met for six weeks, on Mondays and Wednesdays, for three hours in the evening, from 6 to 9 PM. Fifteen students were registered—eight males and seven females. Four of the students were siblings. One student was a recent high school graduate and two students were retired. Two students were from Chile and the rest came from Mexico. All students in the class were fluent in Spanish. Two of the Mexican students stated that Zapotec was their first language but they could communicate in Spanish as a second language. Thus, the use of Spanish in the classroom occurred extensively for clarification and explanation. For the most part, Bengt used Spanish as a medium for instruction.

Julie taught a high-beginning/lower-intermediate grammar class (ESL 040), entitled Beginning Grammar, which covered present simple verb tense, nouns, descriptive and possessive adjectives, and simple sentences. The class met at the same time as Bengt's class for six weeks, two evenings per week. A total of eleven students, all from Mexico, were registered, including four males and seven females, although two of the men never attended. Two of the students were sisters-in-law. The oldest student was a grandmother, approximately 50 years old, whose husband was in Bengt's class. The use of Spanish occurred infrequently and consisted of one-word responses or short, simple sentences, largely because Julie did not speak Spanish fluently.

# Issues that Motivated the Research

## Retention

An important issue in teaching evening ESL classes at satellite campuses of community colleges is retention. Retention involves efforts to "keep learners in programs until they achieve their goals" (U.S. Department of Education, 1992; see also Kerka, 1995, p. 1). Factors identified in the research literature as affecting retention of community college students include personal, demographic, cultural, and institutional characteristics, as well as the institutional climate (Zamani, 2000, p. 96). Many of these issues seemed to be at work at the Canby Extension. On any given night the number of students coming on time (or coming at all) could fluctuate wildly. As each term continued, the numbers would dwindle to just a handful of students showing up on time, if they even came.

## Learning Needs of Migrant Populations

To serve the migrant populations that frequently attend ESL classes at community colleges, a longitudinal relationship with the subject matter has to develop. Students need consistent exposure to language learning experiences over time if instruction is to result in language acquisition. This may especially be the case for second language learners whose lives are conducted primarily in their first language. "If the gap between what is done in the classroom, and what is done outside the classroom, is too great, then the possibilities of learning anything at all are very seriously impaired" (van Lier, 1996, p. 43). Even though these students live in a society where English is the language of the majority, we discovered during informal conversations that few students have the opportunity to use English outside of class. This fact, coupled with the transient nature of the work that migrant populations find themselves a part of, results in their coming and going frequently and suddenly. Thus, addressing their learning needs remains a frustrating challenge.

## Improving Practice through Teacher Reflection

Attempting to circumnavigate some of these frustrations, we decided to take an active and reflective approach to increasing retention as well as consideration of the learning needs of our students. In this approach, teachers "collect data about teaching, examine their attitudes, beliefs, assumptions, and teaching practice, and use the information obtained as a basis for critical reflection about teaching" (Richards & Lockhart, 1994, p. 1).

Our choice for collecting data was to make systematic entries in teaching diaries. Bailey, Curtis, and Nunan (2001) say there are four key benefits of keeping a teaching journal:

> (1) articulating puzzles or problems (including posing hypotheses for further research), (2) venting frustrations, (3) clarifying and reasoning, and (4) stretching ourselves professionally. Almost invariably, articulating puzzles and problems, and venting our frustrations, if we so desire, lead to clarification and possibly to realization, which can result in professional development. (p. 59)

Given the issues motivating our research, teaching diaries seemed to be the best tool on hand for immediacy in consideration of strategies and trouble-shooting techniques we attempted in class, since teaching journals can be useful "as data collection devices in practicing reflective teaching" (Bailey, Curtis, & Nunan, 2001, p. 49).

## Research Questions Addressed

Our research focus emerged from concerns about retaining students in our ESL classes. First, we concentrated on ways to convey the program's attendance policy to the students. We also focused on which strategies would work to increase student retention. We combined these concerns and addressed these research questions:

1. What can we learn about the instructional needs of migrant learners by reflecting on our own practices and assumptions about learner retention?
2. What strategies and approaches can we as teachers use to support learner retention?

## Data Collection Procedures

We used diaries as our method of data collection. In second language research, a diary study is

> an account of a second language experience as recorded in a first-person journal. The diarist may be a language teacher or a language learner—but the central characteristic of the diary studies is that they are introspective: The diarist studies his own teaching or learning. Thus he can report on affective factors, language learning strategies, and his own perceptions—facets of the . . . experience which are normally hidden or largely inaccessible to an external observer. (Bailey & Ochsner, 1983, p. 189)

In using diary entries as a research database, the learners' or teachers' experiences are "documented through regular, candid entries in a personal journal and then analyzed for recurring patterns or salient events" (Bailey, 1990, p. 215).

We collected our thoughts and strategies for improving retention in diary entries that we wrote after class, usually for between ten and fifteen minutes each day. Later, as needed, we would expand an entry if we felt there was more to say. We both wrote our entries in a word processing program, but we kept separate diaries for the entire term. We did not share our diary entries with each other and spoke very little about our strategies for student retention. We refrained from sharing our diaries with colleagues also. Prior to beginning our diaries, we had read an article about teaching diaries that explained, "even if you plan to 'go public', the initial diary entries should usually be written to yourself (or to your most trusted colleagues) in order to avoid prematurely editing or cleaning up the data, or censoring your reflections" (Bailey et al., 2001, p. 58).

## Data Analysis Procedures

We read passages from one another's diaries only after the term ended, when we began collaborating on this chapter. We each analyzed our own diary entries beforehand, concentrating on identifying recurring themes and changes in attitudes over time. This process involved reading and rereading the diaries while making connections as the various themes arose. In the sections that follow, each theme will be illustrated with brief excerpts from our teaching journals.

## Findings

Five principal themes emerged from the analysis of our diary entries on strategies for student retention. These were (a) making time for conversations with our students, (b) changes in our own assumptions and behavior, (c) levels of sponsorship, (d) the impact of circumstantial forces, and (e) the impact of programmatic forces.

### Opening Up "Spaces" for Informal Student-Teacher Conversations

We began to notice that we wrote a good deal about conversations we had with students. Our conversations took place before, during, or even after class and were casual in nature. However, the information gleaned was important as we began to understand the differences between our expectations about attendance and retention and the student-based causes that prevented our expectations from being realized. To get a sense of what attending class meant to the students, we asked them not only what school was like in their home countries, but also their attitudes toward it. Many students' cultural knowledge of attendance, stemming from their concept of time, did not match ours. Several students were embarrassed if they could not attend the class consistently or could not arrive on time, so they felt it was just better to stop attending rather than lose face. The following entry from Bengt's journal illustrates this theme:

> When I asked students to describe school in their native country, I learned that to come to school late was very shameful and teachers often made tardy students objects of ridicule. Since many students had completed only a few years of elementary school, this was the only scholastic paradigm they remembered and could apply to their current endeavors. They felt scared that they again might be humili-

ated for coming late. Even when no humiliation occurred, there was still an ingrained sense of shame. Face-saving was so important for them that it was easier to not show up than to risk embarrassment.

Why, I asked then, would some students come to class so late, say, when there was only a handful of minutes left in a class? Some students explained that getting even a few minutes' worth of knowledge was better than nothing. These students were late because of a justifiable commitment, such as a boss that kept them late at work, and so there wasn't a sense of shame. In addition, the summertime was just a very busy time in the world of agriculture and by late July and August, the imminent harvest took precedence over school, as a great deal of much-needed money could be earned. By asking a few simple questions about their lives, I gained a huge volume of knowledge into my students' worlds.

Bengt concludes, "My goal turned into a concerted attempt to understand my students before having them understand me as a teacher."

## Changes in Our Assumptions and Behavior as Teachers

We grew aware of our own changes in assumptions and behaviors as teachers. Many factors shaped our understanding of retention and why retention was not occurring to our satisfaction. As the instructors, we reviewed the attendance policy many times with the students at the beginning of the term, including explaining the policy in Spanish. As time passed, it became clear that students understood the policy but often could not follow it due to outside constraints and obligations. Realizing this fact helped us to moderate our use of the policy as a reminder. Also, when we understood why students were arriving late, we became less rigid and more understanding with tardiness when our assumptions for it were unfounded. For example, Bengt's diary states,

When I started showing interest, the rapport I had always wanted to build increased ten-fold. Before, my rapport-building questions had been along the lines of what students had done over the weekend or what they thought of the streak of bad weather. Now, by comparison, those questions seem superficial and perfunctory. I stopped writing about myself and my teaching in my diary and instead started writing about how rigid and unyielding the scholastic paradigm might seem to these students—writing about how the U.S. system and Latin American system of education differed and how my expectations as a U.S. community college teacher did not line up with their expectations as Hispanic students studying English.

Another entry stated,

> I feel encouraged further today. I am realizing more and more that as an instructor, I need to understand the students' ideas about coming to school and being a student. A student left me a note in Spanish this morning, that I picked up this evening when I arrived. The note states, "I am sorry that I cannot come to class today. I am having stomach problems. I hope that you are not mad. I hope you will permit me to come back to class."

Finally, our behavior as teachers changed in relation to taking attendance. We discovered that doing so at the end of class instead of the beginning resulted in a more positive experience for the students as their success in attendance was acknowledged. For example, Julie's diary recorded the following observation:

> Sometimes students arrived late for class, but as time progressed, I realized that this was almost always due to an unavoidable scheduling conflict related to a work or family obligation. I decided to emphasize the positive (that they had chosen to attend class) and take attendance at the end. Then I would thank them for coming, describe a productive and fun activity to anticipate for the next class, and casually talk to any students who had questions or just wanted to chat.

## Levels of Sponsorship

Much was happening outside of class that was initially beyond our knowledge, but gradually our diary writing brought it to light. One concept that surfaced was the notion of *sponsorship*, which refers to the fact that students often "arrive in a program with the help and support of a specific person or a few people in their social network. . . . [These people are called] 'sponsors' and the help they provide 'sponsorship'" (Comings & Cuban, 2002, p. 1). We identified two different types of sponsors.

First, there were personal sponsors—people who "are part of a student's everyday life and include relatives, godmothers, children, spouses and partners, neighbors, friends, and co-workers" (Comings & Cuban, 2002, p. 1). Even if students were not showing up, they were still connected to the class by their classmates, who were often friends or family members. One student who was not able to attend class (because his job demands proved excessive) continued learning English through his brother, who would take any extra homework sheets for him to do as time allowed. This same brother also stood in as a surrogate teacher and would explain notes he took in class and then have his absent sibling copy them. Although not an ideal situation, the fact that this support occurred let us know learning could and did take place outside the classroom.

Second, there was an official sponsor, our teachers' aide. In other programs, an example of an official sponsor is "a caseworker who provides a referral to a program and follows up to see how the student's participation works out, [and] gives intermittent, targeted support within a limited time frame" (Comings & Cuban, 2002, p. 1). Our on-site teachers' aide would call students who had stopped regularly attending. The teachers' aide was a native speaker of Spanish and his cultural understanding proved to be essential in retaining students. The sponsorship he provided was invaluable as he was able to communicate any issue of substance and could explain instructor expectations to students with limited English. The following entry from Julie's diary illustrates this point:

> In addition to my personal efforts, the program assistant would call students who had stopped regularly attending. He left voicemails for three male students. Two never attended the course; they registered, but did not come. The third student did come to the next class. I did not learn if the voicemail motivated him to attend. I asked him in English, but he did not understand the question, and I could not phrase my question in Spanish. The program assistant was not available then to ask in Spanish for me.

## Impact of Circumstantial Forces

Although we knew that there were many circumstantial forces at play, their sheer volume and impact had been quite obscure. Work, cultural, and resource factors, such as transportation and child care, played a huge role in determining whether a student could come on time or even attend class at all. For instance, several students had to move to work on farms elsewhere and some others had their work schedules abruptly changed to a time that conflicted with class. Many female students could only attend class if their husbands or boyfriends brought them and these same individuals often worked late and wanted to eat before they brought their wives or girlfriends to study. Other students would have to leave early to handle household-related problems as they often were the only persons available to do so. For example, in Julie's class one student who regularly attended excused herself about two minutes before class started one evening. She had received a call that her husband needed her. He watched their two daughters while she came to class; she didn't say if the call was related to the children. She said that she would come to the next class and did. Another week, a student missed two classes because her baby had a very high fever. One student missed only one class all summer, when there was a special event for the Sunday school children she taught. Julie's diary also documents the case of Juan, who missed class because

> his boss at the woodworking shop switched his schedule from day shift to night shift, leading to a scheduling conflict. Juan told me that his boss tells him that he needs to improve his English skills. I offered to write a letter to Juan's boss, telling him that he had taken my class and worked hard. Juan saw this as a way to avoid going back to the night shift.

Juan left class, telling Julie that he would think about the letter. He planned to attend one last class before transitioning into his new shift at work, but he never returned.

Thus, these circumstantial forces had a profound effect on retention. Clearly, their effect was beyond our control as instructors. We learned to come to terms with the reality of our students' lives and accept this reality as a part of the job.

## Impact of Programmatic Forces

In addition to the circumstantial forces we encountered, there were also programmatic ones. The procedures at the beginning of the term seem to have been confusing for some students, as noted in Julie's diary:

> My first contact with the students took place at Registration Night. Prospective students were asked to come to our satellite campus and enroll in classes. Newcomers to our program took a placement test. I felt concerned because fewer than ten students came to Registration Night and some students were confused and a little disappointed. They thought that it was the first night of classes and were ready to start studying. However, after being tested, they were told to come back later in the week for class.

Classes with low enrollment could be cancelled, and if retention was not possible, the satellite campus program as a whole was in danger of being eliminated. We came face-to-face with this situation when Julie's class was almost cancelled due to enrollment figures that did not meet administrative expectations. Here is a description of the first class:

> There were only three women from Mexico present at the first meeting. These students seemed a bit anxious, asking where the other students were. I didn't know what to tell them. I was a new adjunct instructor, and my password to the program's management system was not functioning. I was waiting for help from the I.T. Department, because I hadn't been able to get into the system and check my roster before class. I just told the students not to worry. However, my concern was that a decision to cancel the course could decrease the students' motivation about the entire program and they might not continue studying at this campus.

> I called the ESL Department Chair and learned that the class could indeed be cancelled. I felt sad because I hadn't realized that there was any chance that a class at the satellite campus could be cancelled. The students, although a small group, were very motivated and I was

eager to work with them. How would this development affect them? I had already strongly encouraged my students to buy the grammar textbook; now my supervisor told me that the students should wait to purchase it. If my class were cancelled, then the students would be split into the lower-level and higher-level classes. At our next class, all three students from the first evening returned and two more students joined.

The final decision to offer the course was not made until the beginning of the third week of the six-week course. While waiting for a decision to be made, the students and instructor were held in limbo. The group dynamics seemed suspended; uncertainty about the class continuing harmed the group's developing cohesion. Furthermore, the students' academic progress was affected because they were told to wait for a final decision before purchasing the course textbook.

It became clear to us as the instructors that there was truly a fine line between accommodating the students and carrying out administrative expectations with regard to retention if the program at our satellite campus was to survive. We began to see that there were other stakeholders, beyond ourselves, involved in the issue of retention. Shouldering the responsibility of student attendance and retention had seemed as if it was ours and ours alone. Subsequently, developing a sense of wider diffusion of that responsibility gave us the knowledge that more dialogue about the issue was necessary and important.

## Implications

Our reflective diary study has focused on strategies for increasing ESL student attendance and retention at a rural satellite campus of a community college in Oregon. As a result of keeping our teaching journals and making concerted efforts to work on these issues, we gained a better understanding of the many factors that come into play where ESL student attendance and retention are concerned. What are the implications of our findings for other ESL teachers and for program administrators?

First, we believe it was helpful to create conversational "spaces" for students where they felt safe talking about their lives and factors that hindered their attendance. In the process, we learned a great deal about their views and experiences. Second, we tried to examine the assumptions and behaviors (both ours and the students') that might be counterproductive to retention. Third, we came to understand that there are many circumstantial factors—both positive and negative—affecting our students' lives outside of class that are beyond their control and ours. As a result, we realized the importance of fostering positive actions—both ours and the students'—in class. For example, as teachers we can work more proactively with the concept of sponsorship, to make sure absent students are supported in their learning. Finally, we realized that in spite of good intentions, programmatic factors may sometimes work against attendance and retention. We hope that raising awareness about these issues will benefit both ESL teachers and program administrators and, ultimately, the students.

This excerpt from Julie's diary symbolizes the complex interaction of factors—those of the students, the teachers, and the program—that can influence attendance, and ultimately retention and learning in community college ESL programs. The diary entry states,

> At our first class, the evening got off to a bumpy start. Our program's assistant, who helps with the students' registration and textbooks, didn't show. When students arrived late for class, because my classroom was at the front of the building, I had to stop teaching, greet the newly arrived students, and take them to a classroom. Some students hadn't been tested, so I took them to the class that seemed the right match for their skill level. We only had three courses, one at each skill level, so it was fairly easy to make the match. However, it took time from my teaching and my students became visibly frustrated as I had to leave several times to handle the on-going interruptions. Later I learned that the building's front door had "relocked" itself. Some students may have arrived for classes but couldn't get into the building. If they thought to knock on my classroom's window, I could have let them in but knocking on the door wouldn't have been heard. Obviously, this situation could only hurt student retention.

We find the image of the relocking door to be a sad but potentially apt metaphor for community college ESL students' attempts to attend class and further their English education. It is almost as if we are trying to unlock the door that continually relocks itself, preventing the students from attending class. We hope that by sharing our experiences of examining student attendance and retention at our campus we may have encouraged other teachers to take similar steps to improve this situation.

# Part 4
## Identity Construction and Development among Community College ESL Students

# Chapter 9

## "My Words Is Big Problem": The Life and Learning Experiences of Three Elderly Eastern European Refugees Studying ESL at a Community College

■ Duffy Galda

T HIS CHAPTER REPORTS ON A STUDY CONDUCTED TO IDENTIFY AND UNDERSTAND common patterns in literacy histories, life experiences, learning strategies, learning goals, and the construction of social identities exhibited by elderly ESL students studying at a community college. Effectively meeting the academic needs of the increasingly diverse ESL student population has proved challenging to instructors and curriculum developers who struggle to accommodate learners with very different experiential and academic backgrounds, learning styles, and learning goals. Today, institutions of higher education are facing extreme demographic changes in student body compositions. In fact, many urban community colleges are serving student populations that exhibit extreme diversity in terms of race, ethnicity, socioeconomic status, and age. Research conducted by the United States Department of Education (The College Board, 2003) reported that sixteen states had concentrations of minority students in higher education ranging from 31 to 40 percent of the total student enrollment. Moreover, eight additional states had more than 40 percent of their total student enrollment comprised of minority students.

Populations of ELLs enrolling in urban community college classes are also becoming increasingly diverse in terms of their educational levels, learning styles, literacies, experiential background, and English language learning goals (Crandall & Sheppard, 2004). In addition, students at various stages of their lives are enrolling in community colleges. Educators working in community colleges struggle to recognize and meet the personal, academic, social, and vocational needs of this dynamic population through curricular development and student services (Liebowitz & Taylor, 2004). Additionally, community college ESL instructors struggle to identify and accommodate learning strategies and modalities through responsive delivery of instruction (Crandall & Burt, 2007). Finally, college administrators and governing boards struggle to appreciate, understand, and address the perspectives, expectations, and needs these students bring to the college.

## Context of the Research

This study was conducted at the Downtown Campus of Pima Community College in Tucson, Arizona, during the Spring semesters of 2005 and 2006. The Downtown Campus is one of six campuses and four learning centers that comprise the Pima County Community College District. In 2006–07, the college had an annual unduplicated student count of 53,147, of which 1,040 were ESL students. The Downtown Campus had an unduplicated annual head count of 18,091, of which 53 were ESL students (i.e., numerous part-time students counted as 53 full-time student equivalencies). The ESL student population is highly diverse, comprised of immigrant, refugee, international, and non–English speaking citizens representing more than 30 language backgrounds.

This chapter summarizes the perspectives shared by three elderly ESL students— Falina, Luda, and Misha (pseudonyms)—who immigrated to the United States from the former Soviet Union as senior citizens. Through their voices, a description of the experiences, issues, and challenges these individuals have faced during their remarkable lives emerges. The participants have provided ESL educators both useful and interesting insights about listening to and working in content classes with adult ESL students like Falina, Luda, and Misha. I hope their perspectives will resonate for instructors, curriculum developers, and decision-makers responsible for meeting the personal, social, and academic needs of ESL students at the community college level.

On the Downtown Campus, approximately 70 percent of the students enrolling in ESL courses are international students, refugees, and immigrants from a wide variety of cultural and linguistic backgrounds. A typical class might include hearing-impaired students, Native American students, immigrants, refugees, and international students, as well as naturalized and native-born American citizens. Linguistic backgrounds represented might include American Sign Language, Apache, Arabic, Chinese, Farsi, French, Hebrew, Hopi, Italian, Japanese, Korean, Navajo, Portuguese, Russian, Slavic, Spanish, Thai, Tohono O'odham, Vietnamese, and Yaqui, as well as various African languages, including Dinka, Fur, Hill Nubian, Maasai, and Nuer. The continuum of ages exhibited by these learners is broad, ranging from the late teens to mid-eighties.

Students in the program also exhibit diversity of experiential and educational backgrounds. Typically these experiences may range from having limited formal education to having earned advanced degrees at universities in non–English speaking countries. Likewise, previous English learning experience varies from limited informal instruction to several months of adult education ESL classes or ESL coursework at the college. Instructors identify several subpopulations of students studying English at the college. Of particular interest is a group of older (retirement age and beyond) immigrants from the former Soviet Union. Most of these students are religious and political refugees who have been offered asylum in the United States. Many are highly educated, and have led rich and rewarding lives, yet at an advanced age find themselves displaced and alienated in a new country with an unfamiliar language and challenging cultural norms and expectations. It is this particular group that forms the focus of this research.

## Issues that Motivated the Research

The research literature on adult English learners in community colleges has been limited. Furthermore, case studies focusing on specific linguistic or cultural sub-populations within this context are even more scarce (Crandall & Sheppard, 2004). So how do community college educators anticipate and meet the needs of their increasingly diverse English language learning populations? This question was posed by ESL faculty members at Pima Community College. To address their question, an investigation was launched to identify and explore the situation of the elderly—one of the diverse student sub-populations they attempt to serve.

In my role as lead faculty in ESL and department chair of languages at the Downtown Campus of Pima Community College, I have interviewed more than two dozen full-time and adjunct ESL instructors, asking what types of information they believe would be beneficial for those who develop and deliver curriculum for diverse student populations. Nearly 70 percent of those interviewed responded that it would be important to identify and understand common patterns in literacy histories, life experiences, learning strategies, learning goals, and the construction of social identities exhibited by their students in order to develop and deliver curricula in a more informed, responsive, and effective manner. In addition, a majority of instructors interviewed believe that policy makers (student services coordinators, administrators, and governing boards) would be better able to make informed administrative decisions if they were made aware of the tremendous diversity of students currently attending ESL classes.

## Research Questions Addressed

This inquiry was guided by the following broad research question: What types of experiences and perceptions do diverse groups of adult English learners bring to the ESL classroom at Pima Community College? Specifically, the project addressed these five research questions:

1. What life experiences do elderly ESL students bring to the ESL classroom?

2. What types of literacy experiences and associated attitudes do elderly ESL students bring to the ESL classroom?

3. What learning styles, learning strategies, and educational experiences do elderly ESL students bring to the ESL classroom?

4. What personal learning goals (applications for English) are identified by elderly ESL students enrolled in ESL courses?

5. How are the personal identities of elderly ESL learners affected by their experiences as English language learners within the new cultural contexts of this country and the ESL classroom?

## Data Collection and Analysis Procedures

I was fortunate to work with three very special students—Falina, Luda, and Misha—in compiling the research data. Although I had worked with each of these students prior to the study, they were not enrolled in my classes during the research period. All three participants were from the former Soviet Union and had emigrated to the United States due to religious persecution. (All are heritage Jews.) They vary in their level of English proficiency, with Falina performing at a high-intermediate level, Luda at a basic level, and Misha at a beginning (no previous knowledge of English) level of proficiency. These students were enrolled in a computer skills course for ESL students when they volunteered to help with this project.

Over the course of the two semesters, I interacted with the student participants individually several times a week, chatting informally, helping each with their computer class assignments, and conducting interviews. Each of the participants took part in open-ended interviews for two hours each week for twenty weeks. These interviews focused on three or four major questions or themes. Many of these questions were "orientation" types of inquiries, ice-breakers chosen to help us all relax and to get to know each other better. Some centered on the participants' life experiences before coming to the United States, in particular, their early memories of their own literacy development during childhood.

To maintain a natural, conversational interaction in the interview sessions, I initially hand-recorded field notes during these conversations. As the participants grew increasingly comfortable with me and the research being conducted, the conversations were audio-recorded and subsequently transcribed within hours of the interviews. In addition, I maintained a research journal that was updated after each interview session to help in the identification and recording of insights and impressions. I utilized the journal to process the conversations and to reflect upon my own thoughts, ideas, and further questions as the project progressed.

Through the open-ended interview sessions, I learned a great deal about the life and literacy experiences that the participants had amassed before coming to the United States. In addition, I gained insights into their perceptions of themselves as learners, as well as some of the personal learning goals identified by each individual. Finally, I managed to uncover self-perceptions held by each and detected some of the social identities constructed by these students as they negotiated their new social, linguistic, and academic environments.

In addition to the interview sessions, I spent one hour per week working with participants in tutoring sessions, helping them with their emerging language skills in computer, writing, and reading applications. The participants eventually consented to being recorded during the tutoring sessions, and these interactions were transcribed within hours of each session. Through the tutoring sessions, I gained insights into learning strategies, learning styles, literacies, and learning experiences exhibited by the participants. I also gathered data concerning the construction of personal identity by each individual in this semi-social, semi-academic context. In order to obtain a more rounded impression of each participant, I attended two full ESL class sessions with the participants each semester. During these visits, I recorded field notes using a divided page technique, which allowed for the recording of observed interactions on one side of the field note page. The other side of the field note page was then available to add additional comments and insights collected from course instructors discussing the observed interactions following the class visits.

Finally, I collected copies of student work and assignments, then examined these materials, mining them for additional data during the course of the semester. Through the examination of student-generated documents, I learned a great deal about the life and learning experiences of the participants. In addition, I was afforded some very personal insights into the perceptions these student participants held of themselves as both learners and as social beings. Finally, through their own carefully considered, self-generated words, I was able to identify additional personal learning goals articulated by the participants.

After working with my co-participants in this project for six months, I had compiled a large amount of raw data. I followed advice from Merriam (1998), who suggests a systematic process of data analysis. I placed the data into a Word document and began coding the information by umbrella categories. I highlighted (with different colors) portions of the data that seemed to fall under these general, umbrella categories. Four umbrella categories emerged from the data: life experiences, literacy and learning, emotions, and identity. I then reviewed the initial research questions and returned to reading—not only the data, but the descriptions of the data. From that point, I continued to identify and code emerging themes that were placed as sub-categories under each of the broad, umbrella categories.

# Learner Portraits

B efore discussing my findings, I will present portraits of the three learners, using their own words to describe their experiences. For each person, I will briefly discuss his or her life experiences, literacy history, learning strategies, learning goals, and social identities.

## Falina

Falina, whose first language is Russian, is a 63-year-old female student who came to the United States from her beloved St. Petersburg, Russia. She left her country in 2002 during the Chechen War, because she believed emigration was the only way she could save the life of her only son, who was sure to be drafted into the conflict.

In terms of her life experiences, Falina was born in Leningrad at the end of World War II, the second of two children. Her mother, an engineer, worked in a military plant. Her father, also an engineer, did not play a significant role in Falina's life, as her parents were divorced and his only role in the family was paying a small amount of child support. Falina lived what she refers to as a "normal" life:

> I had to work in order to help my family. I worked and studied in the evening school. Then I enter the Pedagogical Institute. I married when I was 21. I worked, studied, and had a family. I wasn't happy in my marriage and after 19 years of marriage, we were divorced.

After finishing her studies at the Pedagogical Institute in 1968, Falina worked as a teacher in an elementary school for nearly 30 years until suffering a life-altering stroke in 1997, shortly before she immigrated to the United States:

> After the stroke, I lost much of my memory. I didn't begin to renew and learn to speak again until I came to the college.

Falina's literacy history began when she was a young child. She recalls having very good books at home, and enjoying reading:

> My parents didn't read to me. My mother had no time for reading. I began to read at school. It was a pleasant feeling to read and to learn about the world. I liked to read very much. We had very good books at home.

Falina also commented on her learning strategies. She thinks that several factors have influenced her comprehension and retention of English language skills:

> I worked hard at the lessons, I did my homework, because I was and I am interested in learning more English. Every lesson I learned more and more. The more important thing is that my teacher used the computer on every lesson. The computer helps to learn all the aspects of English—free!

Falina has specific learning goals. She feels she has even more to learn about English, and wants to improve several facets of her communication skills:

> Sometimes, it is very difficult for me to make my thoughts and words in order. I'd like to return the spontaneous speech in both Russian and English languages, to get rid of panic attack when I can't express myself or I can't understand anything.

Falina looks forward to continuing her studies at the college, and dreams that one day her English will be sufficiently fluent to propel her back into the classroom:

> It is my dream, my pipedream, to learn English well enough so that once again I can teach the children. I was born to be a teacher. The special methods, the wonderful ways of my teaching, I wish to share again.

Falina's social identity is a complex issue. She describes her passion for the teaching profession, thus providing insight into one of her core identities, that of a professional educator:

> To teach, to give knowledge, to communicate with student—that was my life. At that time I really made the difference in the life of my students and their parents. I tried to do everything to make them feel comfortable at the lessons, to love learning, to develop their knowledge.

When asked about her future plans for using the computer, Falina discusses specific applications she sees herself using. Her remarks provide insight into an emerging identity, a person who views herself as technologically savvy:

> I think that I will use computer in my future because of my health problems. I can't travel because I am on insulin injections, I have no transportation, I have a very low income. Therefore, my life is very limited. But I am alive yet, and with the help of computer, I can learn

> much about world, important events, books, beautiful places. I hope
> to use my computer for the connection with my daughter's family in
> St. Petersburg. Now, I am computer person!

Falina's strong work ethic and motivation to return to the teaching profession have contributed to her progress in developing English language skills. However, her efforts have been curtailed due to health issues. She looks forward to continuing her studies in the future.

## Luda

In contrast to Falina's commitment to learn English so that she can practice her profession here in the U.S., Luda wants to gain English fluency in order to interact socially with other English speaking seniors residing in her assisted living complex.

Luda is a 75-year-old community college student who came to the United States in 2000 from her native Ukraine. She speaks both Ukrainian and Russian, but utilizes Russian in her daily interactions. Luda was allowed to immigrate to the U.S. under the Family Reunification Plan. Luda's brother, Misha, was already living in the U.S. Coming to the United States was a heart-wrenching decision for Luda, who was forced to choose between gaining refuge in the United States or staying in her troubled homeland to tend to her ailing mother during the last months of her mother's life:

> My beautiful mother was died soon but Immigration say I must
> came now. I no want leave. I love her. But, mine mother no know.
> Mine mother no wake. Nurse say she know never. Nurse say mother
> love. Dah. Mother want Luda safe, go Misha family. Dah. Poor mother.
> I sad. Mine heart break.

Luda has had many difficult life experiences. She was born in Chernigov, a city in the northern part of Ukraine. Chernigov is located about 85 miles northeast of the Ukrainian capital, Kiev, and about 50 miles from the Chernobyl nuclear power plant. Some of Luda's earliest memories are of World War II, a turning point in her life and a devastating family experience.

> When I little girl, my country to wage war with Germany. This was
> very terribly and hart. All men must go war and many people deaded
> of war. The war is very tragedy for all people. The children no go
> school. We no have food and clothes. Many years passed but I not
> forgot War, waiting the letter from mine father.

Luda's family was forever changed by the war, from which her father never returned. Luda worked hard, married the love of her life and had one son. Tragically, Luda lost her husband to cancer at a very young age and never remarried. Tragedy struck a second time when her beloved son, exposed to the radiation from the Chernobyl accident of 1986, also lost his life to cancer. Luda felt alone and frightened:

> This is picture mine son. Petar. Beautiful boy. Here [showing a picture of a man and boy] with very good father, mine husband. Mine son [showing another photo of a strapping young man with a freshly caught fish], mine Petar. Died of Chernobyl [beginning to weep]. Chernobyl taked mine Petar.

In 1998, Luda's brother immigrated to the United States with his family under religious refugee status. Luda was greatly relieved two years later when her own immigration application was approved. Her excitement was described in an essay written for her computer class:

> Letter day oh my God. Letter it arrive from Immigration. Say Luda come. Misha sponsor Luda. I want dance. I want sing. I want cry, mother not come. I believe United States. I believe freedom. I believe safe. I believe future. I believe happiness. I wait to go my new home. Oh my God.

Luda's literacy history was affected by the turmoil of war and its aftermath. After the war, Luda does not remember playing very often, and there was no traditional family time at all:

> Before war, mine father said stories from book. We very, very like. I go school, little girl. I very, very like school. Like learn. But after evacuate, no books, no time read, no time play. All time, work, work. No time school. Is time very bad.

Luda's motivation for taking ESL classes involves wanting to interact more fully in her new home in Tucson. She wants to read books and attend plays written and presented in English. She would like to visit with her neighbors. She does not want to be alienated from the things she enjoys by a language barrier. Luda was encouraged by her sister-in-law, a Pima College student, to attend English classes at the college:

> I go bus early, early. I go morning 6:30. I wait teacher. I wait learn English. All time students no came early. I early. I want study. I learn English.

Luda enjoys the engagement of college life. She plans to continue her studies:

> I live life. I learn all things new. Is good for future. I study computer. I speak American people. I read the book English. Is good for life United State.

Luda's learning strategies combine old fashioned hard work with an awareness and application of her learning styles. Luda seems to be a visual and kinesthetic learner, and exhibits the ability to utilize these strengths to negotiate meaning and develop skills. According to Kress (2003), the interactivity of text, semiotics, and the oral and written word function together to allow for meaning-making. He sees the incidence of a message's "meaning" being realized "spread across" several modes (pp. 35–36). Luda describes the multi-modal nature of her emerging computer skills that help her negotiate meaning in English:

> I like make picture, write little, copy, paste on page. I go Internet. See many, many things. Very, very lot picture. I read, I learn, I see. Is good.

As her English skills continue to grow, so does Luda's confidence:

> I good student. I learn English. I learn computer. I study, mine teacher say, "Practice, practice, practice." I like computer.

In terms of her social identities, Luda seems very interested in mastering a social discourse that will allow her to interact socially with classmates and others as friends. Gee (2004) spoke of discourses enabling empowerment. Luda beams with empowerment when she describes her ability to converse on the phone in English with a native Spanish speaker in their common language of English:

> I friends mine classes. Conchita mine friend. Very, very friend. I go party Conchita house, is big party. I go friends. Conchita say me on telephone, "You my friend, Luda." I very like Mexican friends. I very like college.

Luda now lives in the same assisted living complex as her brother, Misha, who was able to find religious refuge for his family in the United States.

## Misha

Misha is a 78-year-old community college student and Luda's older brother. Misha and Luda are "heritage Jews," people whose families were practicing Jews before the advent of Communism in their native countries. After the fall of Communism, many of these people found themselves victims of hate crimes and discrimination, even though they themselves never practiced a formal religion due to the secular climate of the former Soviet Union. Misha, a civil engineer, experienced discrimination in the workplace. At home, he and his family received anonymous messages threatening their property and their safety. Taking the advice of a friend, Misha applied to the United States for immigration status as a religious refugee.

Like his sister Luda, Misha has had difficult life experiences. His memories of World War II shape his childhood recollections. Misha recalls his childhood:

> All around was war. German very bad atrocities. Father now army soldier go fight on 1941. Father leave family. Fight war. Father no come back. War destroy life my family. Very hard the life for family.

As war disrupted his childhood, Misha's formal educational experiences were also interrupted:

> Father say me take care mother. Take care house. Take care Luda. All time work. Work, make little bit money, give mother. Work garden, grow vegetables to family. No time book, no time study. All time work, work, work.

Things finally improved for the family. Eventually, Misha finished school, earned a degree in engineering, and relocated to Odessa, a city in southern Ukraine. In the Soviet Union, Misha was holding his own, but eventually, time brought tremendous change, once again, to Misha's world:

> Then . . . Glasnost, Perestroika, old ways change, now very much bad, very much hate, very much . . . criminal. No good times. Year, 1991 no is good. Is very, very change.

Misha and his family, faced with religious persecution and living in fear, sought refuge in the United States.

Misha's literacy history was directly impacted by his social conditions. He does not recall having access to books as a boy or anything much about his early literacy development.

> After war, family poor. No money. No school. No book. No read. No write, only work. Is hard life. Mother alone. Work very, very all time. I no play. No study. No time.

Eventually conditions in the Soviet Union improved, and political and economic dynamics resulted in a greater need for an educated populace. Misha was one who benefited since these changing conditions allowed him to develop strong literacy skills:

> Work a lot, a lot year. Many, many year past, then, I go school. I study. I learn very fast. I read, I write. I smart man. Is opportunity very big. I go university. Study. Is good. Misha engineer. Good job. Good wife. Life, OK.

Misha's learning goals are directly related to communication. When he immigrated to the United States, social isolation due to an inability to communicate in English became a big problem. He began to feel as if he was the only person in his world who was not learning English:

Я не говорю по-английски (I don't speak English). Son, Ros go American school. All time talk friends. Say English. All time no talking Russian. Wife, Valentina, sad, say me she go college. Go Mariya and Yulia [neighbors]. Go study English. One years, Luda go college with Valentina. I no want. I old, no learn. Valentina go, learn English much. Valentina, Ros all time practice. Me, no. Friend, Boris, say to me Russian, but in house, in city, I alone. Boris go college, study English. No English, is alone.

Finally Misha enrolled in an ESL class, about which he said, "I take class 60. Study grammar is good. I study."

Misha struggles with high blood pressure and heart disease and frequently misses classes due to doctor appointments and brief hospitalizations. He hopes that his health will allow him to continue with classes in the fall semester: "Dah, study. August, more class. ESL 70. I take test. I see. Study English."

Misha does not mince words when it comes to identifying learning strategies that do not work for him:

No like talk group. No is good. No like. Other students stupid, other students no study. No want leave desk. No want talk, no activities. No talk words good. No like. I say teacher, "No like." Teacher say me, "Misha talk in group." No want talk in group, Misha leave. Strong teacher.

Since Misha was making slow progress in English, his teachers recommended that he enroll in a Russian 101 at the college, which allows Misha to be exposed to contextualized English in a somewhat sheltered environment:

I go class Russian, listen teacher explain grammar. Is good. I learn. I say other students Russian words, they say me English words. Is good. Teacher say how Russian, English different. I learn. (*Smiling*) I good student Russian!

Misha's motivation to study English appears to be directly related to social identity issues. Misha views himself as a highly educated, very competent person who has worked hard to earn the respect of others. He is highly concerned that his limited English influences people's perceptions of him, and that because he has a difficult time interacting and expressing himself in English, others perceive him as uneducated or simple: "I say things American people. American people not know I smart. I engineer. I very big ideas."

Misha's words strike a familiar chord. As I have heard in speaking with Falina and Luda, so much of the personal identities of these students is tied to their abilities to represent themselves as educated, articulate people. Gee (1996) wrote that discourses are indicative of the roles people have in their lives. Being unable to symbolically convey their roles limits not only the personal identity construction of these students, but how they are viewed and understood by others. As Misha so eloquently put it:

> My words is big problem. All people, all American mans no look, no talk, no say me discussion. I am as ghost. No see, no hear, no life. I want say words engineer English. I want say educate English. I educate man, but American mans no see me, Misha no is educate man.

## Findings

An initial summary of the participants' data relative to the five research questions is presented in Table 9.1. The information is organized in terms of the three participants' life experiences, literacy histories, learning strategies and goals, and social identities.

My coding of the data yielded four umbrella categories regarding the learners' experiences as ESL learners: life experiences, literacy and learning, emotions, and identity. These umbrella categories and their sub-categories are presented in Table 9.2 on page 136.

As evidenced through their own words, each participant brings unique experiential and learning backgrounds to the community college. All exhibit a desire to learn English; however, the goals that motivate them are quite different. Each individual is attempting to construct a social identity within a new language and culture. The insights provided by the three participants offer a glimpse into the great diversity of literacy histories, life experiences, learning strategies, learning goals, and the construction of social identities exhibited by ESL students in community college populations. They also underscore the importance of educators creating curriculum and delivering instruction that is highly responsive to the experiences, abilities, and outcomes our student populations exhibit.

The recurring themes reflected through the words of Falina, Luda, and Misha convey volumes. These are people who have lived long, full lives, set against the dramatic backdrop of history and human experience. All were settled into lives in their home countries but were displaced at advanced ages from that settled lifestyle, thrown into an unfamiliar, unsettling cultural and linguistic chaos due to circumstances beyond their control. All have found the inner strength to continue coping and adapting to their life situations as they embrace the opportunity to continue to learn and grow through community college coursework. In their own words, the participants express their experiences, their concerns, their hopes, and their dreams as they strive to build their new lives here in the United States.

**Table 9.1.**

Summary of Participant Characteristics Based on Their Reponses

|  | Falina | Luda | Misha |
|---|---|---|---|
| Life experiences | No recollection of WWII<br>Became a teacher<br>Stroke affected cognitive processing<br>Chechen War refugee<br>Health challenges affecting class attendance and learning: diabetes, partial blindness | WWII childhood<br>Worked in a factory<br>Lost father, husband, child, and mother in separate, tragic situations<br>Immigrated to U.S. under Family Reunification Plan<br>Health challenges affecting class attendance and learning: hypertension, dizziness, respiratory problems | WWII childhood<br>Became an engineer<br>Became a post-Perestroika victim of religious/ethnic discrimination<br>Immigrated to the U.S. as a religious refugee<br>Health challenges affecting class attendance and learning: heart disease and related, repeated hospitalization |
| Literacy history | Solid educational foundation<br>Loved to read<br>Earned a degree in education | War disrupted formal education<br>Returned to school after war<br>Completed secondary school | War disrupted formal education<br>Developed literacy as a young man<br>Earned a degree in engineering |
| Learning strategies | Rigorous study schedule<br>Repetition<br>Use of computer technology to enhance language skills | Multimodal, combining modalities to negotiate meaning | Memorization of grammar rules<br>Translation of material<br>Constant review<br>Exposing himself to sheltered, contextualized English by enrolling in a Russian 101 class at the college |
| Learning goals | Develop English fluency in order to teach in American elementary schools | Develop English skills in order to interact socially with native speakers of English or other immigrants and refugees from diverse language backgrounds | Develop English skills to communicate with native English speakers<br>Develop English skills to elevate status with English speakers |
| Social identities | An innovative, capable, professional educator | A woman capable of developing and maintaining friendships with English-speaking individuals | An educated, articulate person who has much to contribute in a conversation or discussion |

**Table 9.2.**

Umbrella Categories and Sub-Categories in the Data Analysis

| Life Experiences | Literacy and Learning | Emotions | Identity |
|---|---|---|---|
| Trauma | Literacy development | Anxiety | Professional identity |
| Reconciliation to present life situation | Effect of age & health on learning | Isolation | Social identity |
| Family | Desire to expand learning opportunities beyond English skills development | Hope & optimism | Personal identity |
| | Lifelong development | Gratitude | |

### Life Experiences

As the participants discuss their lives, both traumatic incidents and joyful occasions are described. These experiences have helped to form lifelong attitudes and perspectives. For example, Luda reported, "We evacuate from Chernigov in 1941. We drove long time. Children could not go school. We didn't have food and clothes I could not forgot the War."

One life experience the three participants have in common is the reconciliation to their present life situation. Having spent the majority of their lives under Soviet rule during the Cold War, all three were apprehensive about the life that awaited them on this side of the world. Falina's comment sums up her perceptions: "And now I know what it is like, here, on the other side . . . not good, not bad, just different."

A third life experience Falina, Misha, and Luda share is a very strong attachment to their nuclear families, especially their children. Luda lost her only son after Chernobyl, but Misha and Falina both have children living with or near them in Tucson. All three expressed the importance of their children in their lives. Misha expressed this feeling in this way: "I children, Larissa, Ros . . . they future, I love. Life in United States is future, not Misha future, future my children. My son now have future. Work hard, study. Good job, is good life."

### Literacy and Learning

When discussing literacy and learning, all three of the participants discussed the literacy environments of their childhood homes and various aspects of their own literacy development. Each emphasized the importance of their own literacy development experiences, often recalling incidents within their homes or during formal schooling. Once again, Misha's comment is eloquent: "After war, I must work for family, no father, only Misha. Work many years. Many, many years past, then, I go school. I study. I learn very fast. I read, I write. I smart man. Is opportunity very big."

Interestingly, the data contain almost a daily reference to the effects of aging or failing health on each of the participants' ability to learn. During the semesters I collaborated with these three learners, Misha missed almost 25 percent of his classes due to heart and respiratory problems. Falina experienced debilitating problems with one of her eyes related to diabetes. Even Luda battled a round of pneumonia after winter break. In addition to discussing their failing health, the participants' comments often focused on their doubts that their aging minds could keep up with those of younger students:

> I old, slow. These [other] students young. My head is full, not fast. They heads is empty, fast. I too old learn fast. (Luda)

> I think, maybe, I too old learn English. Maybe I learn never . . . I very sick, heart bad. Misha old man. (Misha)

In spite of shared concerns about being advanced-age students, surprisingly, the participants all voiced a strong desire to expand their learning opportunities at the community college beyond English skills development. The data clearly indicate that all three expressed a keen interest in taking mainstream courses in disciplines in which they had specific interests. For example, Luda said, "I go college more. Take class reading. I read American book. I learn American idea, history, more computer. I like."

A final sub-category that emerged from the data under the umbrella category of literacy and learning involved each of the participants' self-perception of being a life-long learner. In spite of their longevity, their health problems, and their monthly social security checks, these individuals believed they still had much to learn about the world around them:

> I think that the computer will complete my life and I wouldn't feel myself lonely and miserable old woman when I wouldn't be able to connect with world in different ways. (Falina)

### Emotions

Often, I was touched by the breadth and depth of emotion expressed by the participants as they discussed their lives, their educational experiences, and their futures. Anxiety often surfaced when the participants reflected on their experiences at the college and in ESL classrooms:

> I know what I want say, but I all time no have words. (Misha)

Feelings of isolation were also routinely expressed as Falina, Luda, and Misha discussed their individual immigrant experiences.

> I work hard, study, every day. It is my "pipe dream" to speak to all people like American person, as if I belong. (Falina)

> I so tired when I invisible. If the people not speak English, they invisible. (Misha)

The participants routinely exhibited a variety of upbeat emotions. An especially poignant theme was the gratitude expressed when discussing immigration to and experiences in the United States.

> After my very big stroke, my American doctors saved my life, and my ESL teachers helped to return my personality. They are all such wonderful people, and I thanks God for them. (Falina)

The participants, when envisioning their futures, often exuded hope and optimism:

> Friends is good. I learn the English, I talking students. I have lot, lot of friends...new friends, new country, new life. Old Luda be new Luda. (Luda)

### Identity

The final umbrella theme that emerged from the data involved identity. This theme not only evidenced how each participant self-identified, but also indicated a concrete concern with the identity they projected to others. In just a few words, Misha describes his professional identity and his current social identity:

> I smart. I engineer. I very big ideas. In Uzbekistan, all people respect. Here, United State, have no words say ideas. Here, all people, no respect . . . here people think I stupid, I man no important, I man have no face. (Misha)

Likewise, Falina indicates her professional and personal identities while discussing life in Russia:

> Of course, I worked hard as a teacher. I was given a special award for my good teaching. I used the new and special methods for teaching the children. I was . . . oh, how to say . . . teacher maestro. I loved my work, but also I loved my own children . . . and now I love my

grandson, Eddie. I was the best mother I could be. I now am the best grandmother for little Eddie. Now, in my life, my son and my grandson, they are my life, it is my responsibility, but it is also my pleasure.

As evidenced through the data, these individuals are learning to balance themselves between two worlds, the world of their past and the world of their present: two worlds, two cultures, two languages, two continents, two lives. A common challenge is learning to move between those two worlds as gracefully and seamlessly as possible. Their strong desire to continue learning and to study new and different things is tempered with the concern that their age and health issues might negatively affect their ability to do so. Gaining competencies in the multiplicity of discourses encountered in new social, cultural, and linguistic contexts is facilitated by their abilities to draw on prior experiences and knowledge and to utilize learning strategies that help them to meet learning goals and to create and re-create their identities.

## Implications

As practitioners in the field, we can take a lesson from the insights so generously provided by Falina, Luda, and Misha. Information garnered from case studies such as these can be valuable to post-secondary institutions and educators as they create policy, develop curriculum, and orchestrate learning experiences addressing the needs of ESL learners.

In particular, this study holds the potential to inform practice at the community college level, especially the practice of those ESL professionals who are responsible for designing and implementing curricula that must meet the needs of extremely diverse populations. The data demonstrate that these three elderly ESL students who came to the United States as religious refugees have "lost" who they once were. Along with the individuals themselves, their very important life experiences and professional identities were displaced as they were torn from the lives they knew and relocated half-way around the world.

But these elderly students who once were "lost" are now in the process of working on who they will become as they enroll in ESL classes at the college. We can remember as we develop and deliver curricula that we are collaborating with a number of our students on the people they will become. In remaining cognizant of that truth, we can continually strive to accommodate our students' unique experiences, abilities, strengths, concerns, and learning goals in our efforts on their behalf.

To more effectively accommodate elderly ESL learners, community colleges should ensure that advisors, counselors, and instructors are made aware of the unique characteristics and needs exhibited by the students being recruited and served. Pima Community College's Downtown Campus has held orientation sessions for student services personnel and adjunct faculty members designed to familiarize college employees with not only the ESL program and policies, but also with the diverse student sub-populations enrolling in ESL courses. Often, college employees have limited experience working with elderly students. When this situation is exacerbated by cultural and experiential differences, colleges run the risk of deterring such students from enrolling in or completing classes by making them feel uncomfortable or unwelcome. After being introduced to inclusive strategies and suggestions, college personnel leave the orientation sessions better prepared to engage and affirm ESL learners.

In addition to orientations for college personnel, fall and spring semester orientations have been held for incoming ESL learners at Pima College. One of the areas of emphasis for these orientations is an explanation of classroom environments, norms, and expectations that may be vastly different from formal learning environments to which the learners may have been exposed in their educational experiences. The orientations provide strategies and suggestions to help students transition into the highly interactive, student-centered courses that are offered. Curricular developers and decision makers should remain cognizant of the learning needs exhibited by their diverse and dynamic student populations. By routinely surveying or interviewing students, curricular leaders will be better prepared to modify curriculum or improve course offerings that more closely reflect learner characteristics and goals.

The data collected in this study offer insight for administrators and policy makers who may not recognize that the traditional concept of a "typical ESL student" and his/her needs and identities might very well be erroneous or outdated. The students served in community college ESL classrooms are a diverse lot, and therefore we risk making critical errors in decision making processes if we base those decisions on sweeping generalizations or erroneous conceptualizations concerning the actual populations we serve.

ESL faculty should ensure that administrators and policy makers are apprised of the characteristics, needs, and learning goals of learners. Additionally, any significant change in the demographics exhibited by the ESL learning population should be noted, to help administrators and policy makers to consider the populations being served when making budgeting and staffing decisions, writing grants, and developing outreach and recruiting materials.

The wealth of educational and experiential backgrounds that elderly ESL learners bring to community colleges should not be overlooked, as they could prove to be valuable resources that could be tapped by college learning communities. At Pima, Holocaust survivors enrolled in ESL classes have been tapped for presentations in history and sociology classes. Russian, Spanish, French, and Arabic speaking students who have enrolled in language classes to enhance their exposure to English have been tapped as language mentors and conversation partners for classmates who are learning the languages. Often, these classmates are significantly younger than their ESL learner mentors and partners, and the intergenerational aspect of the relationships that develop have reportedly benefited the partners in unexpected and positive ways.

My initial review of the research literature indicates that data on specific sub-populations of students who are being served in community college ESL classrooms is limited. Research on elderly ESL students in community colleges is virtually non-existent. Therefore, this study holds the potential of opening a new area of inquiry for researchers working in the realm of ESL and wishing to know exactly who is served by ESL programs at the community college level and how we might better meet their educational needs.

# Chapter 10

# Students' Identity Construction in a Content-Based Instruction Program: Perspectives from a Community College Classroom

■ Hanh thi Nguyen, Francis Noji, and Guy Kellogg

RECENT RESEARCH HAS PAID MUCH ATTENTION TO THE CONCEPT OF IDENTITY AND THE role it plays in language acquisition processes. In this chapter, we closely examine written communications among students in a community college content-based course to investigate issues related to identity construction and language learning.

## Context of the Research

The ESOL (English for Speakers of Other Languages) Program at Kapi'olani Community College in Honolulu, Hawai'i, has been using a sustained content-based curriculum for the past ten years. A *sustained content course* differs in that the content itself is often thematic, whereas another approach to content-based instruction (CBI) is to scaffold learners through a content domain, e.g., "psychology" or "economics" (see Bailey, this volume, and Ravitch, this volume). The course under study was organized around two main content areas: the history of segregation in the southern states and the civil rights movements of the past two centuries, including women's rights, native people's rights, and gay rights in the United States. Through studying these content areas, the students considered concepts such as prejudices and stereotypes in various situations, as well as how to understand, deconstruct, and confront such concepts with intellectual reasoning. The class met every day for four hours and ten minutes per day, divided between two instructors, totaling more than twenty hours per week over a sixteen-week period. It included nineteen international students of English as a second language from Japan, Korea, and Macau, most of whom were recent arrivals to the United States. The average TOEFL® score of the students was 463.35 (paper-based scale). (International students entering the College who score between 400 and 499 TOEFL are admitted to the Intensive Transition Program in ESOL. After this one semester intensive program, students may enter the college's credit ESOL program and begin taking a limited range of other credit classes at the college.) The teacher (Guy Kellogg) was a male Caucasian American who had been teaching English for about fifteen years by the time of data collection.

Content-based instruction in general—that is, "the integration of particular content with language teaching aims" (Brinton, Snow, & Wesche, 1989, p. 2), strives to "acculturate" the student into the discourse community of that content by getting the students to use "some form of the discourse of that content" (Eskey, 1997, pp. 139–140). A *discourse community* has "a broadly agreed set of common public goals" and "mechanism for intercommunication among its members," uses "participatory mechanisms primarily to provide information and feedback" to its members, develops certain genres of speaking and writing as well as specific lexis, and maintains "a threshold level of members with a suitable degree of relevant content and discourse expertise" (Swales, 1990, pp. 25–26). *Discourse,* in this sense, is language use that follows the rules and conventions of a given community.

## Issues that Motivated the Research

*Acculturation* is generally understood as the process in which an individual's language, culture, and values change through interaction with another group. This is in contrast to *assimilation,* the process in which an individual abandons his/her own language, culture, and values to conform to the norms of another group (Richards, Platt, & Weber, 1985). (We will elaborate on the notion of acculturation later in this chapter.) Although acculturation has been thought to be a major advantage for using a content-based approach in the language classroom over the discrete skills approach, to date little is understood about the exact nature of this acculturation process in sustained content-based instruction. This chapter thus aims to gain insights about this process in the context of a sustained content-based course at a community college.

The process in which students become acculturated into the discourse communities of certain content areas is essentially language socialization (Schieffelin & Ochs, 1986), which is the process of learning ways of "acting, feeling, and knowing" (Ochs, 2002, p. 106) in new social groups. These new ways of behaving can be learned as participants display to one another their affective and epistemic stances toward the social action being performed. People's affective stance involves their "mood, attitude, feeling, or disposition as well as degrees of emotional intensity," (p. 109) while their epistemic stance involves their "knowledge or belief, including sources of knowledge and degree of commitment to truth and certainty of propositions" (p. 109). In turn, how someone displays his/her affective stance and epistemic stance can serve to construct his/her social identities, which involve "a range of social personae, including, for example, social roles, statuses, and relationships, as well as community, institutional, ethnic, socioeconomic, gender, and other group identities" (Ochs, 2002, p. 109). Thus, social identities are not something static or fixed, but dynamic, to be performed, displayed, and negotiated in discourse (cf. Butler, 1990; Cameron, 1997; Holmes, Stubbe, & Vine, 1999). Through social interactions in the target language and *in order to* participate in social interactions in the target language, learners construct and transform their social identities in discourse communities using the target language. This perspective prompts us to perceive "acculturation" as a more dynamic process in which the focus is not on the effect of instruction on students, i.e., how instruction acculturates students (following Eskey, 1997), but how students' language and cultural values change through interaction in the target language with peers, teachers, and contents.

In second language acquisition, learners' identities have been found to relate to language learning, especially in the sense that certain identity alignments (e.g., when learners identify themselves with some social groups in the target language, with their peers, or with the goals of the curriculum) may provide the learners with enriching and abundant language learning opportunities, while some other alignments may hinder language learning (e.g., Armour, 2001; Dantas-Whitney, 2002; Lantolf & Pavlenko, 2001; Morita, 2004; Nguyen & Kellogg, 2005; Norton, 2001; Toohey, 2000). The investigation of learners' identity construction is thus highly significant for an understanding of how a second language is learned and, in turn, can yield important implications for instruction. In this chapter, however, rather than trying to find a causal relationship between language learning and identities, we aim to examine on a micro level, through a close analysis of the students' discourse, how identity construction is performed in language learning. In other words, we are interested in second language learners' stance-taking toward the actions being performed in discourse in content-based instructional settings. We believe that there is much to learn by looking at what second language learners say about themselves in written L2 interactions with their peers, but also how they use their emerging L2 skills to enact their social identities (see Gee, 1999).

## Research Questions Addressed

This chapter focuses on these questions:

1. How do second language learners in a content-based course display and negotiate their identities in class discussions online? Specifically, what affective and epistemic stances do they take?

2. How may the learners' identity construction be linked to their language learning? Specifically, is there a relationship between the students' identity performance in discourse with their opportunities for language learning?

We hope that the answers to these questions can provide useful insights into the ways that L2 learning environment shape the identities that learners construct for themselves.

## Data Collection Procedures

An important activity in this particular course, from the second week of class until the end of the semester, consisted of online discussions using WebCT's® message posting forums. WebCT® is a course management software (used by the University of Hawai'i system) that provides a virtual learning environment. In the course under study, WebCT® was used to complement face-to-face instruction, and the key tools utilized were the discussion board, email, and material distribution. The Discussion Tool in WebCT® functions as a bulletin board system with forums for asynchronous message posting. Students may click to view discussions as either threaded or unthreaded.

Students participated in these forums to discuss the course content either as part of a weekly class held in a computer lab or outside of class. In these discussions, the teacher started off a discussion thread by posting a question that either related the materials being covered in class to the students' own lives or elicited the students' reactions to the course materials. The students then responded to these questions but they also responded to one another's comments. A key distinction between this type of discussion and set-up "debate" activities is that in the class under study, the students were not assigned explicit opposing positions to debate that might not have reflected their true beliefs. Rather, in the present data collection, the students were invited to react to the course's content and to one another's comments. It was through these postings that they established their positionings and enacted their identities, as the analysis will reveal below.

The data for this chapter were drawn from a larger collection of 387 synchronous and asynchronous electronic postings from the course's online discussions in one semester. We focused mainly on two exchanges between two pairs of students about stereotypes and prejudices. These extracts were selected because they show the dynamic interrelationship between identity construction and second language learning as the students participated in a discourse centering around the content of the course. Using a microanalytic framework, we examine closely a small amount of data in order to gain in-depth understandings about the phenomena under investigation.

# Data Analysis Procedures

Since we were interested in how the students constructed their identities in social interaction, we utilized discourse analysis and mainly drew on Goffman's (1981) notion of participation framework. According to Goffman, the production of an utterance immediately projects a footing for the speaker, the intended hearer, and possibly a broader audience, making up their participation framework as a whole. Following Goffman, we focused on how the students' utterances in electronic postings indexed their footings (or positionings) for themselves and the recipients. The students' footings served to construct their alignment with or opposition to certain *implicit* values and beliefs. The students' dynamic and emergent identity construction can be observed in their talk about stereotypes and prejudices.

# Findings

As previously mentioned, the key concepts in the course were stereotypes and prejudices. We found that as the students grappled with the meanings of these concepts and how to question and deconstruct stereotypes and prejudices with logical reasoning, they engaged in a discourse that activated their knowledge of linguistic forms and content materials and revealed their senses of self and social relationships. This phenomenon can be seen in two exchanges between two pairs of students (Extract 1 and Extract 2 on pp. 147–148). The context of these exchanges was the teacher's (Guy) initial question in the discussions, one designed to facilitate the conceptual understanding of stereotypes (Message 1). (The message numbers used are the original message numbers in the online discussion, which were assigned automatically in the order of appearance. All the students' names in this discussion are pseudonyms.)

> Message 1 (Guy, September 1, 3:52 pm)
>
> Subject: Personal Experience
>
> definition of "stereotype" [from dictionary.com]
> n: a conventional or formulaic conception or image; "regional
> stereotypes have been part of America since its founding"
> v: treat or classify according to a mental stereotype; "I was
> stereotyped as a lazy Southern European" [syn: pigeonhole]
> Have you ever been stereotyped? What are your personal
> experiences?

It is worth noting that the teacher introduced the dictionary definition of the word *stereotype* before he asked whether the students had been stereotyped in their personal experiences. In doing so, the teacher invited the students to bridge the decontextualized, general, and impersonal meaning of *stereotype* to the context of the students' specific and personal experiences, which provides a means of checking the students' understanding about this word's meaning. As it turned out, the students' responses to this question also revealed a great deal about how they constructed themselves in this class, as can be seen in Extract 1 and Extract 2. (For ease of reference, we have numbered the clauses in this and the other excerpts. We retain all students' unique use of English, punctuation, and spelling.)

### Extract 1: "Why you think you are nerd?"

> Message 2 (Kimiko, September 2, 2:01 pm)
>
> Subject: Stereotypes
>
> (1) I felt stereotypes of nerd (2) when I stay home, (3) no make up on me, (4) wear glasses on me, (5) and doing my homework.

In this posting, Kimiko, a young Japanese woman, described how she was stereotyped, but not by other people as the teacher's question implicitly asked for; rather, it was something she perceived about herself. In the beginning of the message, Kimiko shared that she "felt" that she fit the stereotype of a "nerd" (1) and then gave some details about her habits (2–5) to support her statement. Since being a "nerd" was considered "not cool" by the students in this class, Kimiko's attitude (affective stance) in this message can be considered modest. Regarding her epistemic stance toward the meaning of *stereotype*, her description revealed how she understood the stereotype of "nerd" (i.e., nerds wear glasses, do homework, and do not wear make-up) and that she believed that this stereotype was true. Moreover, Kimiko's writing suggests that this stereotype comprised a part of her social identity construction as a "nerd" and as a modest person.

About a week later, Kimiko's message was responded to by Junko, another young Japanese woman (Message 64), who attempted to deconstruct the stereotype described in Kimiko's message by pointing out the inconsistency among its components. Importantly, this was done as a part of her affiliation with Kimiko.

> Message 64 [Branch from Message 2] (Junko, September 9, 9:16 am)
>
> Subject: Re: Stereotypes from Junko
>
> (1) Why you think you are nerd? (2) I don't think so. (3) If you think you're hard warker of study, (4) it might be true though. (5) But it is steretypes for nerd. (6) You should think you are smart girl. (7) Because, I don't make me up everuday (8) and I wear glasses at night. (9) So do you think am I nerd (10) though I didn't study hard. (11) Or I am other meaning's nerd?

In this message, Junko first questioned Kimiko's claim to be a "nerd" (1) and then disagreed with it (2). As mentioned before, admitting to be a "nerd" might be self-effacing for Kimiko. Thus, Junko's disagreement with Kimiko was actually an attempt to demonstrate alliance with Kimiko. Evidence for this interpretation is that in the next sentences (3–4), Junko agreed with Kimiko about the one positive quality that Kimiko cited about herself (hardworking) and in (6) she complimented Kimiko on this quality. Junko then described two of her own habits that fit Kimiko's original definition of "nerd" (7–9), but then she challenged Kimiko's notion of "nerd" by citing a third habit that did not fit (10). The contradiction among the components of this stereotype was effectively indicated by Junko's use of the concessive connective *though* (10). It is important to note that Junko did not fully question the truth value of the existing stereotype cited by Kimiko, as evidenced in Junko's question in (11) where she posed the possibility that there might be some other meaning of "nerd." This question signaled Junko's tentative stance toward a rejection of the stereotype under discussion. Junko thus managed to avoid opposing Kimiko while problematizing Kimiko's original stereotype. This second action potentially helped both students to realize that stereotypes should be questioned critically, an understanding that could further facilitate the deconstruction of stereotypes and prejudices. This example thus demonstrates that a student's understanding of the concept of a word may not merely be a cognitive state but it can be deeply situated in social actions, in which the student's social identity is co-constructed vis-à-vis the other participants in the class.

We now turn to Extract 2, which is an exchange between Junko and another student, Kanta, a young Japanese man. It started on the same day as Message 64 and continued into the sixth week. Similar to Extract 1, the students in Extract 2 were also concerned with a sense of self and the maintenance of social relationships as they grappled with concepts and social values surrounding stereotypes and prejudices.

## Extract 2: "What is your image about 'OTAKU'?"

Message 19 (Junko, September 9, 8:20 am)

Subject: Stereotpes

(1) I have never met horrible stereotypes (2) but I think everybody have it. (3) For example, some people say (4) "I like to wear the costume in movie." (5) and what do you think the person's hobby. (6) When I said it, (7) my friend was surprised (8) and tell me (9) "You are nerd!!". (10) But I just like the movie and beautiful costume, (11) is it nerd? (12) I think it is stereotypes, (13) what do you think? (14) Am I nerd?

In her response to the teacher's question about the students' experiences of being stereotyped (Message 1), Junko first acknowledged that "everybody" had stereotypes (2). Then, as an example, she recounted how she was stereotyped by a friend due to her hobby of dressing up as characters from movies (3–9). In her story, Junko set up a distinction between the stereotype that her friend applied to her ("nerd" [9]) and what she really was (i.e., she "just like the movie and beautiful costume" [10]). Signaled by the conjunctive "but" (10), this contrast implied her resistance to being categorized to fit an existing stereotype. However, rather than asserting her self-identity, she sought the other class members' opinion about herself (11, 13, 14). Of note, she first asked, "is it nerd?" (11), with the pronoun *it* referring to the habit of wearing costumes from movies. In the second question, "Am I nerd?" (14), however, she changed the subject from *it* to *I*, switching the focus from a single personal trait to her entire self. With this switch, she had also shifted from a neutral stance—putting a type of behavior up for comments from others—to a more involved stance in which her whole identity was open for evaluation. Thus, in this posting Junko not only demonstrated her understanding of what the word *stereotype* meant by giving a personal example of a stereotype, she also focused on her identity construction as defined by the other class members. In other words, this discourse is as much about the course content as it is about the students' social identity construction and co-construction.

A day later, Kanta responded to Junko's posting with Message 65, in which he did not respond directly to Junko's question but discussed both her personal example and a broader understanding about stereotypes.

> Message 65 [Branch from Message 19] (Kanta, September 10, 10:35 pm)
>
> Subject: KANTA to JUNKO
>
> (1) Do you mean (2) peple have a stereotype about "Costume Play"(wearing cosutume) as nerd? (3) Did you feel bad? (4) Yes, Stereotype will make someone upset. (5) It's a sort of prejudice. (6) Therefore they just think (7) that's nerd without their comprehension. (8) However, each person have own idea with their comprehension. (9) If they said to you nerd, (10) you should understand about their idea (11) or you can tell them your idea. (12) You are you !!! (13) Thay are them !!!
> (14) I'm interested in your case, (15) so please tell me more detail.
> (16) Thank you
> (17) KANTA

Kanta first checked his comprehension about the stereotype introduced by Junko (that dressing up as characters from movies was "nerd") and explicitly mentioned the subculture of "Costume Play" (1–2), popular among teenagers and young adults in Japan. (In Japanese, this practice is often referred to as *cosplay*.) While Junko only described what she liked to do in her message ([4] and [10] in Message 15), Kanta used a social label (which he capitalized and put in quotation marks) to refer to the same phenomenon. Thus, while checking his understanding about the stereotype, Kanta simultaneously identified Junko with another recognized social group in their country of origin. The introduction of a new label might help to distance Junko from the other label, "nerd," thus Kanta might be aligning with Junko's positioning in her previous message. Kanta then moved on to address Junko's affective stance toward being labeled as "nerd" ("feel bad") in the next sentence (3). He then aligned with her affective stance by saying "yes" in (4). It is important to note that in this sentence, Kanta shifted the subject to "stereotype" and referred to "someone" in general, effectively linking Junko's personal experience to a general discussion about stereotypes. He continued this impersonal stance with the use of the "dummy" *it* in the next sentence (5). He then indicated his belief that stereotypes were based on a lack of understanding ([6] and [7]) and that ideas varied from person to person (8). Shifting back to the use of second person pronoun, he advised Junko to hold on to her own independent ideas (9–13). Kanta's employment of two series of exclamation marks as he defended Junko's individuality expressed emphasis and strong emotions (12, 13), thus again signaling his alignment with her. Kanta's posting was thus a fine blend of general statements indicating his understanding about stereotypes and interpersonal messages to maintain a positive relationship with his classmate.

This interpersonal aspect was continued in Kanta's closing sentences (14, 15), where he expressed personal interest in Junko's story. Message 191 was Junko's response, in which she showed appreciation of his interest in her personal experience.

Message 191 [Branch from Message 65] (Junko, September 28, 6:39 pm)

Subject: Thanks your reply

(1) Thank for your interest.
(2) In Japanese, "OTAKU (mean nerd)" (2) is not good meaning, I guess. (3) It's kind of stereotypes (4) but I think so. (5) According to KOZIEN, OTAKU means (6) the person who have interest only one thing (7) and don't have common sense. (8) I acknowledge (9) that I know more than general people about this movie (10) but I just like it. (11) What is your image about "OTAKU"? (12) Is it bad one?
(13) I know my friend was joking (14) and I'm not upset. (15) But some people are misunderstanding about "OTAKU" and Mania, I think.
(16) Well, thank you again for reply.
(17) Junko

In her message, Junko introduced the Japanese term *otaku*, which she indicated to be the concept behind the word "nerd" that she had been using from the beginning of this exchange (1–7). (Kimiko's earlier usage of *nerd* was probably also a translation of *otaku*). She first explained that *otaku* did not have a "good meaning" (2), and she acknowledged her own negative stereotype about *otaku* (3–4). She then cited a Japanese dictionary as the authority on the meaning of this word (5–7), thus discussing this stereotype on a general level. (Kōjien [spelled as "Kozien" in Junko's message] is a Japanese dictionary regarded as the most authoritative by many native speakers of Japanese.) Next, she changed the subject to *I* to shift to a personal level (8–10). It is interesting that Junko employed the teacher's very strategy in Message 1 cited above: moving from the dictionary meaning of a word to personal examples in order to understand its concept. Arguably, Junko's use of the teacher's strategy could be additional evidence for her language socialization into the discourse community of an academic class.

In this message, Junko continued to distance herself from the stereotype of *otaku* by using the connective *but* to contrast one detail about her that fit the stereotype (8–9) and another that did not (10). In the next sentences, Junko returned to the impersonal level and asked about Kanta's view on *otaku* (11–12). The interpretation of Junko's question in (12) can be enriched by considering the context of contemporary Japanese society, in which the negative connotations of *otaku* are changing. Her question thus was an effort to seek her classmate's stance toward a concept in her native language. This effort continued in the next sentences where Junko distinguished between *otaku* and another word, *Mania* (15), which, in Japanese, refers to someone with a special interest or hobby and has a less offensive connotation. Junko's pointing out that "some people are misunderstanding" (15) between *otaku* and *mania* implied that for her, these were two separate categories. Since she had distanced herself from the label *otaku*, her invoking of the label *mania* may imply that this was the label she identified herself as. This example also shows how, in a discussion in the second language, first language resources might become necessary for the students to express facets of their identity, which, in many ways, were deeply rooted in their life experiences in the home language and culture.

Kanta responded to Junko's questions about *otaku* a few days later (Message 218), when he discussed his position toward *otaku*, thus directly answering Junko's question.

> Message 218 [Branch from Message 191] (Kanta, October 3, 4:35 pm)
>
> Subject: Kanta to Junko Thanks your reply again
>
> (1) I have good and bad images about "otaku". (2) My good image is the person who parrticularly love or know about the one things. (3) So they know a lot of things. (4) Autually, many company applied "Otaku" (5) because otaku knows about otaku

who like same things as well. (6) The market is really big (7) and they make the effection of economy. (8) Therefore, the copany need their infomation and their psychology. (9) I think generally "otaku" is used as bad image in Japan. (10) My bad image is they stare at only one thing so that it hard for them to accept the other thing. (11) I don't know whether they who are called "otaku" think their "otaku" or not (12) and also don't know the borderline. (13) In my opinion, it is bad to make them bad image by society.

Kanta started his message by declaring first that he had both positive and negative views about *otaku* (1), indicating that he has a balanced viewpoint. He focused on the positive aspect first and related it to the business context (2–8), thus bringing the topic to a larger scale beyond Junko's case. His direct claim of knowledge on this topic can be seen in the absence of any hedges and the use of *actually* to claim access to information new to the recipient. In contrast, when he turned to the negative aspect, he did not claim direct knowledge but rather, referred to what people generally believe about *otaku* in Japan (9). Through these subtle cues, Kanta managed to present two opposite views while also aligning with the positive view and distancing away from the negative view. This alignment can be seen more clearly in his conclusion, when he made a sympathetic statement about *otakus* and blamed society for making this group of people feel bad (13). Since Junko had identified herself as possibly a *mania,* Kanta's balanced and sympathetic view on people with special hobbies served to maintain a positive relationship with Junko. It is also interesting to note that Kanta indicated that he did not know whether *otakus* would consider themselves as such (11), thus implicitly suggesting that a stereotype may be a matter of perspective rather than truth.

While Junko's and Kanta's focus on L1 linguistic forms (*otaku, mania*) may be considered a reflection of their L2 incompetence, we argue that the use of the L1 in fact helped them understand the concepts of the course relating to stereotypes and prejudices. That is, through discussing the social phenomena and meanings exist-ing in their first language and culture, the students confronted existing stereotypes (e.g., about nerds, *otakus,* and *manias*) and analyzed them in English based on available information and reasoning in order to deconstruct them and gain a better understanding about social prejudices.

So far, the analysis has shown that in these two exchanges, the students attended to both the course content and their sense of self related to one another. In other words, their learning about the contents in the second language was intertwined with their identity construction. With an interest in whether these students continued their exploration of stereotypes in further discussions in the course, we looked into their later postings, which will be analyzed.

## Later Postings

The students' understanding about stereotypes in the two extracts examined was evident in their other postings in the online discussions, thus demonstrating that their learning from these exchanges was carried over to other interactions in the class.

For Junko, her understanding about stereotypes as expressed in Extract 2 (pp. 148–152) can be seen again in a posting in another thread (Message 211), sent a day after her second message in Extract 2. In this thread, two other young Japanese women, Michiko and Asada, had shared their experiences in which they witnessed or fought against discrimination toward a friend in their home country, Japan (see Nguyen & Kellogg [2007] for a full analysis). These students and the others who responded had expressed that they felt ashamed of the discrimination by the other Japanese described in those stories, and Junko joined this sentiment.

> Message 211 [Branch from Message 186] (Junko, September 29, 10:47 pm)
>
> Subject: To Michiko and Asada from Junko
>
> (1) I read your experience. (2) These make me disappointed. (3) Fortunately, I didn't meet such situation. (. . .) (4) But, if I met such situation, (5) I'm not sure to do something. (6) I can understand both feeling (7) and I also ashame. (8) I think I and everyone have prejudice. (9) Maybe, although there is no way to disappear prejudice, (10) we can know truth. (11) Truth remove the prejudice. (12) I believe.

In this message, Junko shared that she had not encountered the same kind of situations as Michiko and Asada (3), and acknowledged that she did not know whether she would have fought against discrimination if she were in those situations (4–5). Her alignment with the other students was signaled in her statement that she understood and shared their feelings (6–7). She then moved from this personal and interpersonal level to a broader level in the remainder of the message; this shift being indicated by the use of the compound subject "I and everyone" (8) and continued with the collective pronoun "we" (10). These pronominal expressions may also index solidarity with her classmates. Junko acknowledged the existence and persistence of prejudices (8–9) and expressed her belief that true understanding could help to "remove prejudice" (11). This later posting showed a firmer and clearer position, reflecting a more critical and informed understanding compared to her previous exchanges with Kimiko and Kanta, in which she was only raising questions as she tried to understand the concepts of stereotypes and prejudices together with the other class members. We suggest that this can be considered as evidence of her language socialization into the values adopted in the community of the class, specifically, as shown in this study, the value placed on the students' intellectual exploration of word meanings. Importantly, throughout the discussion including this later posting, we have seen that Junko approached the topic of prejudice on both personal and general levels, effectively managing both social relationships and the course's content.

If Junko transferred her understanding in Extract 2 to another discussion thread, Kimiko on the other hand showed a change of understanding from an earlier exchange, Extract 1, to another posting about three weeks later. In this message (Message 171), Kimiko summarized the discussion on stereotypes. (The summary was an assigned task.)

> Message 171 (Kimiko, September 27, 12:43 pm)
>
> Subject: The summary of Stereotype
>
> Stereotype Thinking
> Kimiko Suzuki
> (1) I agree with everything that everybody said. (2) Stereotype that means an idea of what a particular group of people is like (3) that many people have, (4) especially one that is wrong or unfair. (5) I think most people make stereotype (6) when they do not have enough knowledge about something. (7) Therefore, most people in the class, including me, have some kind of stereotype about people in Hawaii. (8) Nobody really knew that is another country exactly except their own country. (9) One such case is Yume's stereotype. (10) I had same image as her. (11) Hawaiian people are nice, friendly, has dark skins, and big eyes. (12) However once I lived in here, (13) I realized that images were just stereotypes. (14) I'm not talking about Hawaii and Hawaiians, but also any little things. (15) I guess we do a lot of stereotype thinking. (16) Even though it is difficult to notice what a stereotype is, (17) we should still not make stereotype about people, culture, and country. (18) We should be open-minded and see person with individual.

In this posting, Kimiko demonstrated an informed perspective on stereotypes. She first stated that stereotypes were simply "idea(s)" (2), and that these ideas were usually "wrong or unfair" (3), thus indicating her belief that stereotypes were not truths. She went further to express her opinion (via the expression "I think") about the cause of stereotypes, i.e., lack of knowledge (5–6). She then confronted some stereotypes that she and her classmates held (7–13) and generalized it to all cases (14). She acknowledged the existence of "stereotype thinking" (15) but advised against making stereotypes (16–18). From believing in a stereotype in Message 2 to this balanced view in Message 64, Kimiko showed a shift in understanding about the meaning of *stereotype* not only by herself but also by the whole class (as expressed in the reference to "most people in the class" [7] and the collective pronoun *we* [15, 17, 18]). In other words, Junko was able to change her understanding about the meaning of *stereotype* from taking them as truths (Message 2) to considering them as generalizations that need to be evaluated critically (Message 171).

Thus, both Junko and Kimiko showed their socialization into the discourse community of the course, in which stereotypes were not to be taken as given truths but were to be deconstructed with information and reasoning. Further, their efforts to relate personal experiences to general concepts and values in these messages could also be a reflection of their socialization into academic discourse, which has been shown to involve students' extending themselves into "commonplaces" or "culturally or institutionally authorized concept(s) or statement(s)" (Bartholomae, 1986, p. 7). We believe that together with other course materials including extensive readings, presentations, face-to-face discussions, and other online discussions, the exchanges we examined above were part of this language socialization process.

## Implications

The findings of this study first suggest that sustained content instruction provides students with the opportunity for the kind of extended class discussions (in the case of this study, online discussions) in which students can bring in personal experiences that relate to the course materials. It is also possible that in electronic discussions, more students can participate at the same time, thus that their opportunities to share and exchange their personal experiences are increased. (For further discussion about the affordances of online discussion for second language socialization, see Nguyen & Kellogg, 2005).

These extended discussions are powerful in enabling language socialization in a second language and the joint exploration of social identities. Through discussions over a period of time with their peers in which meanings are negotiated and revisited, students can make sense of the concepts and social values associated with specific lexical items in the context of the content used (in the case examined here, *stereotype* and *prejudice*). We have shown that this sense-making process occurs when students integrate new concepts and values into the context of their life experiences. When students are given the opportunity to move continually between the personal level and the general, academic level, as did the students who provided the data for this study, they are also able to construct a sense of self vis-à-vis one another in the second language. This supports the view that successful language learning needs to be experiential (Dewey, 1938/1997; van Lier, 2002).

The findings also demonstrate that as students interact with the course content and with one another, there may be times when, interestingly, they make efforts to understand not only second language concepts but also to revisit first language concepts. This study shows that students' discussion about their native language forms, however, may not compromise second language learning; rather, such discussion can facilitate their understanding of concepts and meanings introduced in discourse communities in the second language. The learning of concepts and social values introduced in the second language thus may transcend linguistic boundaries.

This study also suggests that the language in a sustained content course should not be treated as neutral by students or teachers, but as something that can prompt critical evaluation, challenge, and negotiation. This is because, as mentioned above, when students engage with new content or are prompted to reflect on their own assumptions, they continually construct and re-construct their identities as they reconcile their own existing beliefs (which may be deeply tied to their native languages and cultures) and the values of discourse communities related to the contents under discussion. As content-based instruction becomes more widely accepted in second language classes, language teachers need to be aware that content-based language teaching should not present the target language as a package void of social and political contexts, but should bring students into contact with the language and culture of various discourse communities in the target language. Sustained content-based instruction allows students the time and opportunities to construct their own perceptions of the meanings of words and concepts.

# Part 5
## Defining and Assessing Success in Community College ESL Programs

# Chapter 11

# "To Triumph in My Life":
# ESL Students Define Success

■ Molly J. Lewis

$A$TTENDING ADMINISTRATIVE MEETINGS AT THE COMMUNITY COLLEGE WHERE I WAS A new mid-level manager, I learned early on that year after year, program completion, graduation and transfer rates placed the college toward the back of the community college pack, a trend that obviously did not sit well with college leaders. But I also knew that many of the school's students were non–English speaking immigrants, meeting face-on the challenge of their adopted society and language by enrolling in college ESL classes. I wanted very much to know more about these students, the reasons they enrolled in classes, and the outcomes they envisioned for themselves. It was this curiosity that prompted the study on which this chapter is based.

## Issues that Motivated the Research

$C$ommunity college administrators must make reference to certain agreed-upon indicators in order to discuss the success of ESL learners. Typically cited are scores on placement or proficiency exams, the completion of a level or program, enrollment in for-credit classes, or successful transfer to a four-year school. Such markers share the advantages of being quantifiable and comparable across a range of settings and groups of students. But in using these markers, administrators of community colleges serving communities with large numbers of immigrant, ESL, and first-generation college students often find themselves frustrated by compara- tively low figures for retention, completion, and transfer of their students.

But the power of these outcomes is the challenge they pose to the conventional ways in which many community colleges have framed their missions, and the ways in which immigrant, non–English speaking students have in earlier years been served. Indeed, seeing that the usual ways of measuring success leave institutions, communities, and, often, students themselves shaking their heads in frustration, these outcomes are a clear invitation to examine the ways in which we define and assure student success. All indications are that the need to serve, and serve well, the educational needs of the adult immigrant community will be a defining element of the college mission for many years to come.

For that reason, an ongoing and informed conversation about the motivations and decision making of these learners is required. Interwoven with the conversation on who these students are, motivationally speaking, and what factors impact their involvement with educational institutions, are equally important issues of accountability to all stakeholders, and a primary responsibility to provide the developmental education courses that contribute to workforce development (Nebraska Industrial Competitiveness Alliance, 1999).

The role played by community colleges in developing vocational and job-related general skills will be the likely impetus for college and instructional reform in order to better address the needs and circumstances of adult English language learners. While the academy may concern itself with scholastic measures of student success, government agencies are articulating policy and legislative calls for workforce development, and providing funding for implementation. These calls recognize the complexity of motivations bringing the ESL, first-generation immigrant learner to the classroom. The California Community College Chancellor's Office (CCCCO), in compliance with the federal Perkins Act of 1998 and California's Vocational Technical Education Act (VTEA), is charged with planning and delivering a substantial portion of the training that will bring the state's growing and diverse population into the 21$^{st}$ century. The VTEA mission statement recognizes the complex web of motivations that brings adult ESL learners into the community college classroom, and reflects this complexity in annual reports by including data on four measures of success for targeted students: skill attainment, completions, placement and retention, and gender equity access (California Community Colleges Chancellor's Office [CCCCO], 2000). Data from the Chancellor's Office, 2000–2006, show that the numbers of students retained from one year to the next in basic skills courses such as ESL have declined over this period (CCCCO, 2007). In this context, the concern is that the interdependency between English language skills development and the state's economic engine is compromised. The U.S. Department of Education (DOE) Office of Vocational and Adult Education (OVAE) echoes this concern with attrition, and while stressing the value of retention, acknowledges the influence of the multiple priorities juggled by the non-traditional college student. OVAE offers resources describing the varied ways in which community colleges have responded to the issue (OVAE, 2006).

Though the institution's policy and mission concerns may be far from the mind of the practicing teacher as she prepares for her community college ESL class, the complex lives and motivations of her learners are surely evident to her. The teacher is very aware of the many issues of daily life that impinge on and shape an ESL student's relationship to school and the learning of English. Not only must accessibility to and preparation for classes be considered, but those who work with ESL learners must also realize that these community college students are often older adults, and, therefore, more likely involved in a web of adult responsibilities including work and parenting. If nothing else, learners' multiple roles and obligations often result in part-time enrollment, a status in itself associated with lower completion and retention rates (Wasley, 2007). Add to that mix the fact that these students are often living on the economic margins of the community, and the challenges to regular attendance and re-enrollment at more advanced levels become apparent. For some students, living in the limbo created by an uncertain or undocumented legal status raises additional impediments.

For these reasons, ESL professionals and others may argue that the traditional measures of academic and institutional success must be tempered—if not wholly redefined—for a substantial portion of these non-traditional post-secondary students. One approach may be to see school attendance as only one of a number of roles in which such students engage. As with other part-time students on campus, school attendance defines only one of several sets of obligations that must be fulfilled. For many part-time students in ESL classes, being an English learner and a college student are not primary roles. Nearly always taking precedence, as ESL teachers can report, are family and work responsibilities (see Skillen & Vorholt-Alcorn, this volume). Surely these multiple and often conflicting roles are at the heart of many of the issues resulting in lower retention and completion rates.

In the larger context, the multiple roles of the ESL learner reflect the community served by the school. At a school like Hartnell College in Salinas, California, where this study took place, 73 percent of the 9,400 students are enrolled part-time, a percentage that has varied little over the past several years (Hartnell College, 2005). Across the country, younger, white, financially dependent and better-off students are much more likely to be attending college full-time than the older, independent, minority student—and it is in the latter group that ESL students most frequently are found (National Center for Educational Statistics, 2007, p. 7). For these students, attending class on a regular basis and completing home assignments may in themselves constitute a measure of success. Without discounting the value of a certificate or degree to future career and economic involvement, it also seems reasonable to assess the self-reported purposes and goals that draw these students into the classroom, whether for the first time or intermittently over an extended period, despite the challenges of continuing the education process.

## Research Questions Addressed

This study was primarily an effort to bridge the apparent disconnect between institutional measures of success and ESL learners' perspectives on their learning goals and success as community college students. These qualitative data provide a lens through which to view the motivations and purposes of a small cohort of ESL learners. For the sake of administrators and faculty struggling to bring lower-level students up through the ESL curriculum and into college-level classes, there are two further questions to ask:

1. What goals and motivations do community college ESL students report for taking ESL?

2. As students' English proficiency increases, how do their purposes and goals change, if at all?

## Context of the Research

Hartnell College, founded in 1920, is one of the oldest two-year schools in the California Community College 109-school system. Hartnell's approximately 9,400 students are drawn primarily from the Salinas Valley of Monterey County, a region known internationally for vegetable crop production. Fifty percent of the county's 410,000 residents are Hispanic; 29 percent of county residents are foreign-born; and 47 percent speak a language other than English at home (U.S. Census Bureau, 2000). Reflecting community demographics, 57 percent of Hartnell's student body is Hispanic, and 27 percent report a language other than English—preponderantly, Spanish—as their home language. In the 2005 population, 43 percent of the students were more than 30 years old, and 28 percent attended evening classes only, a number that has dropped over the period since 2000. The percentage of men attending classes at the school has increased steadily during this same period, moving from 45 percent to 53 percent of the student body (Hartnell College, 2005).

## Data Collection Procedures

In the 33 class sections of the various ESL lecture and lab courses offered at Hartnell College in the spring of 2006, there were 1,386 actively enrolled students, in some cases representing a single individual enrolled in multiple classes. This number also includes those enrolled in open-entry lab classes. Ninety-one percent of these enrolled students identified themselves as Hispanic/Latino; 70 percent were women. The class sections were distributed among 21 differently designated ESL courses, at three identified levels of proficiency ranging from beginning English Foundations (with classes numbered in the 120s) through Advanced ESL (classes in the 140 series). At each level, a lab class, a multi-skills class, a vocabulary class, and a reading class are offered. A student who completes this sequence, or who otherwise qualifies (for example, through placement testing), may enroll in courses at the 150 or 160 level, to further develop reading and writing skills, or may move on to English 101F. Successful completion of this course qualifies students to enroll in English 1A, the college-level composition course required for the associate's degree as well as for transfer to most four-year colleges in California.

To frame the general characteristics of ESL students at Hartnell, the typical movement of students through the ESL course sequence was explored. Looking at aggregate data over the semesters from Fall 2004 through Spring 2007, the period that includes the time when this study was conducted, we can character-ize the progress of students through various ESL course sequences. For example, of the 32 students whose first enrollment at the college during this period was in ESL 125, eighteen (just over half) went on to successfully complete the next level (ESL 135), where "success" means completing the course with a grade of "C" or better. Of this group, eight students enrolled in and successfully completed ESL 145. Three of this group then went to complete ESL 155 within this time period. In another sequence, of the 52 students whose initial enrollment was at the ESL 145 level, 49 were successful in the class, with 24 going on to enroll and succeed in ESL 155. One-third of this group (eight students) continued into ESL 165, with the same number subsequently advancing to ESL 101F. Based on data extracted from the Hartnell Executive Information System for the academic years in ques-tion, five students who began at the ESL 145 level during 2004–2007 successfully completed English 1A, the college composition class, in the same period.

Though these data paint a picture all too familiar to college faculty and administrators—few sequence completions, and very few students moving on to college-level work—it is necessary to bear in mind that the completions counted here refer to a time frame that may be too stringent for the part-time adult learner whose motivations and patterns of college class attendance this study elucidates. To learn how this particular group of Hartnell students think about their own future goals—and therefore, how each might measure their ultimate success—a simple questionnaire was developed (see Figure 11.1) and administered to a single class section at each of three levels, ESL 135, ESL 145, and ESL 101F.

As shown in Figure 11.1, students were asked to provide information about their backgrounds, including any previous U.S. schooling experiences and cur-rent employment. They were also asked to respond to a prompt intended to elicit commentary in the writer's own words about what goals or purposes led them to enroll in college classes.

## Data Analysis Procedures

A total of 67 students responded to the survey. Of these, 23 were enrolled in ESL 135, Intermediate English; 23 in ESL 145, Advanced English; and 21 in ESL 101F, Composition and Grammar for ESL. The distribution of these students with regard to background characteristics was remarkably uniform across levels, as summarized in Table 11.1.

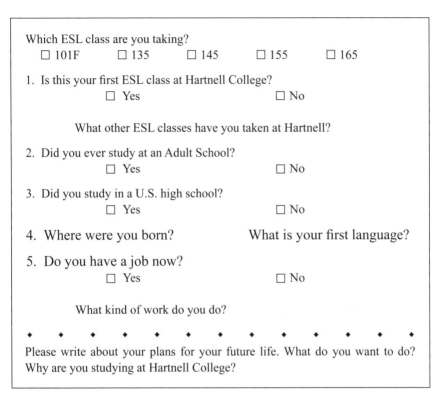

**Figure 11.1.** Student Questionnaire Used to Gather Demographic Information and Data about Student Goals

**Table 11.1.**
Summary of ESL Learner Characteristics (n = 67)

| Class | L1 = Spanish | Attended Adult School | Attended U.S. High School | Taking/Has Taken Other Hartnell ESL |
|---|---|---|---|---|
| ESL 135 (n = 21) | 20 | 14 | 3 | 14 |
| ESL 145 (n = 23) | 22 | 10 | 7 | 11 |
| ESL101F (n = 23) | 21 | 13 | 5 | 13 |
| *Subtotals* | 63 | 37 | 15 | 48 |

In terms of these background characteristics, then, there appears to be a similar demographic profile among students enrolled in the more advanced classes and in the lower level courses.

The next step was to examine the content of the written comments provided in response to the prompt. The 67 responses were read and five coding categories referring to students' reasons for studying in college were defined, based on the range of responses. These five categories of reasons for being in school were (1) to develop a specific skill or knowledge set; (2) to become a practitioner of a particular discipline or profession; (3) to meet academic milestones or goals; (4) to pursue job-related outcomes or goals; and (5) to bring benefits of education to specific family members or the student's family in general.

# Findings

## To Develop a Skill or Knowledge Set

The most frequently expressed student intention or goal (n = 31) was the desire to develop a skill or knowledge set related either to English or to a specific content or discipline area. For example:

| Examples related to learning English | Examples related to a particular discipline |
| --- | --- |
| "I want to speak very good English." | "I will learn all about real estate." |
| "I 'm studing here to better my Inglish." | "I am going to study for nurse." |
| "I'll like to speak, listening and understand English language." | "I want to study something about computers or architecture." |

## To Become a Practitioner in a Particular Discipline or Profession

The second most frequently identifiable goal (n = 23) was phrased in terms of a particular profession—not to study a discipline or skills set in this case, but to become a practitioner: The language used by the respondents seemed to indicate an identification with the person holding a particular knowledge set: *to be a CPA* as opposed to *to study accounting*, for example.

"I'll be come an agronomist."

"Then I will be a CPA."

"After study, I will becaming a good actor."

"My goal in a Bussines man."

## To Attain Specific Academic or Job-Related Outcomes

The third and fourth categories were perhaps the ones that would resonate most clearly with college administrators: many responses reflected academic or work-related outcomes as the reason (or part of the reason) for enrollment. Some of these outcomes were very specific, while others were general in nature.

| Academic Outcomes (n = 23) | Job-Related Outcomes (n = 19) |
|---|---|
| "I want to obtain my AA in ECE" (Early Childhood Education) "I will get a certificate and a license as LVN." | "I must study to get better job." "Then I will work in a school office with good salary and insurance." |

## Benefits to the Family

A fifth goal or measure of success cited by respondents (n = 14) was the benefit education provides to the family, especially to specific family members. For instance, students said:

"I learn to help my husband in his business."

"I learn much more English for talk to my sons."

"Then I help my children with their homework."

"I want a gif to my family better oportunitys."

"I want a help at my brother to make they're homework and take more money to help at my patherns."

Finally, occasionally, and scattered across the three levels, respondents wrote in very general terms about how they view the relation between their schooling and future success (n = 4). Because this category was so small, it was not considered in the further qualitative analysis, but at least anecdotally, it can lend insight to our understanding of student motivations. These comments included the following:

"I study for my satisfaction and for my parents to be proud of me."

"I'll be successful on what I want to be."

"I study to triumph in my life."

The five principal categories provided an effective framework for analysis of students' written responses, creating few outliers. At the same time, it was a minority of students who cited only one reason for being in school: Just as students such as these often have multiple roles to fulfill, and multiple social and economic dimensions to their lives, they most often responded with multiple reasons for being in school. The multidimensional nature of their motivations spoke clearly through their words, interweaving academic, job, and personal or family-related goals as shown in these coded statements:

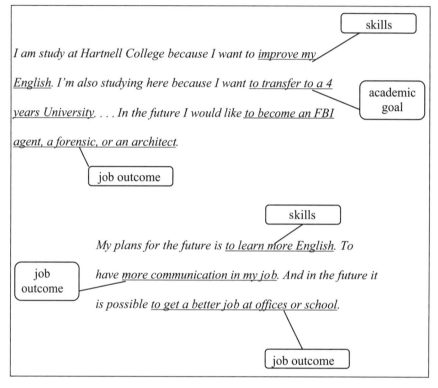

To examine the relationship between the reasons students reported for studying and the level of the ESL class in which they were enrolled, the coded responses to the essay prompt were counted and assigned to cells in a chi-square test. The data are summarized in Table 11.2.

### Table 11.2.
#### Student Goal Responses Based on ESL Class Level (n = 110)

| | ESL 135 (n = 38) | ESL 145 (n = 34) | ESL 101F (n = 38) | Totals |
|---|---|---|---|---|
| Professional | 3 | 8 | 12 | 23 |
| Academic | 3 | 9 | 11 | 23 |
| Job-related | 11 | 5 | 3 | 29 |
| Skills-related | 14 | 11 | 6 | 31 |
| Family benefit–related | 7 | 1 | 6 | 14 |

This distribution of responses is statistically significant since the observed value of chi-square exceeded the critical value of chi-square ($\chi^2_{observed}$ = 22.1755; degrees of freedom = 8; $\chi^2_{critical\ at\ alpha\ =\ .05}$ = 15.5073; p < 0.01). That is, we can be 99 percent sure that this distribution of responses is not due to chance. Beyond that, the distribution suggests that students' reported reasons for studying may vary as their English proficiency increases. For students at the lower level of proficiency, job-related reasons to study and the need to attain discipline-specific skills are more frequently offered as motivation for school participation than is true for students in the higher level classes. To check these interpretations, five one-way chi-square analyses were run to analyze the patterns found in the goal choices of students in the three different ESL courses. None of these comparisons were statistically significant (df = 2; $\chi^2_{critical\ at\ alpha\ =\ .05}$ = 5.99147), perhaps in part because some of the cell sizes are quite small when the students are separated into the three classes. An interesting issue for future research would be whether a larger sample would indeed reveal significant goal differences across the various course levels.

In spite of these non-significant chi-square results, we can speculate that at the upper level of proficiency (e.g., here in the group of English 101F students), these English language learners appear to be more likely to report goals that address their emerging professional identity than is true for the lower-level students. This vision of the self as a practitioner, as a person defined by a set of practices and knowledge, suggests a deeper identification with a future career path and a future self. The student who reports, "I will study accounting" or "I will learn nursing" sees the world in terms of a student identity, while the respondent who states, "I will be a businessman" is positioning himself in a very different context than the academic one in which he currently is active. That future, hoped-for context and identity can only be achieved, the student implies, by successfully moving through a series of academically defined challenges and milestones.

In contrast, the lower-level ESL 135 student who reports as her reason for studying in school that she wants "to get a better job at offices or school" suggests a profile of a student who is probably thinking in terms of better compensation or better working conditions. This kind of response does not appear to reflect the same close identification with a future self transformed by education so much as a current self seeking to reposition herself (and, perhaps, her family) in moderately improved circumstances. There's a transactional or instrumental quality to this kind of goal, while the statement referring to a professional future suggests something more transformational.

The students in the mid-range (in terms of language proficiency) of this sample— students enrolled in ESL 145—fell midway between the other two groups with regard to reporting both job-related and professional motivations. Interestingly, this group was less likely to give multiple reasons for studying, compared to students in the other two classes. The number of ESL 135 students giving more than one reason to be in school was fourteen; in ESL 145, eight; in English 101F, fifteen. Mirroring this pattern, the number of times that benefits to family were cited by ESL 145 students was also fewer than for either other group. Why should this be so?

The by-now conventional approach to understanding learner motivations—referring to instrumental or integrative purposes for learning—does not seem sufficiently multidimensional or complex to describe the pattern we see here. Ullman (1997) notes that such characterizations "assume a static identity and a singular desire on the part of the language learner" (p. 3). But the pattern in this snapshot of Hartnell's ESL students seems anything but static or singular. At each point in their community college experience, these learners are apparently redefining their relationship with English and its various discourses, and resituating themselves in the wider community—Spanish-speaking as well as English-speaking—in which they live. Though learners enrolled in ESL 135 were not necessarily new to the classroom—66 percent had previously completed at least one ESL class at the college—they were at a much different point than were the students in the more advanced classes in negotiating the broader academic and career options that a college experience offers. Those learners who had successfully moved farther along the continuum of developing English proficiency demonstrated by their responses a qualitatively different relationship with academic and professional opportunities.

In itself, this brief discussion of the complex nature of these adult learners' motivations cannot shed light on the unexpected decrease in references to family benefits by respondents in ESL 145. This same group tended to give one reason for study, where the others more frequently gave multiple reasons. Can we guess that these learners identify themselves more exclusively as "students," where their less proficient and less academically experienced peers see themselves more often in terms of bringing their complex outside lives into the classroom? For this latter group, it may be their responsibilities as family members and wage earners that provide the impetus for English learning. However, the mid-range learners at the ESL 145 level seem to demonstrate a focus—Ullman (1997) used the term "investment" (p. 3; also see McKay & Wong, 1996; Norton Pierce, 1995)—on goals related to being successful students. Perhaps students at this mid-range level have made enough gains in their language learning to contemplate new goals for learning English, such as transfer to a four-year university, or job training in a different line of work. Thus, the language of the goals stated by mid-range students reflects a stronger academic focus than the language of the goals offered by the lower-level students. The most proficient students may have completed a redefinition of themselves that again includes family, but by this point they tie family benefits to a future defined in qualitatively different terms, benefits attaching to future activity in a specific career or professional arena.

## Implications

The responses provided by the learners in these ESL classes suggest that along with developing English proficiency, adult ESL learners in the community college experience a shift in the ways in which they define themselves as students. These self-definitions, framed as goals or reasons for studying in a college class, reflect a multidimensional and complex interaction among learners' already full and active non-school lives, their native and adopted cultures and languages, and the array of roles and relationships that the college environment offers, both in the present and in a near-term future.

A study such as this one, limited in scope and intended primarily to illuminate for teachers and administrators this element of student motivation, also raises some key issues for those charged with developing and delivering community college instruction. How can we meaningfully discuss issues of retention and success for this group of learners? How can we define retention and success? The Council for Adult and Experiential Learning (2003) is clearly dismissive of the standard federal benchmark for college student retention. Indeed, how can a standard based on outcomes for a "first-time — full-time student cohort" possibly apply with any validity to these adult students, who will come and go in classes as their other commitments allow them to?

Given that we could agree on a definition, are there ways to encourage adult ESL students to re-enroll, as they are able, by addressing their specific interests and needs? At least in this group of students, the vocational interests of the lower-level learners clustered in a limited number of areas: early childhood education, health care, office skills. This in itself suggests additional questions, including the following: Is there an opportunity here to provide vocation-based language instruction? Are there resources to offer team teaching, with an ESL instructor working in tandem with a discipline- or vocation-specific professional? Are there opportunities to "earn and learn" through on-the-job training programs with a language component? Are classes for these students scheduled during the hours that their school-age children are in class themselves? What provision is otherwise made for child care? Are instructional centers disbursed through the community to remove impediments created by the need to get to a central campus facility? What is the relationship between learners at various levels of proficiency and the utilization of the support services offered by the college, ranging from tutorials and peer study groups to social and academic support for the mature or re-entry student?

In this particular group of students, more than half came to community college after attending an adult education program. How does the community college link with adult education programs? Are adult education programs helping students become aware of the options available through the local community college, and is the college, in turn, supporting the vital role provided by the adult programs?

The pressure is on federal and state governments to prepare a workforce for the 21st century, in a demographic situation characterized by large numbers of immigrants and a growing cohort of elderly students. Community colleges are one of the institutions charged with the development of the requisite vocational and communication skills. The challenge is to flex in response to the realities of immigrant learners' lives, providing the sought-after skills sets, validating the goals and purposes that draw learners into college classes in the first place, and supporting these learners as their academic and vocational options broaden and clarify.

# Chapter 12

# Access to Freshman Composition at Stake: Comparing Student Performance on Two Measures of Writing

■ Cynthia M. Schuemann

IMAGINE THIS SITUATION. A NON-NATIVE SPEAKER OF ENGLISH SUCCESSFULLY completes an advanced ESL writing course at a community college. But then, by virtue of her performance on the Accuplacer® test, she is required to take remedial English writing courses. The student is understandably discouraged, and we as ESL teaching professionals are justifiably concerned.

## Context of the Research

The study reported in this chapter was conducted from 1997 to 1998 at Miami Dade College (MDC) in Florida. It compares student performance on two measures of writing, a standardized, computerized, multiple choice test of sentence skills, and a holistically scored essay exam. The 106 study participants were in their last level of EAP (English for Academic Purposes) at MDC, readying to take freshman-level general education coursework including first-year English composition. Most of the ESL students in this program are immigrant residents. MDC is the largest institution of higher education in the United States, and the academic ESL program accounts for 17 percent of its credit enrollment. Clearly, the college and the students benefit when EAP students successfully complete their language studies and smoothly transition into degree programs.

## Issues that Motivated the Research

In Florida, MDC is part of a 28-member community college system. The Florida Department of Education monitors specific areas of institutional practice for articulation purposes, including course numbering, course descriptions, and student entry placement in the areas of English and math. As community colleges provide open access to higher education, some students are admitted with weaknesses in their academic skills, and are required to take remedial classes. The state has mandated the use of a common basic skills placement test with standard cut scores for placement into freshman composition and exemption from remedial writing, reading, or math. The required placement instrument is the College Board's Accuplacer® test battery, also known as the Computer Placement Test (CPT). The Accuplacer® has two main components, a series of three tests for general college entry assessment and another series of English tests for ESL placement. This study focuses on the sentence skills test for general college entry, not the ESL Accuplacer®. ESL students at MDC take the Accuplacer® sentence skills test at the end of the last level of ESL instruction, level 6. In recent years, the ESL faculty have expressed concerns that this test may inadequately represent the English writing ability of non-native speakers of English (NNS) who are required to take it.

### Background of the Problem

Standardized multiple choice tests are found in all U.S. academic settings. Multiple choice exams are considered highly objective and reliable and can be craftily designed to enhance validity; however, much controversy exists regarding their use as valid measures of writing ability (Crouse, 1997; Hamp-Lyons, 1992; Hughes, 2003; Oller, 1979; O'Malley & Valdez-Pierce, 1996; Weir, 1990; White, 1995). This controversy is due to the fact that multiple choice tests are by their very nature indirect and partial tests of writing; thus, assumptions of writing abilities must be inferred from correct choices on items assessing mastery of writing sub-skills, such as grammatical accuracy or punctuation.

Placement decisions based on Accuplacer® scores affect large numbers of college students. For example, at MDC, of the 8,354 new students tested in Fall Term 2005, 81 percent were not college ready. In fact, 63 percent needed college preparatory coursework, and 18 percent needed EAP (Rodriguez, 2006).

### Statement of the Problem

This study explores the broad research question of how advanced ESL students who are about to transition into mainstream college classes perform on a standardized placement test. Specifically, it probes the relationship between Accuplacer® sentence skills scores and performance on a holistically scored essay exam required of all exiting advanced ESL students. The problem, as noted by ESL faculty, is that the Accuplacer® test components for general college entry are designed to measure basic skills of native speakers of English. Thus, the sentence skills section of the Accuplacer® may be an inaccurate measure of non-native speakers' true writing ability in English and an invalid predictor of their ability to write successfully for regular college classes.

Research in second language acquisition indicates that immigrant students need five to seven years to reach a point of no longer being held back by limited language proficiency issues that affect all areas of their academic careers (Collier, 1989; Cummins, 1992, 2001). To acquire sufficient language proficiency to compete with native speakers in college, NNS students at MDC take intensive English coursework that may last from one to six semesters, depending on their initial level of English proficiency. When these students near the successful completion of the most advanced level of EAP coursework at MDC, they are scheduled to take the Accuplacer®.

Completion of the prescribed coursework could be seen as an indicator of readiness to compete in regular classes. Nevertheless, the score on the 20-item multiple choice writing segment of the Accuplacer® is used to place students into one of the four following "regular" (non-ESL) English composition courses: ENC 1101, ENC 0021, ENC 0020, or ENC 0002. Students who place into the last three do not earn academic credit for these college preparatory writing courses, and other restrictions then apply as to the content courses in which they are permitted to enroll. Moreover, the curriculum for the college-prep courses is designed for under-prepared native speakers of English and focuses on sentence-level writing first, and then single paragraphs; whereas, in the advanced EAP writing course, students are taught essay-writing strategies. A move to an academic setting with much lower expectations can be confusing and demoralizing for these students, as can facing additional requirements before taking field-specific coursework. Since such significant decisions are made based on the Accuplacer® score, it is vital that the score is a truly valid and reliable measure of this student population's writing ability.

## Research Question Addressed

In response to the concerns expressed, this study asks, *Is there a significant relationship between Accuplacer® writing scores and holistically scored essay exams of advanced ESL students at the community college level?*[1] To answer the question, this study compares the use of the Accuplacer® as a placement mechanism to the use of holistically scored essays.

---

1. The complete dissertation also includes a pilot study report for comparison and findings from an alternative-forms assessment which probed Accuplacer®'s test reliability for the population. The test was found to be reliable, and pilot results supported the final study findings of reliability and validity.

This investigation will enable us to bring an informed stance to discussions of the merit of administering the Accuplacer® sentence skills test for the purpose of evaluating the writing ability of advanced ESL students. A positive relationship is anticipated, as both the Accuplacer® and the essay exams intend to measure the same construct, writing proficiency; of concern, however, is the strength or weakness of the relationship, and the degree to which variations in one score are associated with variations in the other.

## Data Collection Procedures

This correlational study examines the relationship between scores earned on two distinct writing assessment instruments taken by the same student population within a close time frame. As Brown (1996) explains, "The purpose of correlational analysis in language testing is to examine how the scores on two tests compare with regard to dispersing, or spreading out, the students" (p. 151). In other words, a correlational study compares the distributions of two sets of scores. This investigation compares placement decision patterns, across four different ENC levels, based on data from two placement instruments.

### Sample

The study evaluated test results from students enrolled in seven course sections of advanced ESL writing at one MDC campus. The sample included 106 students.[2] Except for seven students, the participants were all from Central and South America and the Caribbean. They spoke Spanish, Portuguese, and Haitian Creole as their first languages. Their mean age was 27, with the youngest being 17 and the oldest 57. The participants were 65 percent female and 35 percent male. Only those students who took both a departmental final essay in December 1997 and the Accuplacer® between the end of October 1997 and the first week of January 1998 were included. All participants took both exams within a maximum seven-week period.

### Time Frame

First, I carried out a pilot study to establish procedures during the summer term. The format and administration procedures were the same for both studies although the sample size for the pilot was smaller (n = 68). Then, the actual study followed in the fall term. The participants took three examinations in the following order: PASS, Accuplacer®, and essay. The PASS (Placement Articulation Software Services)

---

2. The college-wide total number of students enrolled in advanced ESL writing at all campuses was 758 for that term. Of the 218 students enrolled at the selected campus, only 106 (49%) met the criterion of having taken both the Accuplacer® and final departmental essay exam within the timeframe. Thus, the sample size for the study was 106.

test is an equivalent-forms practice version of the actual Accuplacer®. Following the three exams, Accuplacer® scores were collected from online MDC records in early 1998, and final holistic scoring of the essay exams was also carried out at that time.

## Instrumentation and Procedures

The first tests taken by the participants, the practice PASS and the actual Accuplacer®, were adaptive tests. Ward, Kline, and Haugher (1991) note that the Accuplacer® battery of computerized adaptive tests is based on Item Response Theory design. He explains that individual test items presented vary in adaptive tests, according to the students' prior responses. The first questions are drawn randomly from the item bank. Then, the computer estimates a projected score and selects the next question at an appropriate difficulty level and continues automatically re-estimating the expected score until a specified number of questions has been given.

The Accuplacer® includes five independent exams: reading comprehension, sentence skills, arithmetic, elementary algebra, and college-level mathematics. This study investigated only the sentence skills test. College Entrance Examination Board and Educational Testing Service (1997) test manuals state that the Accuplacer® tests range from twelve to twenty items and produce scores with a reliability of .90 or more. They assert that more than twice this number of items would be needed for similar results with a well-designed non-adaptive test.

The Accuplacer® sentence skills test contains twenty multiple choice items. It includes two types of questions: choosing the correct substitute for an underlined sentence portion and choosing the best rewording of a given sentence. To illustrate, questions included in the student guide are reprinted here (The College Board, 2007).

---

**Question 1: (Sentence Correction Question)**

Select the best version of the underlined part of the sentence. The first choice is the same as the original sentence. If you think the original sentence is best, choose the first answer.

When you cross the street in the middle of the block, this is an example of jaywalking.

    A. When you cross the street in the middle of the block, this

    B. You cross the street in the middle of the block, this

    C. Crossing the street in the middle of the block

    D. The fact that you cross the street in the middle of the block

**Question 2: (Construction Shift Question)**

Rewrite the sentence in your head following the directions given below. Keep in mind that your new sentence should be well written and should have essentially the same meaning as the sentence given you.

In his songs, Gordon Lightfoot makes melody and lyrics intricately intertwine.

Rewrite, beginning with <u>Melody and lyrics . . .</u> Your new sentence will include

A. Gordon Lightfoot has

B. make Gordon Lightfoot's

C. in Gordon Lightfoot's

D. does Gordon Lightfoot

In both of these sample-test items there are elements of cultural bias that make them inappropriate for testing an NNS population. Bachman (1990) states that test bias is evident when there are "systematic differences in test performance that are the result of differences in individual characteristics, other than the ability being tested, of test-takers" (p. 271). Cultural bias in testing can occur when test items include cultural, regional, or generational references that interfere with the test's ability to measure the construct of interest, in this case writing ability. In the first item, "jaywalking" is a low-frequency, non-academic vocabulary item that might be confusing, and in the second item, "Gordon Lightfoot" is a cultural reference to a Canadian folk singer, popular in the '70s, that would be unfamiliar to most NNS students. In both cases, a student could use knowledge of language structure and an awareness that being concise in English is valued to guess that "C" and "C" are the correct answers; however, NNS students face a different challenge here than native English speakers. Further, lack of familiarity with the term "jaywalking" or the cultural figure "Gordon Lightfoot" does not have any relationship to lack of writing ability.

The first test, the practice Accuplacer® PASS test, was administered to the advanced ESL writing class sections in a formal test setting one week before the classes were scheduled to take the actual Accuplacer®. (See Schuemann, 1998, for a full discussion of study procedures.) They took the PASS to become familiar with the test style and to reduce anxiety. From my experiences at MDC, I know that the Accuplacer® typically causes these ESL students great stress due to the significant placement decision arrived at from its results, as well as its computerized, multiple choice nature.

Next, the Accuplacer® was administered to class groups by the campus testing department. Upon completion of the un-timed Accuplacer® battery, students were referred to the academic advisement department. There they were aided in interpreting their scores and registering for appropriate courses for the following semester. I later accessed MDC online student records to collect Accuplacer® score data.

The final essay exam was administered at the end of the semester. During the last class period before the exam, instructors discussed their expectations for the students' performance on the essay test and distributed a common reading to the students. Throughout the semester students had written essays following units with thematic readings and discussions. To keep consistent with this practice and to parallel the format of the midterm, the campus course coordinator, an EAP faculty member, provided instructors with an article for students to read and think about prior to receiving the topic choices on the exam date. The rationale for eliciting text-based essays is well expressed by White (1995), who states, "Many writing courses focus primarily on reading and writing about given texts: essays, literature, or anthologized readings. If a course is text-bound and most of your instruction relates to writing about texts, then a text-based essay is appropriate" (p. 74).

A *Newsweek* "My Turn" article, "Crimes of Compassion" (Huttmann, 1983/1998), was distributed to the students. In sum, it told the story of a nurse who struggled with making a decision not to call for a resuscitation team. Her patient was close to death from cancer and had asked her to not press the code blue button again. Huttmann reflected on the dilemma our society must face as technological advances are prolonging lives with diminished qualities.

Students did not know the essay topics in advance. The four prompts were distributed to the students at the final exam session. Students were allowed to use dictionaries and/or thesauruses, but they were not allowed to discuss the topics or receive any assistance from the instructor or their classmates. Basically, they were asked to write a response to one of four topics: (1) describe a difficult decision to act or not act, (2) compare cultural norms concerning death, (3) discuss harmful or beneficial effects of technological advances, or (4) discuss Huttmann's use of emotional appeal.

Although limiting the participants to only one topic, rather than giving them four options, might have boosted inter-rater scoring reliability (Hughes, 2003), the validity of the writing assessment would have been questionable. Presented with only one topic, certain students without a strong knowledge base on that topic would be placed at a possible disadvantage unrelated to the writing construct being measured (Reid, 1990); thus, four prompts offered the student writers alternatives.

Following the exam administration, I met with each of the instructors to evaluate the essays. I had been trained by ETS in holistic scoring procedures and was an official Test of Written English (TWE) reader. I followed the methods used by ETS to train the instructor/readers. Raters previewed and discussed the scoring guide, anchored scoring behaviors, and then rated the essays. Each essay was scored by two evaluators, the instructor and myself.

The holistic scoring guide used combined elements from the 6-level TWE scoring guide and an 8-level essay scoring guide used by the English department. I had developed the scoring rubric in collaboration with another ESL faculty member, the campus course coordinator for advanced writing. It was designed to reflect the writing proficiency range of advanced ESL students. The rubric had been adopted by the campus ESL department two semesters prior to the semester in which the study was carried out. It had proven effective for evaluating essays at this level. The essays were rated as demonstrating clear competence, 6 points; competence, 5 points; minimal competence, 4 points; developing competence, 3 points; suggesting incompetence, 2 points; and incompetence, 0–1 point.

When two raters gave identical scores, the essay was assigned that score. If there was a difference of one point, a half-point (0.5) score between the two was assigned. (For example, if one rater assigned a 4 and the other a 5, the score awarded was 4.5.) In the rare instance that the scores were two points apart, a discussion of the criteria ensued and in the end the instructor's judgment was used in determining the final grade on the essay, which counted as one-third of the final grade for the course.

It is important to note that these scores were not those used for the statistical procedures performed in this study. They were used to assign grades. All of the essay exams were later independently evaluated following the same procedure by two outside readers who were trained by ETS and were official TWE readers. The outside readers' scores were the ones used in the statistical procedures. This process helped to limit any chance that instructor knowledge of the students and their handwriting could have influenced score decisions. Further, the first round of holisitic scores could be later be compared with the second round by outside raters as an added reliability check.

During the round of scoring by the outside raters, there were only five instances out of 106 cases with scores being off by two points, and these five essays were assigned an average score. There were no instances of scores being off by more than two points. This is clear evidence of high inter-rater reliability as it indicates a 90 percent scorer agreement within one point on a six-point scale. However, there were seven instances in which the TWE-trained raters had scored the essays at a two to three point difference from the previous instructor/researcher score. These seven essays were read by a third TWE-trained reader, and then the third score was averaged in with the other independent rater scores as part of the final score.

## Variables and Statistical Treatments

The data collected and treated in stage two of this study included students' essay scores, Accuplacer® sentence skills scores, and demographic data on their first language, gender, and age. To set the stage, I first analyzed the demographic data. First language was categorized as Spanish-Portuguese, French-Creole, and Other. Gender was categorized as male or female. Age was run first as continuous data to determine a mean age, standard deviation, and range. It was then collapsed into two categories: 17–25 and 26–57.

Of direct relevance to the research question addressed in this chapter, a Pearson product moment correlation coefficient, $r$, was calculated. This statistic (expressed in terms of a coefficient between −1 and +1) provides an index of the relationship between the Accuplacer® sentence skills scores and the essay scores. A positive correlation closer to +1.00 would provide evidence that strong and weak performances on the Accuplacer® are associated with strong and weak performances on the holistic writing example.

To determine percentages and placement ranges I collapsed Accuplacer® scores into four categories based on the cut-off scores for the four ENC (regular English) courses: (1) ENC 0002, (2) ENC 0020, (3) ENC 0021, or (4) ENC 1101. I then used the cross-tabulation procedure to test for differences in placement in contrast to ranked essay scores from 1 to 6.

Finally, I ran independent-samples *t*-tests to test for differences between gender, age, and language groups on the Accuplacer® results and on the essay exam. These tests were conducted to increase background understanding of the students in the sample.

# Data Analysis Procedures

## Demographic Description of the Sample

As shown in Table 12.1, the number of female participants was almost double the number of males (69 to 37). In addition, Spanish/Portuguese was spoken by the majority of participants (70 percent). The next largest group, Haitians, spoke French/Creole (23 percent). Only 7 percent of the participants spoke a language other than Spanish/Portuguese or French/Creole. Spanish and Portuguese were considered one group because of the similarities between the two languages and because there were too few Portuguese speakers to create a separate group (n = 3).

***Table 12.1.***
Demographics of ESL Study Sample Drawn at Miami-Dade College, Fall 1997
(n = 106)

| Attribute | Category | n | Percent |
|---|:---:|:---:|:---:|
| Gender | Male | 37 | 35% |
|  | Female | 69 | 65% |
| Age | 17–25 | 53 | 50% |
|  | 26–57 | 53 | 50% |
| 1st Language | Spanish/Portuguese | 74 | 70% |
|  | French/Creole | 25 | 23% |
|  | Other | 07 | 7% |

Age was first analyzed in continuous form. The mean age was 27 with a standard deviation of 7.3. The range was 40 years, with the minimum age being 17 and the maximum 57. The greatest concentration of cases was found in the range of 20–24 (n = 36, or 34 percent of the cases), with the second largest being 25–29 (n = 28, or 26.4 percent of the cases). Age was later collapsed into two groups, 17–25 and 26–57, as depicted in Table 12.1. Two groupings were made so that 50 percent of the participants fell into each category.

## Description of Test Results

For the second stage of the study, I analyzed the two test scores: Accuplacer® sentence skills test, and the holistically scored essay exam. Frequencies and descriptive statistics of these test scores are summarized in Table 12.2.

As shown in Table 12.2, the mean score for the Accuplacer® was 75.87 with a standard deviation of 22.76. The maximum score earned was 117 (out of 120 possible points) and the minimum score earned was 31. On the essay test, the mean score was 4.61 with a standard deviation of 0.88. The maximum score was 6, with 4 and above being a passing score and 3 and below being a failing score. Data collected from the two instruments, Accuplacer® and the essay exams, were normally distributed with no outliers. Normality for both test results is further evidenced in the slight numbers for skewness and kurtosis ($-.055$ and $-.959$ for Accuplacer®, and $-.158$ and $-.763$ for the essay). These numbers are all close to 0, indicating normal distributions with somewhat narrow curves, skewed slightly right for the essay data.

## Analysis of the Relationships among Exam Scores

The appropriate application of inferential parametric statistical tests rests on three assumptions: normal distribution, homogeneity of variance, and continuous depen-

***Table 12.2.***

Frequencies and Descriptives of Accuplacer® and Essay Scores, Fall 1997

| Statistic | Accuplacer® | Essay |
|---|---|---|
| N | 106 | 106 |
| M | 75.87 | 4.61 |
| SD | 22.76 | 0.88 |
| Range | 86 | 3.5 |
| Minimum | 31 | 2.5 |
| Maximum | 117 | 6.0 |
| Skewness | $-.055$ | $-.158$ |
| Kurtosis | $-.959$ | $-.763$ |

dent variables (Gay, 1987). As illustrated, these three assumptions were met; thus, it was appropriate to investigate the level of association between the Accuplacer® and essay scores with the Pearson product-moment ($r$) linear correlation coefficient. The results are shown in Table 12.3.

The correlations are significant at the 0.01 level. Thus, the finding with respect to the primary research question is affirmed. There *is* a significant correlation between Accuplacer® sentence skills test scores and holistically scored essay exams of advanced college-level ESL students.

The Pearson product moment correlation comparing the Accuplacer® and essay scores was .611 for the fall study. The .611 correlation indicates that there is a moderate correlation between Accuplacer® and essay scores, evidencing a substantial relationship. According to Haist (1993), correlations of .40 to .70 fall into this category. The .611 correlation is on the high end. This correlation is higher than the .49 determined by Haist (1993) in a study contrasting Accuplacer® sentence-skills scores with writing samples of 800 regular college students. The .611 correlation is within the range of correlations, .55 to .66, found by ETS (1996) in other studies comparing the TOEFL (Test of English as a Foreign Language) section 2 scores and TWE scores. Both of these ETS instruments, indirect and direct, are designed for non-native speakers of English.

With respect to overlapping variance, Table 3 shows that 37 percent of the variation in writing proficiency was common to both the Accuplacer® and essay exams. The .37 r-squared value means that the two procedures are measuring something in common, but they are also both contributing unique variance.

To further probe the extent to which Accuplacer® sentence skills data can be used for appropriate ENC (non-ESL English composition classes) placement decisions for advanced ESL students, essay scores were contrasted with Accuplacer®/ ENC placement levels at MDC utilizing cross-tabulations. The cross-tabulation procedure is used to show how groups differ on a measure. Table 12.4 shows the frequencies of both ENC placement groups based on Accuplacer® cut-off ranges and 106 essay scores. The four ENC placement groups are shown across the top of the table and the essay scores are shown on the left side. ENC 0002 is the most remedial writing class and instruction concerns sentence-level writing. ENC 0020

**Table 12.3.**
Correlations of Accuplacer® and Essay, Fall 1997

| Statistic | Accuplacer® & Essay |
| --- | --- |
| $r$ | .611 |
| $r$ squared | .37 |
| N | 106 |

p>.01; Two-Tailed Test for Significance.

***Table 12.4.***
Frequency Distribution of ENC Placement and
Essay Scores Cross-Tabulation, Fall 1997

| | *Accuplacer* Score Ranges and ENC Placement | | | | | |
| | (26-50) | (50-71) | (71-82) | (83-120) | | |
| Essay Score | ENC 0002 | ENC 0020 | ENC 0021 | ENC 1101 | Total | % |
|---|---|---|---|---|---|---|
| 6.0 | | | 4 | 8 | 12 | 11.3 |
| 5.5 | | 3* | 3 | 11 | 17 | 16.0 |
| 5.0 | 1* | 3* | 5 | 9 | 18 | 17.0 |
| 4.5 | 1* | 7 | 6 | 7 | 21 | 19.8 |
| 4.0 | 5* | 7 | 4 | 4 | 20 | 18.9 |
| 3.5 | 4 | 4 | | 2* | 10 | 09.4 |
| 3.0 | 3 | 4 | | | 7 | 06.6 |
| 2.5 | 1 | | | | 1 | 00.9 |
| Total | 15 | 28 | 22 | 41 | 106 | |
| % | 14.2 | 26.4 | 20.8 | 38.7 | | 100% |

*Possible cases of inappropriate placement

introduces students to writing eight- to ten-sentence paragraphs of description and narration. ENC 0021 introduces students to writing four- to five-paragraph essays, still focused on description and narration. ENC 1101 is the only course of the four that is classified as non-remedial, college level. In ENC 1101 students continue to master essay writing skills, but at a more sophisticated level, with additional rhetorical modes, and under stricter time restraints. The essay scores shown on Table 12.4 range from 2.5 to 6. A score of 4 is considered minimal competence.

Table 12.4 clearly illustrates the marked relationship and symmetrical association between essay scores and ENC placement based on Accuplacer® scores. The data show evidence of an association, from which we can interpret that there appears to be a placement range corresponding to the distribution of Accuplacer® scores. It indicates a generally effective placement range from Accuplacer® scores.

In column four, however, there are two surprising cases of students with essay scores of 3.5 being placed in ENC 1101. Of greater concern, in column one, is one case of a 5 essay being placed in ENC 0002, one case of a 4.5, and five cases of 4 essays being placed in ENC 0002. Also of concern, in column two, are three cases of 5.5 essays and three cases of 5 essays being placed in ENC 0020. While the reason for this inconsistency is unknown, it represents a margin of error if the Accuplacer® is the sole determinant of placement. Nonetheless, the number of surprising placements totals only 14, or 14.2 percent of the 106 cases. Overall, the Accuplacer® sentence skills assessment appears to be a fair and accurate tool for placing advanced ESL students into regular English writing classes with the essay scores being used as a further basis for judgment.

To illustrate the ramifications of placement, I would like to include examples of feedback I have received from former ESL students who continued in ENC classes. They have characterized their experiences in ENC 1101 as very challenging. For example, one student who had earned an A in advanced ESL writing struggled to achieve a C in ENC 1101. Other students have shared stories of having to repeat ENC 1101 several times. Most former advanced ESL writing students who placed in ENC 0021 have reported feeling comfortable and successful, appreciating the essay review. On the other hand, those having to take ENC 0020 report being bored, and those in ENC 0002 report feeling very uncomfortable being mixed in with American students with extremely weak academic skills. Thus, the misplacements of greatest concern would be the seven students in column one who demonstrated competency on the essay exam, but were placed in ENC 0002 based on their Accuplacer® score.

Overall, the results of the study indicate that misplacements are rare. Cross-tabulation revealed an 86 percent appropriate placement rate, supporting the validity of the Accuplacer sentence skills test as a placement measure of writing ability. In cases where a student's grade record in an advanced ESL writing course indicates possible misplacement into a low level, the student should be able to petition to be considered for an alternative writing assessment for placement, e.g., an essay. Such a request should include a recommendation from the ESL writing instructor.

## Analysis of the Variables Gender, Age, and First Language

As a further check on the interpretation of these results, I ran independent-samples $t$-tests to test for differences between gender, age, and first language groups on the Accuplacer® and on the essay exam. These tests were performed to increase confidence in the instruments. Independent-samples $t$-tests calculate the probability that observed differences in two means result from sampling error. The observed $t$ values indicated no significant difference in Accuplacer® or essay score related to gender, age, or first language. First, the difference between the mean scores on the Accuplacer® for gender, where scores can range from 26 to 120, was only 2.11. The difference for age was 1.24, and 2.54 for first language. The "other" category of languages was excluded from this statistical procedure as it only included seven cases and the languages were not a cohesive group. They included Japanese, Vietnamese, Mandarin Chinese, and Russian. Second, the difference between the mean scores on the essays (where scores ranged from 2.5 to 6.0) is only 0.25 for gender, 0.04 for age, and 0.1 for language. Both instruments appear unbiased in terms of gender, age, or first language.

# Implications

Language placement tests serve an important function for programs of higher education. In particular, they facilitate curricular planning to meet the instructional needs of students by placing them into relatively homogeneous ability levels (Brown, 1996). Most standardized placement or admissions tests in the United States are multiple choice, indirect measures.

The main purpose of stage two of the study was to determine the validity of the Accuplacer® sentence-skills test for a non-traditional and growing segment of the Accuplacer® test-taking population, non-native speakers of English. The Pearson product moment correlations indicated a substantial relationship between Accuplacer® and essay scores, supporting its validity. These results were inconsistent with the hypothesis that the Accuplacer® scores may inadequately represent NNS true academic writing proficiency in English.

As a placement instrument, the Accuplacer® sentence-skills test is effective at discriminating among the various levels of student writing ability at MDC. It is appropriate for preliminary screening and placement of both native speakers of English (Rich, 1993) and non-native speakers who are at the advanced level. This finding may indicate that advanced ESL students have increased similarity in some ways to general entry-level college students. As adult students acquire a second language, they experience various states of interlanguage development along the continuum from first language to second language (Brown, 1996). The findings of this study imply that advanced ESL students have reached a language level wherein they are struggling with some writing issues that are common to both the native and non-native English speaking population.

In comparing essay scores to levels of English course placement as determined by Accuplacer® scores, it was found that 86 percent of the advanced ESL students were appropriately placed. These findings are similar to those of Rich (1993), who investigated the performance of the general student population entering MDC in fall 1992 on the Accuplacer® and an essay exam. In Rich's study (1993), approximately 85 percent of 5,291 students were judged as being appropriately placed by the Accuplacer®. The similar percentages are another indication of how the advanced ESL population may approximate the standard population of test takers.

Another favorable conclusion concerning the Accuplacer® that can be drawn from the findings is that the Accuplacer® sentence-skills test discriminated equally among second language, gender, and age groups included in this study. Although the range of language groups represented in this study was limited, these findings lend support to the assumption that the Accuplacer® is as effective and appropriate as holistic essay scores as a placement mechanism. These findings suggest that the Accuplacer® taps into meaningful differences in advanced ESL students' writing skills that are independent of language background.

The findings of this study also substantiate the truth that there is no perfect testing instrument for placing students. The exceptional cases of concern here were the students who had demonstrated skill at writing essays, a contextualized productive task, while scoring poorly on the Accuplacer®, a set of decontextualized, receptive tasks.

A case example from this group can help to illustrate the consequence of assessment error. One woman who was an A student in level 6 writing, scored 5.5 out of 6 points possible on her final essay, yet she was placed into ENC 0020, the second-level remedial course, by her Accuplacer® score. She was so discouraged, she actually left the college and studied at another Florida institution, eventually earning a B.A. in English, followed by a M.S. in TESOL. This person is now a full-time ESL faculty member at MDC. Clearly, her English ability, needs, and potential were misdiagnosed by the Accuplacer® test. Her case serves to remind us of the importance of having procedural mechanisms in place to meet the needs of students with similarly high ESL grades but low Accuplacer® results.

No one academic assessment instrument can provide a perfect reflection of a test taker's true abilities. These must be demonstrated over time in a classroom setting. The multiple choice Accuplacer® sentence-skills test has unique strengths and weaknesses, as do holistically scored essay exams. These advantages and disadvantages should be weighed when making a decision as to the most effective instrument for a particular purpose.

The Accuplacer® is economical, untimed, adaptive, and computerized, and it has immediate reporting mechanisms. It is also valid and reliable. Much thorough research by ETS, the College Board, and others has affected its design. On the other hand, one of the greatest drawbacks to over-reliance on multiple choice measures to assess writing is negative washback (Hughes, 2003). Washback results as elements of instruction begin to reflect increased "practice" for the test. Multiple choice exercises and test items are devoid of meaning-rich contexts that enhance learning.

Essay exams, conversely, result in positive washback by encouraging increased amounts of authentic writing as students prepare for tests that demand actual writing. Scoring, however, is costly and time-intensive. As shown in this study, scores given by trained raters can be demonstrated as reliable. Yet careful procedures must be followed to ensure such reliability. Neither the holistically scored exit essays nor the Accuplacer® as they are used at MDC provide students with error feedback.

Finally, this study would not be complete without a call for further research. There are five areas that could be further investigated as a result of this study.

First, the success rates of this particular sample in regular English courses should be investigated to support or question the findings of this study. Such a study should be both quantitative and qualitative as data concerning placement, retention, and performance could be analyzed, and individual students could be formally interviewed about their experiences. The results could inform advisors, educators, and future students facing similar circumstances.

Second, factors contributing to the attrition rate in the advanced writing sections should be investigated to determine why 48 percent of the originally enrolled students did not take both the Accuplacer® and final exam. Both exams are integral to successful transfer into associate degree programs. Understanding factors that contribute to attrition would be valuable for institutions concerned with curriculum development and retention.

Third, it is hoped that this study will be replicated in other settings with ESL students who take the Accuplacer® sentence-skills test. This replication is vital as it is the first study of its kind with such a population. Such research can contribute to our understanding of the educational needs of this group.

Fourth, the present study involved advanced-level ESL students. It should be replicated with intermediate-level students to gain insights into the point at which the Accuplacer® might be considered inappropriate. Some institutions use the Accuplacer® as a generalized placement instrument for all entering students. Low-level ESL students should not be tested with the Accuplacer® because their limited knowledge of English would cause them to score low on the test and experience frustration. The purpose of the Accuplacer® general entry tests is to distinguish among remedial-level placements or exemptions. ESL students are not remedial students.

Finally, it would also be beneficial for educators to learn if the Accuplacer® reading comprehension test and the Accuplacer® mathematics/algebra tests are valid and reliable for the advanced ESL population. Many standardized reading comprehension tests designed for native speakers of English include generic passages with vocabulary and contexts familiar to someone growing up in the United States, but unfamiliar to many adult immigrants. It would be important to determine whether or not the reading passages reflected academic prose consistent with freshman-level college texts. Also, although math and algebra exams are less language dependent, Accuplacer® could include word problems or directions that are unfamiliar to nonnative speakers who studied these subjects in another language. Again, it is essential to have confidence in Accuplacer® scores as the placement decisions derived from their results greatly impact student career tracks.

A final practical consequence of this study has been the creation of a one-page summary of the findings that is now distributed to advanced ESL writing students and faculty. This practice has helped to ease test anxiety by assuring students of the fairness of the test, and it has helped them to interpret their scores more effectively.

To conclude, this study provides some preliminary evidence that the Accuplacer® sentence-skills test is as effective an instrument as holistically scored essays for placement purposes with advanced-level ESL writing students in most cases. Moreover, this study can serve as a basis for further studies concerning standardized testing instruments and ESL populations.

# Chapter 13

# Student Learning Outcomes and ESL Student Success in the Community College Classroom

■ Marit ter Mate-Martinsen

"Students have to be able to understand SLOs, because SLOs are written for the students and not the teacher. I found that a lot of people were writing SLOs more for colleagues to understand. So keeping the language really, really basic was the biggest challenge." This comment is from Jane (pseudonym), one of two ESL community college teachers featured in this chapter, speaking to one of the many critical challenges facing ESL departments at many community colleges. This chapter illustrates the teachers' key learnings and ongoing struggles as they create meaningful student learning outcomes (SLOs) and assessment tools. The teachers' conversations with colleagues and their own personal reflections provide insights into the evolving definition of "student success" in the community college ESL context.

## Issues that Motivated the Research

Community colleges across the United States have been charged with developing student learning outcomes (SLOs) and corresponding assessment tools, which impact ESL programs at community colleges as well. Accreditation agencies require evidence of student success, and the measurement and accomplishment of student success directly impacts federal and statewide funding. The Academic Senate for California Community Colleges defines SLOs as "overarching specific observable characteristics developed by local faculty that allow them to determine or demonstrate evidence that learning has occurred as a result of a specific course, program, activity, or process" (Snowhite, Adams, Gilbert, Reilly, Welch, & Rheinheimer 2005, p. 8). In other words, SLOs are outcomes of what a student will have accomplished by the end of a course that will be of use to the outside world. The term *outcome* is different from an objective, which places the emphasis solely on what happens in the classroom (Stiehl & Lewchuk, 2002). In addition, outcome-based education emphasizes what a learner "could do at the end of a course rather than what content the instructor would be expected to cover" (Webster, 2001, p. 16). Thus, the use of SLOs represents a shift in thinking as it places the focus on the student rather than the teacher. According to WASC, the accreditation agency for the Western Area Schools and Colleges, the central questions are: "What did students learn and leave being able to do? How do we know?" (as cited in Ferrer & Rondowski, 2006, p. 13). The use of SLOs also represents a shift in the way learning outcomes should be articulated, since there is an expectation that SLOs will be understood not only by the community college faculty and administration, but also *by the students* themselves. As this chapter will demonstrate, the expectation that ESL students should understand the SLOs are both a source of innovation and struggle for the faculty charged with SLO development. To help community colleges move toward an outcome-based, curricular approach that places the student at the center, incentive grants have been made available, and as a result, many community colleges have hired consultants to facilitate SLO training for community college faculty.

## Context of the Research

Since 2004, different groups of faculty at Santa Barbara City College (SBCC), a community college on the south central coast of California, have gone through year-long SLO training sessions in preparation for the 2009 WASC accreditation. These SLO training sessions are referred to as the Student Learning Outcomes (SLO) Development & Implementation Project. The training includes attending one large and one small meeting a month to create, revise, and complete three to seven SLOs for a course and a rubric for an assignment. Although a few ESL faculty members participated in the training before 2006, the largest group of ESL faculty started the SLO training during the 2006–2007 academic year.

The ESL faculty at SBCC were faced with the challenge of making SLOs and rubrics comprehensible to students who are still developing their English language skills. For this reason, attention to the language used in the SLOs and rubrics remained a central issue in the process of developing the outcomes. In addition, the ESL faculty needed to grapple with the reality that transfer rates into regular coursework are often viewed as the prevailing measure of ESL student success at the community college.

Since little research has been conducted on ESL teachers' challenges and rewards in the development of SLOs and rubrics for community college ESL students, this study aims (1) to report on the journey two ESL community college faculty members undertook to develop SLOs and rubrics, and (2) to share the faculty's struggles and triumphs in an effort to improve student success. I hope that this research will inform future dialogue on issues related to the development and implementation of SLOs and rubrics in the community college ESL classroom.

## Research Question Addressed

This study addressed this research question:

> 1. What challenges did two community college ESL teachers encounter in developing and presenting SLOs and rubrics to their students, and how did the teachers overcome them?

## Data Collection and Analysis Procedures

Two ESL teachers participated in the study, whom I will refer to as Jane and Barbara (pseudonyms). Both are full-time ESL instructors at the same community college on the south central coast of California (SBCC). Jane holds an MA in TESOL and has been training teachers and teaching ESL and EFL around the globe for 28 years. She has been an ESL community college instructor for sixteen years. Barbara has an MA in TESOL also and has taught ESL for twenty years, of which eighteen years have been within the community college setting.

Jane received her initial SLO training in 2004–2005 and has continued to work on developing SLOs and rubrics, while Barbara started the training two years later during the 2006–2007 academic year. Throughout their training cycles, Jane and Barbara met with full-time and adjunct ESL faculty members who developed SLOs and rubrics for some of the same courses they taught. Jane created SLOs and rubrics for two classes—a high-beginning and a low-advanced course focused on "Reading, Speaking, and Listening." Barbara worked on developing SLOs and rubrics for a beginning level ESL writing course.[1]

The exploration of my research question was based on informal discussions, monthly SLO meetings, and interviews with the two participants over the course of the 2006–2007 academic year. Being part of the SLO project enabled me to take field notes during faculty meetings and learn how teachers varied in their processes of writing the SLOs and rubrics, as well as their sources of struggle. Over time, I was also able to glean some important insights about the ways the teachers viewed the impact of the SLOs on the students' learning.

---

1. The ESL program offers five levels (beginning-advanced) with three core courses at each level: "Reading, Speaking, and Listening," "Writing," and "Grammar."

Once the 2006–2007 academic year ended, I conducted in-depth interviews with Jane and Barbara. The questions centered on the process Jane and Barbara took and the difficulties they faced in generating SLOs and rubrics, the manner in which they presented these learning tools to their students, and the improvement of student learning as a result of using SLOs and rubrics. I invited Jane and Barbara to participate in this study because they are both very familiar with the curriculum at SBCC, and they have a background in TESOL methodology and pedagogy. They were also very willing to participate. Because Jane had more experience with learning outcomes and rubrics than Barbara, I anticipated that their responses to the interview questions would shed light on the way teachers vary in their work with SLOs and rubrics depending on their level of experience with these learning tools. I also collected copies of SLOs and rubrics from Jane and Barbara and studied them with a focus on student comprehension. In addition, I met with the campus-wide SLO facilitator, and through this interview I learned a great deal about the mandate for SLOs within the community college setting.

To analyze the data, I carefully looked through the materials I collected, read through my field notes, and transcribed the final interviews with Jane and Barbara. I then coded my data based on the following categories: (1) Jane and Barbara's process in creating SLOs and rubrics, (2) challenges they encountered, and (3) the value of SLOs and rubrics and the impact on student success. After I grouped information based on recurring themes within these three main categories, sub-categories emerged such as the emphasis on student comprehension of SLOs.

## Findings

In my exploration of the trends, I have used Jane and Barbara's own comments, as well as my interpretations of the data, to portray their processes of developing SLOs and rubrics. The research question was, what challenges did two community college ESL teachers encounter in developing and presenting SLOs and rubrics to their students, and how did the teachers overcome them?

As noted earlier, Jane worked on developing SLOs and rubrics for her high-beginning and low-advanced "Reading, Speaking, and Listening" courses (see Figures 13.1 and 13.2, pages 190–191). By the time I began this study, she had already piloted these materials. She developed her own set of SLOs and rubrics for her high-beginning course but collaborated with another teacher on the low-advanced course SLOs and rubrics since the other teacher had already developed SLOs for this level.

Jane shared the SLOs with her students during the first week of class. She explained that each class at the college would eventually be linked to SLOs. She also told her students that they would be able to fully comprehend the learning outcomes by the end of the course.

Looking back on the process of developing the SLOs and rubrics for her students, Jane indicated that one of her main goals was to ensure that her students would

By the end of this course students will be able to:

1. Demonstrate reading skills of previewing, predicting, skimming and scanning for main ideas and information.

2. Identify basic parts of speech (nouns, verbs, adjectives, adverbs) and correct usage of words in context.

3. Use new vocabulary in speaking and writing activities.

4. Research, prepare and present an oral group presentation on an assigned topic, using visual aids, which informs the class about the topic.

5. Use an American English dictionary to identify parts of speech and meanings of vocabulary.

*Figure 13.1.* SLOs Developed for a High-Beginning Course in "Reading, Speaking, and Listening"

be able to comprehend the SLOs and accomplish them by the end of the course, so she tried to keep the language "basic." For Jane, keeping the language basic entailed repeating certain words, such as "use," in an effort to reduce the lexical complexity of the statements and help the students understand concretely what kind of behaviors the SLOs intended to address (see Figure 13.1).

During the follow-up interview, Jane commented:

> They [The SLO training facilitators] want you to use Bloom's tax-onomy, but the students can't really understand a lot of those [words used to describe behaviors]. So is that for the benefit of other students or other teachers? I don't care if I repeat the verb. They [the students] don't have much language at the low level.

Here Jane addresses an important source of struggle for many of the ESL teach-ers—namely, how to write the SLOs and rubrics in a way that make sense to students who are still in the process of developing proficiency in English. Jane underscored the importance of ESL students as important stakeholders in the process of devel-oping SLOs, adding that:

> Students have to be able to understand SLOs, because SLOs are written for the students and not the teacher. I found that a lot of people were writing SLOs more for colleagues to understand. So keeping the language really, really basic was the biggest challenge.

While Jane chose to avoid Bloom's Taxonomy, it seems that the use of this cat-egorization system is a hallmark of the SLO genre. For example, a website on

## Group Animal Research Project
## Grading Rubric

*Student Learning Outcome: By the end of the course students will be able to: Research, prepare and present an oral group presentation using visual aids on an assigned topic which informs the class about the topic.* The Animal Research Project and Presentation is worth 100 points. You will be graded on the following criteria. Each group member will receive an individual grade.

| Criteria | Excellent (A) | Good (B–C) | Unacceptable (D–F) |
|---|---|---|---|
| **Animal research completed. Specific sources are provided (encyclopedia, books, Internet).** *30 points* | All questions were answered. Information is complete and accurate. Sources are given. (27–30 points) | Most information is complete and accurate. Sources are given. (21–26 points) | Information is not complete and/or accurate. Sources are not given. (0–20 points) |
| **Poster (and other visual aids)** *30 points* | Interesting and well-organized poster. The above information is clearly and neatly written. Few or no spelling or grammar mistakes. Excellent pictures and artwork. (27–30 points) | Good poster. The above information is written, but not as clearly and neatly as it could be. Some spelling and grammar mistakes. Pictures are good. (21–26 points) | Incomplete poster. The above information is not written clearly or neatly. Many mistakes in spelling and grammar. Pictures are not good. (0–20 points) |
| **Oral presentation** *20 points* | Speaks very clearly and slowly. Uses words people can understand. Voice is loud for everyone to hear. Good pronunciation. Practice is evident. (18–20 points) | Speaks well, but some improvement is needed. Difficult to understand at times. Practice is not evident. (14–17 points) | Does not speak clearly. Very difficult to understand. Practice is not evident. (0–13 points) |
| **Group cooperation and participation** *20 points* | Works very well with group members. Cooperation and participation in planning the presentation is evident. (18–20 points) | Works well with group members but more cooperation and participation in planning is necessary. Needs to be more active. (14–17 points) | Does not work well with group members. Does not cooperate or participate in planning the presentation. Was absent or missed the presentation. (0–13 points) |

<u>**Comments:**</u>

**Total Points:**
**Grade:**

***Figure 13.2.*** Sample of an SLO and Corresponding Assessment Rubric for a High-Beginning Class in "Reading, Speaking, and Listening"

SLOs developed by Laney College, a community college in Oakland, CA, stipulates that:

> SLOs use action verbs from Bloom's Taxonomy with an emphasis on higher-order thinking skills. . . . SLOs should be written in language that students (and those outside the field) are able to understand. ("How to write student learning outcomes," n.d., p. 1)

This same website gave sample SLOs for an ESL Grammar 1 course:

> STUDENTS WILL BE ABLE TO: Understand and follow oral and written directions. Also demonstrate basic aural comprehension by responding appropriately to spoken questions, statements and prompts. . . . Function as productive members of a group by cooperating in interactive learning tasks. . . . Develop sound test-taking strategies and study skills. ("How to write student learning outcomes," n.d., p. 3)

Although teachers may be expected to rely on Bloom's Taxonomy, it's not clear how appropriate this expectation is for writing SLOs for ESL students. Jane commented: "It's really hard to write SLOs for level 1 students, because a true level 1 student doesn't have any English." Jane's concerns prompt important questions about the comprehensibility of SLOs: If a beginning-level ESL student is actually able to comprehend the Grammar Level 1 SLOs mentioned above, would he or she belong in a beginning-level ESL course? Is there really a way to make SLOs clear and meaningful to a true beginning-level ESL community college student? Ultimately, for whom are SLOs being written at the beginning levels?

Jane emphasized that teachers need to scaffold their students' comprehension of the SLOs. Otherwise, the SLOs would be useless; Jane commented, "Basically, we're recycling and adding, we're constantly building . . . they have to be connected, level 1 through 5. We need to be looking across the board that we're using the same language and make sure our students can understand." Thus Jane, who had tested her SLOs and rubric for the low-level course, was confident that her students would be able to carry out the SLOs but uncertain they would be able to understand the language used to write the SLOs.

Like Jane, Barbara identified the language of SLOs as a source of struggle but described it as a challenge of "visual consistency," as highlighted here:

> SLOs should be really easy, so it is easy to navigate for the students. We don't want to do whole new things at each level. . . . So in level 1 you start with certain level vocabulary, and in level 2 you just add more vocabulary, but you're staying with the same visual format. It's kind of like brainstorming. Are we going to agree as a department to use lists in level 1? Are we going to do lists and add bubbles in level 2?

Thus, Barbara suggested that the language or "visual consistency" for SLOs should be carefully scaffolded between course levels. For instance, students might learn how to use clusters for brainstorming in a beginning level writing course, and in the next level they continue to practice clusters but also learn how to make lists. The same principle could be applied to SLOs.

Whereas Jane worked on SLOs and rubrics for a lower and a higher level "Reading, Speaking and Listening" course, Barbara wrote SLOs for two different core courses: a beginning-level writing class and an advanced-level grammar course. Barbara had taught the advanced-level grammar course for many years and was thus very familiar with the course content and student ability at this level. She had also taught beginning-level students, so she knew what to expect from students at this level. Still, Barbara struggled to write SLOs and rubrics for her low-level writing courses since she was writing them for students at an even lower level of English proficiency than students in Jane's high-beginning course.

Although Barbara received guidelines for how to write SLOs by the campus-wide SLO facilitator, the learning outcomes concept remained "unclear." What eventually helped her was to consider what will be most beneficial to her students. Barbara stated, "I had to step back: What is going to help my students? What is going to help them learn English? That was my roadmap."

Like Jane, Barbara tried to use simple language in her SLOs for her low-level ESL course since this course generally enrolls some true and some false beginning-level students. She also worked together with a group of adjunct colleagues who had taught the beginning-level writing course for years, and together they developed SLOs for this course, as shown in Figure 13.3 on page 194.

In the small group meetings and final interview, Barbara frequently raised questions about whom the SLOs are written for and how they can be made meaningful for the students. In her year-end interview, she compared her beginning-level ESL class to a group of students studying sign language for the first time ever and stated:

> Let's think about sign language. Let's use that as a paradigm. You've never probably signed language before, so now I'm going to give you SLOs, but I'm going to give them in signs. So if you look at the signs, do you know what you will have accomplished by the end of the course?

Like students of beginning sign language, beginning-level ESL students have virtually no (English) language skills, which makes it difficult for them to comprehend the language associated with SLOs. Barbara also questioned how she could discuss pedagogical ideas with a student who had never finished high school or had been out of school for more than twenty years. This issue demonstrates the importance of a shared understanding of academic goals between teachers and students, which can be difficult to cultivate in the beginning-level classroom. In fact, Robishaw (1993) explains that one cannot assume that adult ESL learners have a schema

By the end of this course students will be able to:

1. write a simple sentence using capitalization, a subject, a verb, punctuation and legible penmanship.
2. write simple affirmative, negative and interrogative sentences using:

    a. simple present, present continuous, and simple past sentences

    b. *like* + infinitive, *need* + infinitive, *want* + infinitive and *have* + infinitive

    c. subjects and verbs in appropriate order.
3. use the writing process to respond to correction symbols (S=subject; V=verb; C=capitalization; P=punctuation) and produce:

    a. pre-writing organization

    b. preliminary drafts

    c. final copy
4. attempt to write a short, rudimentary paragraph of five to eight sentences containing:

    a. title

    b. topic sentence

    c. body sentences

    d. concluding sentence
5. use a word processing program to complete course assignments.

*Figure 13.3.*  Sample SLOs for Beginning-Level Writing Course

for goals-driven learning since goal setting can be viewed as representative of a Western middle-class mindset.

Barbara observed that it was much easier to share her SLOs with her advanced-level class. Her advanced-level students could communicate in English, and since they had generally been attending college for at least a semester, they had been oriented to an academic skills context. Barbara noted that despite her use of complex metalanguage, she often could find a way to explain and illustrate the grammar points that were part of her SLOs to her students and emphasize that students would be able to apply these grammar points by the end of the course. However, when she presented her SLOs to her low-level class, Barbara was met with blank faces: "Level-1 students just sat there. I thought, 'I'm not going here again'."

During one group meeting, some ESL teachers, including Barbara, wanted to know how the Modern Languages Department had dealt with writing SLOs for beginning-level language students. Had the foreign language faculty struggled with keeping the language simple in Spanish, so a beginning-level Spanish student could understand the SLOs in Spanish? When the ESL faculty asked the Spanish department this question, the Spanish language instructors explained that they had written all their SLOs and rubrics in English; they felt that were they to write them in Spanish, the SLOs would not have been comprehensible to their beginning-level Spanish students. Thus, by writing SLOs in English, the Spanish faculty could ensure that SLOs would be comprehensible to the beginning and advanced Spanish language student. Interestingly, one of the first ESL faculty members to go through the campus-wide SLO training had dealt with this situation in the same manner as the Spanish department: since all his beginning-level students were Spanish speakers, he translated his SLOs and rubrics into Spanish. However, this was not a lasting solution since some international students placed into beginning-level classes as well, and most of them were not Spanish speakers. In the small group meetings, Barbara often brought up the point that it must be much easier for the rest of the campus faculty to write SLOs since they did not have to deal with students learning English.

Barbara continued to be concerned with making beginning-level SLOs clear, comprehensible, and meaningful to her students. Eventually, she wondered, "Are we benefiting the students or are we wasting their time, and who are we writing these SLOs for?" At another group meeting, she argued that SLOs at the beginning level should be written for the teacher and that the rubrics should be for the students. Eventually the campus-wide SLO facilitator agreed that perhaps SLOs for level-one ESL courses are more for the teachers than the students. He stressed, however, that the rubrics had to be for the students since each assignment had to be spelled out clearly, and students needed to know in advance how they would be graded.

Instead of presenting level-one ESL students with a list of SLOs, Barbara thought that it would be better to model to her beginning-level students what they would need to accomplish by the end of the course. For instance, she could write a sentence with a capital letter, subject, verb, and period on the board to show that students would be able to achieve this by the end of the course, and thus students would know what would be expected of them. Nevertheless, even with this approach, there could be challenges since a true beginning-level ESL student may not be able to differentiate when the teacher was demonstrating a learning outcome versus teaching a language lesson. Barbara worried that the student might think the SLO demonstration was a part of the day's lesson and leave the first class thinking it was too challenging and not return to the next class.

Therefore, SLOs need to be carefully scaffolded from level to level, so students can comprehend them and a clear progression of English skills can be observed. However, as Jane and Barbara's experiences reveal, it is challenging to accomplish this goal, as the Spanish department discovered. They achieved this goal by writing their SLOs in English—their students' native language.

Although Barbara had originally tried to collaboratively develop SLOs for her advanced grammar course as well, she quickly realized that her understanding and approach to teaching grammar clashed with those of her colleague. This challenge of differing opinions among faculty was also identified by Webster (2001), who conducted a case study of 23 ESL community college faculty members as they were moving toward an outcome-based curriculum. As a result, Barbara and her advanced-level grammar colleague decided to work on their SLOs individually.

All faculty members were instructed to develop at least one rubric during the 2006–2007 academic year. Barbara chose to write one for her low-level writing course. Together with her low-level writing colleagues, she created a rubric for the entire course. According to Barbara, the rubric "totally bombed. I was very off target. My first rubric didn't work out very well. [The students] spent a lot of time figuring out what it meant." She later discovered that each rubric should be designed for a specific assignment. As a result, she changed her approach and began to experiment with checklists, another type of rubric, according to the campus-wide SLO project facilitator. For instance, after students learned that each sentence begins with a capital letter, Barbara included a question about capital letters in her assignment checklist such as "Did you begin each sentence with a capital letter?" and students circled "Yes, I did" or "No, I didn't."

Barbara thought it was critical to introduce the assessment checklists *after* students had had a chance to generate a short composition about a specific topic. However, the campus-wide SLO facilitator instructed her to hand out the checklist first, so students could use it as a guide and know what they would be graded on in advance. Barbara feared that giving the checklist to her students first would make them feel inhibited about writing. In response to the SLO facilitator's feedback, Barbara indicated that in future semesters, she would create a form that featured the checklist on one half of the paper and lines for writing the assignment on the other half.

Jane and Barbara also participated in developing departmental SLOs, a joint effort among all the ESL full-time faculty members. The department had decided that it would be beneficial for the full-time faculty members to reach consensus first before opening up the discussion of program-wide SLOs to the entire department. To write SLOs, the faculty members considered three central questions: Who are our students, what are they doing, and what are their goals? Student goals might include moving into a vocational or academic program, or helping a child with his homework. As Barbara emphasized, "We want to make sure that our SLOs are written to address our students' needs. When students learn a language, they have a reason."

Another source of struggle in developing SLOs was the need (at least initially) to take into account the administration's emphasis on ESL transfer rates into academic and vocational programs on campus as the primary marker of success. Thus, if a student finishes levels one through four in a five-level ESL program but stops before taking Level 5, he is not considered a success, based on administration standards. However, the ESL teachers concurred that by finishing four levels of English, it was possible that a student could succeed in what he set out to do (see Lewis, this volume). Once the department started to think more in terms of their student population's needs and less about the administration's measure of ESL student success, the full-time ESL faculty identified three types of student goals, and thus three roads toward student success. The department came up with the SLOs shown in Figure 13.4.

These SLOs represent a major shift in how ESL student success would be measured by the ESL program. While the ESL Department would continue to collect data on ESL transfer rates, it would also be able to monitor progress on benchmarks

---

The successful ESL student will fit into one of the three goals below:[*]

1. Educational goals: Upon successful completion of the ESL credit program, a successful student will be able to:

   • Demonstrate both written (writing/reading) and spoken (oral/aural) academic language skills necessary to enter English Skills courses[2]

   • Demonstrate basic computer skills

   • Identify campus resources as well as career and academic opportunities

   • Demonstrate communicative competence necessary for classroom success

2. Career goals: Upon completing ESL coursework necessary to meet a student's career goals, a successful student will accomplish one or more of the following:

   • Meet workplace language goals to improve career and job opportunities

   • Transfer into a vocational program

   • Demonstrate basic computer literacy skills

3. Personal goals: Upon completing ESL coursework necessary to meet a student's personal goals, a successful student will accomplish one or more of the following:

   • Meet student's personal and/or familial language goals

   • Demonstrate basic computer literacy skills

[*]Some ESL students may move from one goal to another with exposure to education (e.g., a student may enter higher education for the first time, accomplish Goal #3, and then move to Goals #1 and/ or #2).

---

**Figure 13.4.** Department-Level SLOs Generated by Full-Time ESL Faculty

---

2. The next level after ESL is English Skills, a basic skills program.

that directly tapped into other markers of student success, such as computer literacy, job placement, or academic readiness. Jane declared:

> What we produced in our meeting was great, very beneficial. . . . We know we have students with different purposes. If you're wanting to head into an academic major, there is a different track or [if you] want to go shopping without getting embarrassed, when to ask a question, there is another track.

Barbara was enthused as well: "This is a community college. I love it how our SLOs came right back to our students." Developing program-wide SLOs allowed the full-time faculty to re-envision the program, its mission and the curriculum. The next challenge is for the department to revise its ESL curriculum to be in sync with the program-wide SLOs.

## Implications

This study suggests that SLOs and rubrics benefit both the teacher and the student. Jane and Barbara both appreciated what the SLO process had done for the ESL program. It had started a dialogue on pedagogy, learning outcomes, and classroom assignments among colleagues. However, making SLOs clear and meaningful for beginning-level ESL community college students remains a challenge. Thus, further research should be conducted on how ESL programs at community colleges across the United States deal with the SLO process for beginning-level ESL students.

Jane and Barbara were able to observe an enhanced level of student success. Jane noted:

> I found it very motivating. [The students] really all want to do the best they can, and in the rubric it is exactly spelled out what they have to do. So for the animal poster project, the students were just following the rubric to get a top grade. The posters were better than ever. In general, 90 percent of the students did a really excellent job as opposed to 50 percent.

However, it would also be useful to research ESL students' perspectives on SLOs and rubrics to discover if students found these beneficial and if they noticed an improvement in their work as a result of them. Interestingly, Jane and Barbara were both handed a generic SLO student evaluation by the campus-wide SLO project facilitator. Since ESL students had a difficult time making sense of the evaluation due to the language, Jane and Barbara were unable to receive any helpful feedback from the students. Thus, in determining whether SLOs help ESL students, it would be necessary to develop an assessment tool that would be comprehensible for beginning to advanced ESL students.

It would also be beneficial for TESOL programs to prepare future ESL teachers on how to develop learning outcomes and rubrics, so they are better prepared for the ESL community college classroom. Most importantly, ESL programs at community colleges across the United States should be in dialogue with each other and share strategies for making SLOs and rubrics effective to enhance ESL student success.

# REFERENCES

Abriam-Yago, K., Yoder, M., & Kataoka-Yahiro, M. (1999). The Cummins model: A framework for teaching nursing students for whom English is a second language. *Journal of Transcultural Nursing, 10*(2), 143–149.

Aduwa-Ogiegbaen, S., & Iyamu, E. (2006). Factors affecting quality of English language teaching and learning in secondary schools in Nigeria. *College Student Journal, 40*(3), 495–504. Retrieved December 19, 2006, from Academic Search Premier database.

Alamprese, J. (2004). Approaches to ABE transition to postsecondary education. *Focus on Basics, 6*(D), 26–29.

Alghazo, I. M. (2006). Student attitudes toward web-enhanced instruction in an educational technology course. *College Student Journal, 40*(3), 620–630. Retrieved December 18, 2006, from ezproxy.pc.maricopa.edu

Al-Jarf, A. (2002). *Effect of online learning on struggling ESL college writers.* San Antonio, TX: National Educational Computing Conference. (Retrieved April 9, 2007, from OCLC FirstSearch database, ERIC Document Reproduction Service No. ED475920)

Allison, H. A. (2006). Immigration + new literacy studies + digital technologies = ESL for a new south. In C. Machado (Series Ed.) & M. Spaventa (Vol. Ed.), *Perspectives on community college ESL: Vol.1: Pedagogy, programs, curricula, and assessment* (pp. 47–60). Alexandria, VA: TESOL.

American Association of Community Colleges. (2007). *AACC facts about allied health professionals.* Retrieved April 5, 2007 from www.aacc.nche.edu

American Council on Education. (2004). *Reflections on twenty years of minorities in higher education and the ACE annual status report.* Washington, DC: American Council on Education.

Anzaldúa, G. (1999). Preface. In G. Anzaldúa (Ed.), *Borderlands/La frontera* (pp.19–20). San Francisco: Aunt Lute Books.

———.(2002). Now let us shift . . . the path to conocimiento . . . inner work, public acts. In G. Anzaldúa & A. Keating (Eds.), *This bridge we call home* (pp. 540–578). New York: Routledge.

Aragon, S. (Ed.). (2001). *Beyond access: Methods and models for increasing retention and learning success among minority students: New directions for community colleges, no. 112.* San Francisco: Jossey-Bass.

Armour, W. S. (2001). 'This guy is Japanese stuck in a white man's body': A discussion of meaning making, identity slippage, and cross-cultural adaptation. *Journal of Multilingual and Multicultural Development, 22*(1), 1–18.

Attewell, P., Lavin, D., Domina, T., & Levey, T. (2006). New evidence on college remediation. *Journal of Higher Education, 77*(5), 886–924.

Babbitt, M., Mlynarczyk, R., Murie, R., & Wald, M. (2004). *Designing content-based programs for college success.* Paper presented at the TESOL Conference, Long Beach, CA.

Bachman, L.F. (1990). *Fundamental considerations in language testing.* Oxford: Oxford University Press.

Bailey, K. M. (1990). The use of diary studies in teacher education programs. In J. C. Richards & D. Nunan (Eds.), *Second language teacher education* (pp. 215–226). New York: Cambridge University Press.

Bailey, K. M., Curtis, A., & Nunan, D. (2001). *Pursuing professional development: The self as source.* Boston: Heinle.

Bailey, K. M., & Ochsner, R. (1983). A methodological review of the diary studies: Windmill tilting or social science? In K. M. Bailey, M. H. Long, & S. Peck (Eds.), *Second language acquisition studies* (pp. 188–198). Rowley, MA: Newbury House.

Baker, T. L., & Vélez, W. (1996). Access to and opportunity in postsecondary education in the United States: A review. *Sociology of Education, 69*, 82–101.

Barakzai, M. D., & Fraser, D. (2005). The effect of demographic variables on achievement in and satisfaction with online coursework. *Journal of Nursing Education, 44*(8), 373–380. Retrieved December 19, 2006, from Wilson Web database.

Bartholomae, D. (1986). Inventing the university. *Journal of Basic Writing, 5*(1), 4–23.

Beglar, D., & Hunt, A. (1999). Revising and validating the 2000 word level and university word level vocabulary test. *Language Testing, 16*(2), 131–162.

Belack, J. (2005). Threatening our diversity. *Journal of Nursing Education, 44*(5), 199–120.

Benesch, S. (2001). *Critical English for academic purposes: Theory, politics, and practice.* Mahwah, NJ: Lawrence Erlbaum.

Blumenthal, A. (Ed.). (2006). *Students, mission, and advocacy.* Vol. 2 in C. Machado (Series Ed.), *Perspectives on community college ESL.* Alexandria, VA: TESOL.

Boesel, D., Alsalam, N., & Smith, T. (1998). *Educational and labor market performance of GED recipients: Research synthesis.* Washington, DC: National Library of Education. (ERIC Document Reproduction Service No. ED982033)

Bok, D. (2006). *Our underachieving colleges: A candid look at how much students learn and why they should be learning more.* Princeton, NJ: Princeton University Press.

Boudett, K. P., Murnane, R. J., & Willett, J. B. (2000). 'Second-chance' strategies for women who drop out of school. *Monthly Labor Review, 123*, 19–32.

Branch, M. (2001). Recruitment of minorities into the nursing profession. *Minority Nurse Newsletter, 8*(2), 4.

Braxton, J. (2000). *Reworking the student departure puzzle.* Nashville, TN: Vanderbilt University Press.

Brickman, A., & Braun, L. (1999). *Existing models for post-secondary transition programs: Research findings*. Boston: Massachusetts Community College Executive Office.

Brinton, D. M., & Holten, C. A. (2001). Does the emperor have no clothes? A re-examination of grammar in content-based instruction. In J. Flowerdew & M. Peacock (Eds.), *Research perspectives on English for academic purposes* (pp. 239–251). Cambridge: Cambridge University Press.

Brinton, D. M., Snow, M. A., & Wesche, M. (1989). *Content-based second language instruction*. New York: Newbury House.

————.(2003). *Content-based second language instruction: Michigan classics edition*. Ann Arbor: University of Michigan Press.

Brown, J. D. (1996). *Testing in language programs*. Upper Saddle River, NJ: Prentice Hall.

Brutza, C. J., & Hayes, M. (2006). Whose technology is it anyway? In C. Machado (Series Ed.) & M. Spaventa (Vol. Ed.), *Perspectives on community college ESL: Vol. 1: Pedagogy, programs, curricula, and assessment* (pp. 125–133). Alexandria, VA: TESOL.

Butler, J. (1990). Performative acts and gender constitution: An essay in phenomenology and feminist theory. In S. Case (Ed.), *Performing feminisms: Feminist critical theory and theatre* (pp. 270–282). Baltimore: Johns Hopkins University Press.

Buttaro, L. (2001). Second language learning and language arts. *The Community College Enterprise, 8*(1), 81–101.

Calderon-Young, E. (1999). Technology for teaching foreign languages among community college students. *Community College Journal of Research and Practice, 23*(2), 161–169. Retrieved December 19, 2006, from Academic Search Premier.

California Community Colleges Chancellor's Office. (2000). *California state plan for vocational and technical education: Executive summary*. Retrieved July 13, 2007 from www.cccco.edu/divisions/esed/voced/resources/library/State-Plan-Word/5.00execsum.doc

————. (2007). *Program/retention success rates*. Retrieved July 30, 2007, from misweb.cccco.edu/mis/onlinestat/ret_sucs.cfm

Cameron, D. (1997). Performing gender identity: Young men's talk and the construction of heterosexual masculinity. In S. Johnson & U. Meinhof (Eds.), *Language and masculinity* (pp. 47–64). Oxford: Blackwell.

Cameron, J., & Heckman, J. (1993). The non-equivalence of high school equivalents. *Journal of Labor Economics, 11*(1), 1–47.

Campinha-Bacote, J. (1998). Cultural diversity in nursing education: Issues and concerns. *Journal of Nursing Education, 37*(1), 3–4.

Carmona, J. (Ed.). (2008). *Faculty, administration, and the working environment*. Alexandria, VA: TESOL.

Carnevale, A. P., & Desrochers, D. M. (2001). *Help wanted . . . credentials required: Community colleges in the knowledge economy*. Princeton, NJ: Educational Testing Service.

Carrasquillo, A. K., & Rodriguez, V. (1996). *Language-minority students in the mainstream classroom*. Clevedon, UK: Multilingual Matters.

Chae, J. E. (2000). *Student departure from U.S. community colleges: A competing risks survival analysis.* Cambridge, MA: Harvard University, Graduate School of Education.

Chapelle, C. A. (2005). Computer-assisted language learning. In E. Hinkel (Ed.), *Handbook of research in second language learning and teaching* (pp. 743–755). Mahwah, NJ: Lawrence Erlbaum.

Chisholm, I. (1995/96). Computer use in a multicultural classroom. *Journal of Research on Computing in Education, 28*(2), 162. Retrieved December 18, 2006, from Academic Search Premier database.

Chisman, F. P., & Crandall, J. (2007). *Passing the torch: Strategies for innovation in community college ESL.* New York: Council for the Advancement of Adult Literacy.

Clifford, R. (1998). Mirror, mirror, on the wall: Reflections on computer-assisted language learning. *CALICO Journal, 16*(1), 1–10.

Cohen, A., Glasman, H., Rosenbaum-Cohen, P. R., Ferrara, J., & Fine, J. (1988). Reading English for specialized purposes: Discourse and analysis and the use of student informants. In P. L. Carrell, J. Devine, & D. E. Eskey (Eds.), *Interactive approaches to second language reading* (pp. 152–167). Cambridge, UK: Cambridge University Press.

The College Board. (2003). *Higher education landscape.* Retrieved April 1, 2006, from www.collegeboard.com/highered/res/hel/hel.html

————. (2007). *Accuplacer® sample questions for students.* New York: College Board.

College Entrance Examination Board and Educational Testing Service. (1997). *Accuplacer® test administration manual.* Princeton, NJ: College Entrance Examination Board and Educational Testing Service.

Collier, V. P. (1989). How long? A synthesis of research on academic achievement in a second language. *TESOL Quarterly, 23*, 509–531.

Comings, J., & Cuban, S. (2002). *Sponsors and sponsorship: Initial findings from the second phase of the NCSALL persistence study.* Boston, MA: National Center for the Study of Adult Language and Literacy.

Corson, D. (1997). The learning and use of academic English words. *Language Learning, 47*(4), 671–718.

Council for Adult and Experiential Learning. (2003). *How well are we serving our adult learners? Investigating the impact of institutions on success and retention.* Retrieved August 14, 2007, from www.cael.org/pdf/Reenrollment_Study.pdf

Coxhead, A. (2000). A new academic word list. *TESOL Quarterly, 34*(2), 213–238.

Crandall, J., & Burt, M. (2007). *Issues in literacy for adult English language learners.* Retrieved April 17, 2007, from userpages.umbc.edu/~crandall/Issues_in_Literacy_ for_ Adult_English_Language_Learners

Crandall, J., & Kaufman, D. (2002). *Content-based instruction in higher education settings.* Alexandria, VA: TESOL.

Crandall, J., & Sheppard, K. (2004). *Adult ESL and the community college.* New York: Council for the Advancement of Adult Literacy.

Crawford, J. (1997). *Best evidence: Research foundations of the Bilingual Education Act* (NCBE Report). Washington, DC: National Clearinghouse for Bilingual Education.

Crist, J., & Tanner, C. (2003). Interpretation, analysis, and methods in hermeneutic interpretive phenomenology. *Nursing Research, 52*(3), 202–205.

Crouse, J. (1997). Essay versus multiple-choice tests: Does test format make a difference for course placement in college? *ACT Information Brief* (No. 97-1). Iowa City, IA: ACT Research Division.

Cummins, J. (1992). Language proficiency, bilingualism, and academic achievement. In P. A. Richard-Amato & M. A. Snow (Eds.), *The multicultural classroom* (pp. 16–26). White Plains, NY: Longman.

————. (2000). *Language, power, and pedagogy: Bilingual children in the crossfire.* Clevedon, UK: Multilingual Matters.

————. (2001). *Negotiating identities: Education for empowerment in a diverse society* (2nd ed.). Los Angeles: California Association for Bilingual Education.

Cummins, J., & Schecter, S. R. (2003). Introduction: School-based language policy in culturally diverse contexts. In S. R. Schecter & J. Cummins (Eds.), *Multilingual education in practice: Using diversity as a resource* (pp. 1–16). Portsmouth, NH: Heinemann.

Dantas-Whitney, M. (2002). Critical reflection in the second language classroom through audiotaped journals. *System, 30*(4), 543–555.

del Bueno, D. (2005). A crisis in critical thinking. *Nursing Education Perspectives, 26*(5), 278–282.

Dewey, J. (1938/1997). *Experience and education.* New York: Simon & Schuster.

Diekelmann, N., & Lampe, S. (2004). Student-centered pedagogies: Co-creating compelling experiences using the new pedagogies. *Journal of Nursing Education 43*(6), 245–248.

Diekelmann, N., & Magnussen-Ironside, P. (1998). Hermeneutics. In J. Fitzpatrick (Ed.), *Encyclopedia of nursing research* (pp. 243–245). New York, NY: Springer.

Donnelly, R., & Fitzmaurice, M. (2005). Collaborative project-based learning and problem-based learning in higher education: A consideration of tutor and student role in learner-focused strategies. In G. O'Neill, S. Moore, & B. McMullin (Eds.), *Emerging issues in the practice of learning and teaching.* Retrieved October 28, 2005, from www.aishe.org/readings/2005-1/donnelly-fitzmaurice-Collaborative-Project-based-Learning.html

Draud, B., & Brace, S. (1999). *Assessing the impact of technology on teaching and learning: Student perspectives.* Retrieved February 3, 2006 from www.mtsu.edu/~itconf/proceed99/brace.html

Dreyfus, H. L. (1994). Preface. In P. Benner (Ed.), *Interpretive phenomenology: Embodiment, caring, and ethics in health and illness* (pp. vii–xi). Thousands Oaks, CA: Sage Publishing.

Educational Testing Service. (1996). *TOEFL test of written English guide* (4th ed.). Princeton, NJ: Author.

Elbow, P. (1981). *Writing with power.* New York: Oxford University Press.

Ellis, R. (Ed.). (2000). *Learning a second language through interaction.* Amsterdam: John Benjamins.

Eskey, D. E. (1997). Syllabus design in content-based instruction. In M. A. Snow & D. A. Brinton (Eds.), *The content-based classroom: Perspectives on integrating language and content* (pp. 132–141). White Plains, NY: Longman.

Farrell, P. (1990). *Vocabulary in ESL: A lexical analysis of the English of electronics and a study of semi-technical vocabulary.* Dublin, Ireland: Centre for Language and Communication Studies. (ERIC Document Reproduction Service No. ED332551)

Feldman, R. S. (2000). *Essentials of understanding psychology.* Boston: McGraw-Hill.

Ferrer, M. & Rondowski, S. (2006). *Student learning outcomes (SLO) development & implementation website.* Retrieved September 10, 2006, from frc.sbcc.edu/slo/rubric/resourceslinks/pdf/011805insvcprsnt.pdf

Ferris, D., & Hedgcock, J. S. (1998). *Teaching ESL composition: Purpose, process, and practice.* Mahwah, NJ: Lawrence Erlbaum.

Ferris, D., & Tagg, T. (1996). Academic oral communication needs of EAP learners: What subject-matter instructors actually require. *TESOL Quarterly, 30*(1), 31–58.

Fillmore, L. W., & Snow, C. E. (2000). What teachers need to know about language. *Center for Applied Linguistics Special Report.* Retrieved September 13, 2004, from www.cal.org.htm

Fletcher, A., Beacham, T., Elliott, R.W., Northington, L., Calvin, R., Hill, M., et al. (2003). Recruitment, retention and matriculation of ethnic minority nursing students: A University of Mississippi School of Nursing approach. *Journal of Cultural Diversity, 10*(4), 128–133.

Flinn, J. B. (2004). Teaching strategies used with success in the multicultural classroom. *Nurse Educator, 29*(1), 10–12.

Gass, S. M. (1997). *Input, interaction, and the second language learner.* Mahwah, NJ: Lawrence Erlbaum.

Gay, L. R. (1987). *Educational research: Competencies for analysis and application* (3rd ed.). Columbus, OH: Merrill.

Gebhard, J. G. (2006). *Teaching English as a foreign or second language.* Ann Arbor: University of Michigan Press.

Gee, J. P. (1996). *Social linguistics and literacies: Ideology in discourses.* New York: Routledge.

———. (1999). *An Introduction to discourse analysis: Theory and method*: New York: Routledge.

——— (2004). Learning language as a matter of learning social languages within discourses. In M. Hawkins (Ed.), *Language learning and teacher education: A sociocultural approach* (pp. 13–31). Buffalo, NY: Multilingual Matters.

Goffman, E. (1981). *Forms of talk.* Philadelphia: University of Pennsylvania.

Grabe, W., & Stoller, F. L. (1997). Content-based instruction: Research foundations. In M. A. Snow & D. M. Brinton (Eds.), *The content-based classroom: Perspectives on integrating language and content* (pp. 5–21). White Plains, NY: Longman.

Greenleaf, C., Schoenbach, R., Cziko, C., & Mueller, F. L. (2001). Apprenticing adolescent readers to academic literacy. *Harvard Educational Review, 71*(1), 79–129.

Grubb, W. N. (Ed.). (1999). *Honored but invisible: An inside look at teaching in community colleges.* New York: Routledge.

Guhde, J. A. (2003). English-as-a-second language (ESL) nursing students: Strategies for building verbal and written language skills. *Journal of Cultural Diversity, 10*(4), 113–117.

Gutierrez, R. (2002). Beyond essentialism: The complexity of language in teaching mathematics to Latina/o students. *American Educational Research Journal, 39*(4), 1047–1088.

Hagedorn, L. S., Chi, W., Cepeda, R. M., & McLain, M. (2007). An investigation in critical mass: The role of Latino representation in the success of urban community college students. *Research in Higher Education, 48*(1), 73.

Haist, C. (1993). A comparison of *Accuplacer®* and writing sample scores with communication course grades and GPA's. In R. Girowc & S. Susini (Eds.), *Computerized placement testing* (pp. 49–56). Etobicoke, Ontario: Ontario Accuplacer® Consortium.

Hamilton, J. (1998). *First-time students entering a two-year public college with a GED, Fall 1991 to Fall 1996.* Gainesville, GA: Gainesville College.

Hamp-Lyons, L. (1992). *Holistic writing assessment of LEP students.* Proceedings of the Second National Research Symposium on Limited English Proficiency Students' Issues: Focus on evaluating and measurement, Vol. 2. Washington, DC: U.S. Department of Education, Office of Bilingual Education and Minority Language Affairs. (ERIC Document Reproduction Service No. ED349830)

Hanson-Smith, E. (1997). *Technology in the classroom: Practice and promise in the 21st century.* Alexandria, VA: TESOL.

Hartnell College. (2005). *Student characteristics/full-time, part-time status.* Retrieved July 30, 2007 from www.hartnell.edu/irp/efactbook/efactbook_2003/fa2005-pdf/t14-partime-fulltime-fa05.pdf

Hasan, R. (1980). What's going on: A dynamic view of context in language. In C. Cloran, D. Butt, & G. Williams (Eds.), *Ways of seeing, ways of meaning* (pp. 37–50). London: Cassel.

Hassouneh-Phillips, D. (2003). An education in racism. *Journal of Nursing Education, 42*(6), 258–268.

Heidegger, M. (1968/1993). *Basic writings* (Rev. ed.). San Francisco, Harper.

———. (1969). *Identity and difference.* New York: Harper & Row.

Helsing, D., Broderick, M., & Hammerman, J. (2001). A developmental view of ESOL students' identity transitions in an urban community college. In R. Kegan, M. Broderick, E. Drago-Severson, D. Helsing, N. Popp, & K. Portnow (Eds.), *Toward a new pluralism in ABE/ESOL classrooms: Teaching to multiple "cultures of mind"* (pp. 79–225). Cambridge, MA: National Center for the Study of Adult Learning and Literacy.

Higgins, J. J. (1966). Hard facts: Notes on teaching English to science students. *ELT Journal, 21*, 55–60.

Hmelo, C. E., & Evenson, D. H. (2000). Problem-based learning: Gaining insights on learning interactions through multiple methods of inquiry. In C. E. Hmelo & D. H. Evenson

(Eds.), *Problem-based learning: A research perspective on learning interactions* (pp. 1–16). Mahwah, NJ: Lawrence Erlbaum.

Holmes, J., Stubbe, M., & Vine, B. (1999). Constructing professional identity: 'Doing power' in policy units. In S. Sarangi & C. Roberts (Eds.), *Talk, work, and institutional order: Discourse in medical mediation and management settings* (pp. 351–385). Berlin, Germany: Mouton de Gruyter.

Hughes, A. (2003). *Testing for language teachers* (2nd ed.). Cambridge: Cambridge University Press.

Huttman, B. (1983/1998). A crime of compassion. In P. Eschholz & A. Rosa (Eds.), *Models for writers: Short essays for composition* (pp. 293–296). New York: St. Martin's Press.

Institute of International Education. (2005). *Open doors 2005: Report on international educational exchange.* New York: Institute of International Education. Retrieved June 22, 2006, from opendoors.iienetwork.org/?p=69689

Ironside, P. M. (2004). "Covering content" and teaching thinking: Deconstructing the additive curriculum. *Journal of Nursing Education, 43*(1), 5–12.

Jackson, D. K., & Sandiford, J. R. (2003). *Predictors of first semester attrition and their relation to retention of generic associate degree nursing students.* Paper presented at the Council for the Study of Community Colleges, Dallas, Texas.

Jiang, B., & Kuehn, P. (2001). Transfer in the academic language development of postsecondary ESL students [Electronic version]. *Bilingual Research Journal, 25*(4), 417–436.

Jourdenais, R. M., & Shaw, P. A. (2005). Dimensions of content-based instruction in second language education. In R. M. Jourdenais and S. E. Springer (Eds.), *Content, tasks and projects in the language classroom: 2004 conference proceedings* (pp. 1–12). Monterey, CA: Monterey Institute of International Studies.

Kasper, L. F. (Ed.). (2000). *Content-based college ESL instruction.* Mahwah, NJ: Lawrence Erlbaum.

———. (2002). Technology as a tool for literacy in the age of information: Implications for the ESL classroom. *Teaching English in the Two Year College, 30*(2), 129–145.

Kelley, M. L., & Fitzsimons, V. M. (2000). *Understanding cultural diversity: Culture, curriculum, and community in nursing.* New York: NLN Press.

Kennedy, M. L., Kennedy, W. J., & Smith, H. (2003). *Writing in the disciplines: A reader for writers* (5th ed.) Englewood, NJ: Prentice Hall.

Kerka, S. (1995). *Adult learner retention revisited.* Columbus, OH: ERIC Clearinghouse on Adult Career and Vocational Education. (ERIC Document Reproduction Service No. ED389880)

Kern, R. (2006). Perspectives on technology in learning and teaching languages. *TESOL Quarterly, 40*(1), 183–210.

Klisch, M. L. (2000). Retention strategies for ESL nursing students: Review of literature 1990–1999 and strategies and outcomes in a small private school of nursing with limited funding. *Journal of Multicultural Nursing & Health, 6*(1), 21–29.

Kress, G. (2003). *Literacy in the new media age.* New York: Routledge.

Kuehn, P. (1996). *Assessment of academic literacy skills: Preparing minority and limited English proficient (LEP) students for post-secondary education.* Fresno: California State University. (ERIC Document Reproduction Service No. ED415498)

Kumaravadivelu, B. (2006). *Understanding language teaching: From method to postmethod.* Mahwah, NJ: Lawrence Erlbaum.

Labbo, L. D. (2006). Literacy pedagogy and computer technologies: Toward solving the puzzle of current and future classroom practices. *Australian Journal of Language and Literacy, 29*(3), 199–209.

Lai, C., & Kritsonis, W. (2006). The advantages and disadvantages of computer technology in second language acquisition. *National Journal for Publishing and Mentoring Doctoral Student Research, 3*(1). Retrieved April 9, 2007, from OCLC FirstSearch database. (ERIC Document Reproduction Service No. ED492159)

Lam, Y. (2000). Technophilia vs. technophobia. A preliminary look at why second-language teachers do or do not use technology in the classroom. *Canadian Modern Language Review, 56*(3), 389–420.

Lantolf, J., & Pavlenko, A. (2001). (S)econd (L)anguage (A)ctivity theory: Understanding second language learners as people. In M. Breen (Ed.), *Learner contributions to second language learning: New directions in research* (pp. 141–158). London: Longman.

Lave, J., & Wenger, E. (1991). *Situated learning: Legitimate peripheral participation.* Cambridge, UK: Cambridge University Press.

Levin, J. S. (2000). *The re-fashioned institution: The community college in the age of globalization.* Unpublished manuscript.

Liebowitz, M., & Taylor, J. (2004). *Breaking through: Helping low-skilled adults enter and succeed in college and careers.* Boston: Jobs for the Future and National Council for Workforce Education.

Logan, J. R., & Deane, G. (2003). *Black diversity in metropolitan America.* Albany, NY: Mumford Center for Comparative Urban and Regional Research. Retrieved October 17, 2007, from mumford1.dyndns.org/cen2000/BlackWhite/ BlackDiversityReport/Black_Diversity_final.pdf

Long, M. H. (1996). The role of the linguistic environment in second language acquisition. In W. C. Ritchie & T. K. Bhatia (Eds.), *Handbook of research on language acquisition: Vol. 2. Second language acquisition* (pp. 413–468). New York: Academic Press.

Lopez, K. A., & Willis, D. G. (2004). Descriptive versus interpretive phenomenology. Their contributions to nursing knowledge. *Qualitative Health Research, 14*(5), 726–735.

Machado, C. (2006). Series editor's preface. In C. Machado (Series Ed.) & M. Spaventa (Vol. Ed.), *Perspectives on community college ESL: Vol. 1: Pedagogy, programs, curricula, and assessment* (pp. v–vi). Alexandria, VA: TESOL.

Machado, C., & Solensky, S. (2006). From marginalized to integrated: ESL placement testing goes mainstream. In C. Machado (Series Ed.) & M. Spaventa (Vol. Ed.), *Perspectives on community college ESL: Vol. 1: Pedagogy, programs, curricula, and assessment* (pp. 187–199). Alexandria, VA: TESOL.

Malu, K. F., & Figlear, M. R. (1998). Enhancing the language development of immigrant ESL nursing students: A case study with recommendations for action. *Nurse Educator, 23*(2), 43–47.

Marshall, S., & Gilmour, M. (1993). Lexical knowledge and reading comprehension in Papua New Guinea. *English for Specific Purposes, 12*, 69–81.

Maxwell, J. A. (2005). *Qualitative research design: An interactive approach* (2nd ed.). Thousand Oaks, CA: Sage Publications.

McKay, S., & Wong, S. (1996). Multiple discourses, multiple identities: Investment and agency in second-language learning among Chinese adolescent immigrant students. *Harvard Educational Review, 66*(3), 577–608.

Menager-Beeley, R. (2001). *Student success in web based distance learning: Measuring motivation to identify at risk students and improve retention in online classes.* Paper presented at the 10th International Conference on World Wide Web, Orlando, FL. Retrieved April 9, 2007, from OCLC FirstSearch database. (ERIC Document Reproduction Service No. ED466608)

Merriam, S. B. (1998). *Qualitative research and case study applications in education.* San Francisco: Jossey-Bass.

Mikol, C. (2005). Teaching nursing without lecturing: Critical pedagogy as communicative dialogue. *Nursing Education Perspectives, 26,* 86–89.

Morita, N. (2004). Negotiating participation and identity in second language academic communities. *TESOL Quarterly, 38*(4), 573–603.

Moss, R. L., & Young, R. B. (1995). Perceptions about the academic and social integration of underprepared students in an urban community college. *Community College Review, 22*(4), 47–61.

Mulready-Shick, J. (2005). *Caring for this nation by addressing the nursing shortage: Lessons learned from regulatory impact on students of multicultural backgrounds in the U.S.* Paper presented at the First International Congress of Qualitative Inquiry, Urbana-Champaign, IL.

―――. (2008). *The lived experiences of students as English language learners in the nursing classroom: A critical hermeneutic inquiry.* Unpublished doctoral dissertation, University of Massachusetts, Boston.

Murnane, R., & Levy, F. (1996). *Teaching the new basic skills: Principles for educating children to thrive in a changing economy.* New York: Free Press.

Murphy, J., & Stoller, F. (2001). Sustained-content language teaching: An emerging definition. *TESOL Journal, 10*(2/3), 3–5.

Nation, I. S. P. (1983). Testing and teaching vocabulary. *Guidelines, 5,* 12–25.

―――. (1990). *Teaching and learning vocabulary.* Boston: Heinle.

―――. (2001). *Learning vocabulary in another language.* Cambridge, UK: Cambridge University Press.

National Advisory Council on Nurse Education and Practice. (2000). *A national agenda for nursing workforce racial/ethnic diversity.* Retrieved May 4, 2004, from www.bphr/hrsa.gov/nursing/nacnep

National Center for Education Statistics. (2007). *Part-time undergraduates in post-secondary education, 2003–04: Post-secondary education descriptive analysis report.* Retrieved August 23, 2007, from nces.ed.gov/pubs2007/2007165.pdf

National Clearinghouse for English Language Acquisition and Language Instruction Educational Programs. (2006). *NCELA FAQs*. Retrieved July 5, 2007, from www.ncela.gwu.edu/expert/faq/08leps.html

Nebraska Industrial Competitiveness Alliance. (1999). *Building the foundations of workforce development: A business and community guidebook.* Retrieved July 29, 2007, from www.neded.org/files/businessdevelopment/library/BldngFndtns.pdf

Newman, M., & Williams, J. (2003). Educating nurses in Rhode Island: A lot of diversity in a little place. *Journal of Cultural Diversity, 10*(3), 91–95.

Nguyen, H. T., & Kellogg, G. (2005). Emergent identities in online discussions for second language learning. *The Canadian Modern Language Review, 62*(1), 111–136.

———. (2007). *Second language socialization in content-based instruction.* Unpublished manuscript.

Norton, B. (2001). Non-participation, imagined communities, and the language classroom. In X. Bonch-Bruevich, W. Crawford, J. Hellermann, C. Higgins & H. T. Nguyen (Eds.), *Selected proceedings of the second language research forum* (pp. 167–180). Somerville, MA: Cascadilla Press.

Norton Pierce, B. (1995). Social identity, investment, and language learning. *TESOL Quarterly, 29*(1), 9–31.

Ochs, E. (1993). Constructing social identity: A language socialization perspective. *Research on Language and Social Interaction, 26*(3), 287–306.

———. (2002). Becoming a speaker of culture. In C. Kramsch (Ed.), *Language acquisition and language socialization: Ecological perspectives* (pp. 99–120). London: Continuum.

Office of Vocational and Adult Education (OVAE). (2005). *Adult Education and Family Literacy Act: Program facts.* Washington, DC: U.S. Department of Education. Retrieved Feb. 12, 2006, from www.ed.gov/about/offices/list/ovae/pi/AdultEd/index.html

———. (2006). *Increasing student retention.* Washington, DC: U.S. Department of Education. Retrieved July 13, 2007, from www.ed.gov/about/offices/list/ovae/pi/cclo/reten.html

———. (2007). *Transitions to postsecondary education.* Washington, DC: U.S. Department of Education. Retrieved Oct. 18, 2007, from www.ed.gov/about/offices/list/ovae/pi/AdultEd/transition.html

Oller, J. (1979). *Language tests at school.* London: Longman.

Olson, D. R. (1997). Talking about text and the culture of literacy. In B. Davies & D. Corson (Eds.), *Oral discourse and education* (pp. 1–9). Boston: Kluwer.

Omaggio, A. C. (1982). The relationship between personalized classroom talk and teacher effectiveness ratings: Some research results. *Foreign Language Annals, 14*(4), 255–269.

O'Malley, J. M., & Valdez-Pierce, L. (1996). *Authentic assessment for English language learners.* Reading, MA: Addison-Wesley.

Pally, M. (2000). *Sustained content teaching in academic ESL/EFL: A practical approach.* Boston: Houghton Mifflin.

Pardue, K. T., Tagliareni, M. E., Valiga, T., Davison-Price, M., & Orehowsky, S. (2005). Substantive innovation in nursing education: Shifting the emphasis from content coverage to student learning. *Nursing Education Perspectives, 26*(1), 55–57.

Pascarella, E. T., & Terenzini, P. T. (1991). *How college affects students: Findings and insights from twenty years of research.* San Francisco: Jossey-Bass.

Peters, P. (1986). Getting the theme across: A study of dominant function in the academic writing of university students. In B. Couture (Ed.), *Functional approaches to writing: Research perspectives* (pp. 169–185). London: Frances Pinter.

Phillippe, K. A., & Patton, M. (2000). *National profile of community colleges: Trends and statistics* (3rd ed.). Washington, D.C.: American Association of Community Colleges.

Phoenix College. (2007). *Institutional research data warehouse.* Retrieved April 27, 2007, from www.maricopa.edu

Pica, T. (1994). Research on negotiation: What does it reveal about second-language learning conditions, processes, and outcomes? *Language Learning, 44*, 493–527.

Preston, R. (1994). *The hot zone.* New York: Anchor.

Rance-Roney, J. (1995). *Transitioning adult ESL learners to academic programs.* Washington, DC: National Clearinghouse for ESL Literacy Education. (ERIC Reproduction Service No. ED385173)

Reder, S. (2000). Adult literacy and postsecondary education students: Overlapping populations and learning trajectories. In J. Comings, B. Garner, & C. Smith (Eds.), *Annual review of adult learning and literacy: Vol. 1* (pp. 111–157). San Francisco: Jossey-Bass.

Reid, J. (1990). Second language writing: Assessment issues. In B. Kroll (Ed.), *Responding to different topic types* (pp. 191–210). Cambridge, UK: Cambridge University Press.

Rendón, L. I. (1999). Toward a new vision of the multicultural community college for the next century. In K. M. Shaw, J. R. Valadez, & R. A. Rhoads (Eds.), *Community colleges as cultural texts: Qualitative exploration of organizational and student culture* (pp. 195–204). Albany: SUNY Press.

Rendón, L. I., Jalomo, R. E., & Nora, A. (2002). Theoretical consideration in the study of minority student retention in higher education. In J. M. Braxton (Ed.), *Reworking the student departure puzzle* (pp. 127–156). Nashville, TN: Vanderbilt University Press.

Rhoades, G. (1998). *Managed professionals: Unionized faculty and restructuring academic labor.* Albany: SUNY Press.

Rich, J. (1993). *Can a writing sample improve placement in English courses?* Research Report No. 93-13 R. Miami, FL: Miami-Dade Community College Institutional Research.

Richards, J., Platt, J., & Weber, H. (1985). *Longman dictionary of applied linguistics.* London: Longman.

Richards, J. C., & Lockhart, C. (1994). *Reflective teaching in second language classrooms.* Cambridge, UK: Cambridge University Press.

Richardson, J. R. C., & Skinner, E. (1992). Helping first-generation minority students achieve degrees. In L. S. Zwerling & H. B. London (Eds.), *First-generation students: Confronting the cultural issues* (pp. 29–43). San Francisco: Jossey-Bass.

Robishaw, D. (1993). The case for pre-goal setting. *Adventures in Assessment, 5,* 93.

Rodriguez, S. (2006). *Miami Dade College information capsule: Basic skills assessment results fall terms 2001 through 2005.* I.C. No. 2006-0C3. Miami, FL: Miami Dade College Institutional Research.

Santos, M. G. (2003). *Three empirical studies on the academic vocabulary knowledge of U.S. language-minority community college students.* Unpublished doctoral dissertation, Harvard University, Cambridge, MA.

————. (2004). Some findings on the academic vocabulary skills of language minority community college students. *Focus on Basics, 6*(D), 7–9. Retrieved June 26, 2004, from www.gseweb.harvard.edu/ncsall/fob/2004/santos.html

Saxon, D. P., & Boylan, H. R. (1999). *Characteristics of community college remedial students.* Retrieved November 13, 2007, from www.ncde.appstate.edu/reserve_reading/student_characteristics.htm

Scarcella, R. (2001). Some key factors affecting English learners' development of advanced literacy. In M. J. Schleppegrell & M. C. Colombi (Eds.), *Developing advanced literacy in first and second languages: Meaning with power* (pp. 209–226). Mahwah, NJ: Lawrence Erlbaum.

————. (2003). *Academic English: A conceptual framework.* Irvine: University of California Linguistic Minority Research Institute.

Scarcella, R., & Rumberger, R. W. (2000). Academic English—Key to long-term success in school. *UC LMRI Newsletter, 9*(4), 1–2.

Schieffelin, B. B., & Ochs, E. (1986). Language socialization. *Annual Review of Anthropology, 15*, 163–191.

Schleppegrell, M. (2001). Linguistic features of the language of schooling. *Linguistics and Education, 12*(4), 431–439.

Schleppegrell, M., & Christian, D. (1986). *Academic language proficiency.* Paper presented at the Meeting of the American Anthropological Association, Philadelphia, PA.

Schmidt, R. W., & Frota, S. N. (1986). Developing basic conversational ability in a second language: A case study of an adult learner of Portuguese. In R. R. Day (Ed.), *Talking to learn: Conversation in second language acquisition* (pp. 237–326). Rowley, MA: Newbury House.

Schuemann, C. (1998). *An investigation into the comparable effectiveness of two tests of writing administered to college-level English as a Second Language students: The Computerized Placement Test and holistically-scored essay exams.* Unpublished doctoral dissertation, Florida International University, Miami. UMI Dissertation Service Number 9903434.

Schuyler, G. (Ed.). (2000). *Trends in community college curriculum: New directions for community colleges, no. 108.* San Francisco: Jossey-Bass.

Schwendeman, R. (1999). *A review of thirteen transitional education projects or programs.* Worcester, MA: Office of SABES.

Shaw, K. M., Valadez, J. R., & Rhoads, R. A. (1999). Community colleges as texts: A conceptual overview. In K. M. Shaw, J. R. Valadez, & R. A. Rhoads, *Community colleges as cultural texts: Qualitative explorations of organizational and student culture* (pp. 1–13). Albany: SUNY Press.

Skehan, P. (1989). *Individual differences in second-language learning.* London: Hodder-Arnold.

————. (2003). Focus on form, tasks, and technology. *Computer Assisted Language Learning, 16*(5), 391–411. Retrieved December 19, 2006, from Academic Search Premier database.

Smith, B. A. (1999). Ethical and methodologic benefits of using a reflexive journal in hermeneutic-phenomenologic research. *Journal of Nursing Scholarship, 31*(4), 359–370.

Smith, T. M. (2003). Who values the GED? An examination of the paradox underlying the demand for the general educational development credential. *Teachers College Record, 105*(3), 375–415.

Snow, M. A. (2001). Content-based and immersion models for second and foreign language teaching. In M. Celce-Murcia (Ed.), *Teaching English as a second or foreign language* (3rd ed., pp. 303–318). Boston: Heinle & Heinle.

Snowhite, M., Adams, J., Gilbert, G., Reilly, B., Welch, L., & Rheinheimer, S. (2005). *Working with the 2002 accreditation standards: The Faculty's Role.* Retrieved September 10, 2006, from www.asccc.org/Publications/Papers/AccreditationStandards2005.html

Spanos, G., Rhodes, N. C., Dale, T. C., & Crandall, J. (1988). Linguistic features of mathematical problem solving: Insights and applications. In R. R. Cocking & J. P. Mestre (Eds.), *Linguistic and cultural influences on learning mathematics* (pp. 221–240). Mahwah, NJ: Lawrence Erlbaum.

Spaventa, M. (Ed.). (2006). *Pedagogy, programs, curricula, and assessment.* Vol. 1 in C. Machado (Series Ed.), *Perspectives on community college ESL.* Alexandria, VA: TESOL.

Stasinopoulos, J. (2006). The power of personal narrative: What we can learn from our students. In C. Machado (Series Ed.) & A. Blumenthal (Vol. Ed.), *Perspectives in community college ESL: Vol. 2: Students, mission, and advocacy* (pp. 151–162). Alexandria, VA: TESOL.

Stiehl, R., & Lewchuk, L. (2002). *The outcomes primer: Reconstructing the college curriculum.* Corvallis, OR: Learning Organization.

Stoller, F. L. (2002). Promoting the acquisition of knowledge in a content-based course. In J. Crandall & D. Kaufmann (Eds.), *Content-based instruction in higher education settings* (pp. 109–123). Alexandria, VA: TESOL.

Stoller, F. L., & Grabe, W. (1997). A six T's approach to content-based instruction. In M. A. Snow & D. M. Brinton (Eds.), *The content-based classroom: Perspectives on integrating language and content* (pp. 78–94). White Plains, NY: Longman.

Stone, Y. (2006). Conflicting or complementary agendas? Community colleges and ESL students. In C. Machado (Series Ed.) & A. Blumenthal (Vol. Ed.), *Perspectives in community college ESL: Vol. 2: Students, mission, and advocacy* (pp. 163–176). Alexandria, VA: TESOL.

Stovall, M. (2000). Using success courses for promoting persistence and completion. In S. R. Aragon (Ed.), *Beyond access: Methods and models for increasing retention and learning among minority students* (pp. 45–62). San Francisco: Jossey-Bass.

Stryker, S. B., & Leaver, B. L. (1997). Content-based instruction: Some lessons and implications. In S. B. Stryker & B. L. Leaver (Eds.), *Content-based instruction in foreign language education* (pp. 282–312). Washington, DC: Georgetown University Press.

Swain, M. (1995). Three functions of output in second language learning. In G. Cook & B. Seidlhofer (Eds.), *Principle and practice in applied linguistics: Studies in honour of H. G. Widdowson* (pp. 125–144). Oxford, UK: Oxford University Press.

———. (1996). Integrating language and content in the immersion classrooms: Research perspectives. *Canadian Modern Language Review, 52*(4), 529–548.

Swales, J. (1990). *Genre analysis: English in academic and research settings.* Cambridge, UK: Cambridge University Press.

Szelenyi, K., & Chang, J. C. (2002). ERIC review: Educating immigrants: The community college role. *Community College Review, 30*(2), 55–73.

Tinto, V. (1993). *Leaving college: Rethinking the causes and cures of student attrition* (2nd ed.). Chicago: University of Chicago Press.

———. (1996). Persistence and first-year experience at the community college: Teaching new students to survive, stay, and thrive. In J. N. Hankin (Ed.), *The community college: Opportunity and access from America's first-year students.* Columbia, SC: National Resource Center for the Freshman Year Experience and Students in Transition.

Toohey, K. (2000). *Learning English at school: Identity, social relations and classroom practice.* Clevedon, UK: Multilingual Matters.

Trueba, E. T., & Bartolomé, L. I. (Eds.). (2000). *Immigrant voices: In search of educational equity.* New York: Rowman & Littlefield.

Tyler, J., Murnane, R., & Willett, J. (2000). Do the cognitive skills of school dropouts matter in the labor market? *Journal of Human Resources, 35*(4), 748–754.

———. (2003). Who benefits from a GED? Evidence for females from "high school and beyond." *Economics of Education Review, 22*(3), 237–247.

Tyler, J. H. (2005). The General Educational Development (GED) credential: History, current research, and directions for policy and practice. In J. Comings, B. Garner, & C. Smith (Eds.), *Review of adult learning and literacy, Vol. 5* (pp. 45–84). Mahwah, NJ: Lawrence Erlbaum.

Ullman, C. (1997). *Social identity and the adult ESL classroom.* Retrieved July 13, 2007, from www.cal.org/caela/esl_resources/digests/socident.html

U.S. Census Bureau. (2000). *Quickfacts: Monterey County, California.* Retrieved July 30, 2007, from quickfacts.census.gov/qfd/states/06/06053.html

U.S. Department of Education. (1992). *Model indicators of program quality for adult education programs.* (ERIC Document Reproduction Service No. ED352499)

———. (1998). *The Carl D. Perkins vocational and allied technical education act of 1998 federal definition of limited English proficiency.* Retrieved July 5, 2006, from frwebgate. accedd.gpo.gov/cgi-bin/getdoc

———. (2004). *President Bush proposes record $57 billion for FY 2005 education budget.* Press release. Retrieved Mar. 15, 2007, from www.ed.gov/news/press releases/2004/02/02022004.html

———. (2006). *Report to Congress on state performance, adult education, and the Family Literacy Act FY 2003–2004.* Washington, DC: Office of Vocational and Adult Education.

Valentine, J. F., Jr., & Repath-Martos, L. M. (1997). How relevant is relevance? In M. A. Snow & D. M. Brinton (Eds.), *The content-based classroom: Perspectives on integrating language and content* (pp. 233–247). White Plains, NY: Longman.

van Lier, L. (1996). *Interaction in the language curriculum: Awareness, autonomy and authenticity.* New York: Longman.

————. (2002). An ecological-semiotic perspective on language and linguistics. In C. Kramsch (Ed.), *Language acquisition and language socialization: Ecological perspectives* (pp. 140–164). London: Continuum.

————. (2005). The bellman's map: Avoiding the "perfect and absolute blank" in language learning. In R. M Jourdenais and S. E. Springer (Eds.), *Content, tasks and projects in the language classroom: 2004 conference proceedings* (pp. 13–21). Monterey, CA: Monterey Institute of International Studies.

Vernez, G., & Abrahamse, A. (1996). *How immigrants fare in U.S. education.* Santa Monica, CA: RAND. (ERIC Document Reproduction Service No. ED399320)

Ward, W., Kline, R., & Haugher, J. (1991). Using microcomputers to administer tests. In *College Board computerized placement tests background readings* (pp. 107–122). Princeton, NJ: ETS.

Warschauer, M. (1999). *CALL vs. electronic literacy: Reconceiving technology in the language classroom.* Retrieved January 27, 2006, from www.cilt.org.uk/research/papers/resfor2/warsum1.htm

————. (2005). Sociocultural perspectives on CALL. In Joy L. Egbert (Ed.), *CALL research perspectives* (pp. 41–44). Mahwah, NJ: Lawrence Erlbaum.

Wasley, P. (2007). Part-time students lag behind full-time peers, study finds. *The Chronicle of Higher Education, 53*(45), A25. Retrieved July 31, 2007, from chronicle.com/weekly/v53/i45/45a02502.htm

Webster, J. M. (2001). *Faculty development for outcome-based curriculum reform in the community college.* Unpublished doctoral practicum, Oregon State University, Eugene.

Weir, C. J. (1990). *Communicative language testing.* Englewood Cliffs, NJ: Prentice Hall.

Wesche, M., & Skehan, P. (2002). Communicative, task-based, and content-based language instruction. In R. Kaplan (Ed.), *Oxford handbook of applied linguistics* (pp. 207–228). Oxford, UK: Oxford University Press.

Wetzel, K., & Chisholm, I. (1998). An evaluation of technology integration in teacher education for bilingual and English as a Second Language education majors. *Journal of Research on Computing in Education, 30*(4), 379. Retrieved December 18, 2006, from Academic Search Premier database.

White, E. (1995). *Assigning, responding, evaluating: A writing teacher's guide* (3rd ed.). New York: St. Martin's Press.

Whitehurst, G. (2002). *Evidence-based education* [Archived slideshow presentation]. Washington, DC: U.S. Department of Education. Retrieved November 10, 2007, from www.ed.gov/nclb/methods/whatworks/eb/edlite-slide001.html

Wiley, T. G. (1993). *Access, participation and transition in adult ESL: Implications for policy and practice.* Washington, DC: Southport Institute for Policy Analysis. (ERIC Document Reproduction Service No. ED421897)

Wong-Fillmore, L., & Snow, C. (2000). *What teachers need to know about language.* Washington, DC: U.S. Department of Education, Office of Educational Research and Improvement. (ERIC Document Reproduction Service No. ED444379)

Wrigley, H. S. (2007). Beyond the life boat: Improving language, citizenship, and training services for immigrants and refugees. In A. Belzer (Ed.), *Toward defining and improving quality in adult basic education* (pp. 221–240). Mahwah, NJ: Lawrence Erlbaum.

Yang, H. (1986). A new technique for identifying scientific/technical terms and describing scientific texts. *Literary and Linguistic Computing, 1*(2), 93–103.

Yoder, M. (1997). The consequences of a generic approach to teaching nursing in a multi-cultural world. *Journal of Cultural Diversity, 4*(3), 77–82.

Zachry, E. M. (2008). *Case studies of promising instructional and professional development in non-credit ESL programs: An examination of non-credit ESL programs at Bunker Hill Community College.* Alexandria, VA: TESOL.

Zafft, C., Kallenbach, S., & Spohn, J. (2006). *Transitioning adults to college: Adult basic education program models.* Boston: World Education. Retrieved January 15, 2007, from www.ncsall.net/index.php?id=26

Zamani, E. M. (2000). Sources and information regarding effective retention strategies for students of color. In S. Aragon (Ed.), *Beyond access: Methods and models for increasing retention and learning among minority students* (pp. 95–104). San Francisco: Jossey-Bass.

Zamel, V., & Spack, R. (Eds.). (1998). *Negotiating academic literacies: Teaching and learning across languages and cultures.* Mahwah, NJ: Lawrence Erlbaum.

Zhao, Y. (2003). Recent developments in technology and language learning: A literature review and meta-analysis. *Calico Journal, 21*(1), 7–27.

# CONTRIBUTORS

**Kathleen M. Bailey** received her Ph.D. in Applied Linguistics from the University of California, Los Angeles. Since 1981 she has worked at the Monterey Institute of International Studies, where she is a professor in the TESOL and the Teaching Foreign Language (TFL) master's degree programs. She is currently the faculty advisor to the Language Program Administration certificate students and the Peace Corps Masters Internationalist candidates. Her research and teaching interests include language assessment, teacher education and supervision, the teaching of speaking and listening, content-based instruction, and research methodology—particularly in language classroom research. In 1998–1999 she was the president of the international TESOL association.

**Maricel G. Santos** received her Ed.D. in Human Development and Psychology (Language and Literacy) from the Harvard Graduate School of Education. She also has a master's degree in TESOL from the Monterey Institute of International Studies. She is currently an assistant professor of English at San Francisco State University where she teaches second language acquisition theory, research, and methods; adult ESL literacy; and curriculum development. She previously worked as a research associate with the National Center for the Study of Adult Learning and Literacy. Her current research examines the role of immigrant learners as agents of change in health care.

**LaTesha Charbonnet** is a graduate of the TESOL master's degree program at the Monterey Institute of International Studies. She received her B.A. in Spanish, with a minor in International Studies, from Southeastern Louisiana University in Hammond. LaTesha has previously taught Spanish at the elementary, high school, and college levels in the United States and English at the elementary level abroad. She is currently teaching ESL at the Intensive English Program at the University of New Orleans. Her research interests include sociolinguistics and teacher education and supervision.

**Emily Dibble** received her Ph.D. in Cognitive Psychology from the University of Washington (Seattle). She is currently Executive Dean of Institutional Effectiveness at Bunker Hill Community College in Boston, where she drives the strategic planning process linked to the college budget, generates institutional data for improving the college, and serves as Project Director for a federally funded initiative to build learning communities at the college. Her interests include making high quality adult education universally available.

**Duffy Galda** is a doctoral candidate in Language, Reading, and Culture at the University of Arizona. She holds master's degrees in Curriculum and Instruction, Bilingual/Multicultural Education, and Special Education from Northern Arizona University. Since 1997, she has been a faculty member at Pima Community College, where she has served as department chair of languages and lead faculty member in ESL. She enjoys teaching both ESL and education courses. Her research and teaching interests include adult language learners, indigenous language revitalization, technology in the language classroom, developmental education, and identity expression on social networking websites.

**Guy Kellogg** received his master's degree in Teaching Foreign Languages from the Monterey Institute of International Studies in 1991. His research interests include learner discourses in computer-mediated environments, content-based instructional approaches in IEP settings, and the sociocultural contexts of EL teacher training in countries where English is spoken as an "other" language. Guy has taught both French and English at the post-secondary level in the United States. From 2004 to 2006 he facilitated several teacher education workshops for university lecturers in Vietnam. He is an associate professor at Kapiʻolani Community College.

**Molly J. Lewis** received a master's degree in Anthropology from the University of California Los Angeles, and a master's degree in TESOL from the Monterey Institute of International Studies. She taught in, designed, and administered intensive ESL programs at MIIS before joining Hartnell College, a community college in Salinas, California. There she served as Coordinator, International Education Programs, in the Center for International/Intercultural Education. Additionally, she directed Hartnell's GEAR UP project in the Soledad (CA) Unified School District, working with partners there to create and support a college-going culture in the community.

**JoAnn Mulready-Shick** completed her Ed.D. in Higher Education at the Graduate College of Education at the University of Massachusetts, Boston, where she also is faculty and undergraduate program director in the College of Nursing and Health Sciences. She has held nursing faculty and administrative positions in urban community colleges for over twenty years. She recently was a research team member on the Community College Student Success Project, which characterized best practices for assessment of community college student outcomes. Her current research interests include critical and phenomenological inquiry into student experience in learning, success, and leadership development.

**Hanh thi Nguyen** received her Ph.D. in English Language and Linguistics from the University of Wisconsin, Madison. She is currently an assistant professor in the TESL Programs at Hawaiʻi Pacific University. Her research interests include the development of interactional competence, identity construction in social interaction, pharmacist-patient communication, and Vietnamese applied linguistics. In 2007 she served as the co-organizer of the International Conference on Pragmatics and Language Learning held at the University of Hawai'i, Manoa.

**Frank Noji** received his master's degree in ESL from the University of Hawai'i at Manoa and is presently a professor at Kapi'olani Community College. He developed and coordinates the ESOL content-based program at Kapi'olani. His present interests are curriculum design of content-based courses and the use of reading in content-based instruction. He is also creating an online database that can be used as a source of materials for content-based courses.

**Lara Ravitch** received her master's degree in Teaching Foreign Languages from the Monterey Institute of International Studies. She currently teaches English as a Second Language at Truman College in Chicago and is the Dean of Concordia Language Villages' Russian immersion program. She has also taught English as a Foreign Language in Russia and graduate-level English for Academic Purposes in California.

**Cristie Roe** received her Ph.D. in Higher Education from the University of Arizona in 2002. She is also a graduate of the Monterey Institute of International Studies in California with a master's degree in TESOL. From 1980–1990, she taught English in Haiti and at Texas Southmost College, a community college now partnered with the University of Texas at Brownsville on the Texan/Mexican border. Since 1990, she has taught English composition, English as a Second Language, and developmental English at Phoenix College in Arizona.

**Cynthia M. Schuemann** earned an Ed.D. in Higher Education Instruction and a master's degree in TESOL from Florida International University. She is a professor at Miami Dade College, teaching ESL and linguistics. She has been with the college over twenty years, and has served as a chairperson the Department of ESL and Foreign Languages. She regularly presents at local and international conferences and has conducted teacher training in Brazil, Ecuador, and China. Recent publications include the *English for Academic Success* series with Heinle Cengage. She is a TESOL affiliate board member, works with the Florida Community College EAP Consortium, and was an Interest Section Chair for TESOL International.

**Bengt Skillen** received his master's degree in TESOL from the Monterey Institute of International Studies in 2001. From 2002 to 2007, he worked in the Portland, Oregon, area teaching ESL at several community colleges, high school bridge programs, and at Portland State University. In his present position, he designs and develops technical training programs in the health care profession. His research and teaching interests include content-based instruction, adult education, intercultural communication, and second language education and he has served on the Oregon TESOL board.

**Marit ter Mate-Martinsen** holds a master's degree in TESOL with Distinction from the Monterey Institute of International Studies. She has taught ESL and trained teachers from around the globe since 1997. Since 2002, she has taught ESL at Santa Barbara City College, a community college in California, where she is an assistant professor. Her teaching and research interests include computer-assisted language learning, project-based learning, cooperative learning, content-based instruction, integrated skills, materials development, and teacher training. She coordinates the Los Padres CATESOL Chapter, and as a non-native English speaker from the Netherlands, she was recently awarded the TESOL Leadership Mentoring Program Award.

**Julie Vorholt-Alcorn** received her master's degree in TESOL from the Monterey Institute of International Studies. She is currently an ESL lecturer at Lewis & Clark College. She recently taught at Clackamas Community College. Her teaching career began as a high school English teacher. She then taught EFL in Turkey for three years and chaired the Foreign Languages Department at a combined middle school and high school. She later taught ESL/EFL to children and teenagers in Minnesota and to adults in China, California, and Indiana. In 2006–2007 she was the chair of the international TESOL association's Materials Writers Interest Section.

**Elizabeth M. Zachry** received her Ed.D. in Human Development and Psychology from the Harvard Graduate School of Education. She is currently a Research Associate at MDRC (formerly, Manpower Demonstration Research Corporation), where she serves as Project Director for MDRC's evaluation of Achieving the Dream, a national initiative to improve student achievement in community colleges. She has previously served as a researcher for the National Center for the Study of Adult Learning and Literacy, the Council for the Advancement of Adult Literacy, the Change Leadership Group, and the National Institute for Literacy. Her research and teaching interests include adult literacy and developmental education in community colleges.

# SUBJECT INDEX

# AUTHOR INDEX